'Reporting For

Twenty Five Years
Of
Policing the West Midlands

1974 - 1999

By
Michael Layton & Stephen Burrows

First published in 2019

Dedication

To all of the police officers and police staff in the West Midlands, many of whom have, and do, put themselves routinely in harm's way to protect, and serve the public. Also, in memory of David Cross (R.I.P) who did so much as the Curator of the West Midlands Police Museum to preserve the history of the Force.

Figure 1 Dave Cross with Lord Knights. Courtesy of D Menzel

Front Cover Picture

The picture was taken by Mr Bernard Hess, Chief Photographer of the Birmingham Post and Mail Group, in August 1976. It features former PC Derek Rowe of the West Midlands Police in Newton Street, Birmingham City Centre, and was taken to mark the demise of the last gas street-lamps in Birmingham. It is reproduced with kind permission of Chris Adams Syndication Editor from BPM Media.

We are also particularly grateful to the Express & Star newspaper for their assistance in relation to research and the provision of a significant number of images which have added real value to this book.

Figure 2 Michael Layton, Adam Phillips (Express & Star) & Stephen Burrows at the Express & Star offices in Wolverhampton, courtesy of S Burrows

Author Biographies

Michael Layton QPM joined the British Transport Police as a Cadet on the 1st September 1968, and after 3 years, was appointed as a Police Constable in 1971, serving at Birmingham New Street Station. In 1972 he transferred to Birmingham City Police, which amalgamated in 1974 to become the West Midlands Police, where he eventually reached the rank of Chief Superintendent in 1997. Whilst much of his service was spent in the Criminal Investigation Department, for the next 6 years he was responsible for the policing of half of the Borough of Walsall.

On retirement from that Force in 2003, he went on to see service with the Sovereign Bases Police in Cyprus, and then returned to the British Transport Police in 2004, initially as a Detective Superintendent (Director of Intelligence). He spent his last two years as the Operations Superintendent at Birmingham, where he continued with his passion for combating football violence, until finally retiring again in 2011.

In the January 2003 New Year's Honours List, he was awarded the Queen's Police Medal for distinguished police service. He is the author, or co-author, of a number of factual books, predominantly police-related, as well as historical crime fiction books. Michael is also a self-employed consultant engaged predominantly with crime and community safety issues, and is a resident of Bromsgrove. He is a member of the British Transport Police Independent Advisory Group in the Midlands area, and a Trustee of the British Transport Police History Group.

Stephen Burrows joined West Midlands Police in 1983, working in Birmingham, Wolverhampton and Walsall. He performed a wide variety of roles in ranks up to and including Detective Superintendent. These included uniform command, complaints and discipline, (including internal and cross-Force enquiries) and CID command, (including Serious Crime Investigation, Child Protection and Head of Intelligence).

In 2002 he transferred to Warwickshire Police as Chief Superintendent (Area Commander), and then became Detective Chief Superintendent, (Head of Protective Services), for the Force, a post held for 5 years. He was trained as Senior Investigating Officer, in Kidnap command, and all levels of Firearms Command amongst other skills. He retired in 2013 following 30 years' service, 11 of which were spent at Chief Superintendent rank.

He currently works for The Home Office in the field of Communications Data.

Books by Michael Layton & Stephen Burrows

Fiction:

'Black Over Bill's Mother's'

'Keep Right On'

'Pretty Thing' (Stephen Burrows)

Non-fiction:

'Top Secret Worcestershire' (Published by Brewin Books)

'The Noble Cause'

'Tara-A-Bit, Our Kid', a little book of slang used in Birmingham.

'One In For D&D', a little book of Police slang.

'It's a Blag'. Police tricks and funny stories

'Walsall's Front Line Volume One'

'Walsall's Front Line Volume Two'

'Hunting The Hooligans' (Michael Layton)

'Police Dog Heroes' (Michael Layton)

'Tracking The Hooligans' (Michael Layton)

'The Hooligans Are Still Among Us' (Michael Layton)

'Violence In The Sun' (Michael Layton)

'Birmingham's Front Line' (Michael Layton)

Visit our Website and Facebook page for more information
www.bostinbooks.co.uk
www.facebook.com/BostinBooks

Figure 3 Michael Layton & Stephen Burrows circa 2002, courtesy of M Layton

Contents

Foreword

This book details many of the important, complex, and interesting investigations and events, during the first 25 years of West Midlands Police, and includes tributes to those West Midlands Police officers who have lost their lives on duty during those years.

'West Midlands Police, The First Twenty-Five Years', is a fascinating read not just for police officers, and those employed by the Force during those years, but to everyone in the West Midlands, and beyond, as policing in one form or other features daily in all our lives.

From the early days of school-crossing duties, to dealing with burglaries, assaults and more, the investigation of murders, serious and organised crime and through to terrorism, the West Midland Police have been at the forefront of protecting and keeping safe the people of this great conurbation. There have been many outstanding acts of bravery and numerous extremely difficult but successful investigations over the years.

The book can only provide a synopsis of what happened each year, during those 25 years, but together with some wonderful pictorial memories I am sure readers will at the conclusion only wish there had been room for more!

With such a diverse policing responsibility covering so many aspects of everyday life it would be wrong to suggest that West Midlands Police has always done everything right. There have been times when things have gone wrong, and sometimes despicable crimes have been committed and those responsible have not been brought to justice.

To take just one case Alice and Edna Rowley, two elderly sisters, were murdered at their corner shop in Sparkhill, Birmingham over Christmas 1987. I was the Senior Investigating Officer and to this day, over 30 years later, I still wonder if we missed a vital clue which would have solved those murders.

The authors have tried their utmost to ensure that the history of the first 25 years provides the reader with a balanced, but informative, reflection of those years.

Finally, I know the authors would wish to thank everyone who has contributed towards making this book the excellent read it is. I also know that the families of those who have, over those 25 years, lost their loved ones in the performance of their duties, will be grateful that this book creates another lasting memory for them.

Michael J Foster QPM

Introduction

Following plans to amalgamate 3 police forces into one, a steering committee was formed comprising the Chief Constables of the City of Birmingham Police, Warwickshire Police and the old West Midlands Constabulary. The new force was initially to be called the *'West Midlands Metropolitan Police'* and on the 23rd August 1973, it was announced that Sir Derrick Capper would be the Chief Constable (Designate) of the new Force.

Sir Derrick Capper originally moved to Birmingham in 1959, after being appointed as an Assistant Chief Constable in the City of Birmingham Police, and later became the Force's Chief Constable in 1963. He was awarded the Queen's Police Medal in 1960 and made a Knight Bachelor in 1968.

During his service he was made the President of the Association of Chief Police Officers and was a keen player of golf, rugby football, and athletics sports.

Retired officer Leo Harris recalls that Derrick Capper believed strongly that police sports teams were a good way of engaging positively with local communities.

Figure 4 'Derrick Capper's Tug of War Team', circa 1967 - courtesy of L Harris

In 1973 he was described as 6' 4" tall in *'policeman's boots'*!

On the 1st September 1973, a planning team was formed to assist in bringing about a smooth transition to the proposed amalgamations.

In his first report to the Police Authority for the West Midlands Metropolitan County on the 15th October 1973, Sir Derrick stated that the realistic establishment for the new Force should be 7,295 officers, but accepted that the actual establishment on amalgamation would be that of the combined strength of the 3 Forces, which was in fact considerably less.

The new Force was to be made up of the City of Birmingham Police, the West Midlands Constabulary, 1,033 officers from the Solihull, Chelmsley Wood and Sutton Coldfield Divisions of Warwickshire and Coventry Constabulary, plus 127 officers from the Stourbridge Division of West Mercia Police, and 97 officers from Aldridge and Brownhills Sub-Division of Staffordshire and Stoke-on-Trent Police.

The numbers in the senior command team of the new Force were set at a Chief Constable, a Deputy Chief Constable and 7 Assistant Chief Constables.

The Home Office, when approving the establishment for the new Force, authorised an Assistant Chief Constable and a Superintendent (Staff Officer) as an Inspectorate, to be held supernumerary for one year in order to ensure that procedural changes were carried out uniformly.

A 'Metropolitan' style helmet was eventually decided upon for the new Force, and it was agreed that officers would wear a black and white diced headband on their caps, bringing them into line with the style adopted by most other Forces in the country at that time.

On Sunday the 24th June 1973, the last Annual Parade of the City of Birmingham Police took place at Cannon Hill Park, when sections of the Force were inspected by the HMI, Mr George Fenwick. The last church parade and service for the Force took place on Sunday the 14th October 1973, at St Martins Parish Church in the Bull Ring, with Roman Catholic members attending a Mass at St Chads Cathedral in Birmingham.

Other events were held to commemorate the passing of the City of Birmingham Police, including a match played between the City of Birmingham Police rugby team and a 'Sir Derrick Capper's 15' made up of players from local rugby clubs. Retired officer David Millichamp remembers the event well and describes it as a 'very good open game which the police side lost narrowly.' He went on to spend 17 years involved with the team, much of it as the captain or coach.

Figure 5 The two rugby teams in March 1974. Courtesy of D Millichamp

The last officer to join the City of Birmingham Police was Police Constable Robert Duncan Wiltshire who enrolled on the 4th March 1974.

***

On the 1st April 1974, the *'West Midlands Police'* was formed, and on that date control and responsibility for policing the *'Midland-Links'* motorways was transferred to the new Force. At the point where the M5 and M6 merge, it was estimated that during the summer months vehicle flows of up to 100,000 vehicles per day were recorded, making the area particularly busy for traffic officers.

Initially, the policing of the Birmingham area continued in much the same way, with the only notable change being the incorporation of the Royal Town of Sutton Coldfield into the *'D'* Division.

When the Force was 'born' it had an actual workforce of 5,226 police officers and there were 1,245 vacancies.

The West Midlands comprised of two cities, namely Birmingham and Coventry, 4 major towns, Dudley, Solihull, Walsall and Wolverhampton, and a large number of smaller towns including Stourbridge, Halesowen, West Bromwich, Bloxwich and Aldridge.

Some of the inner-city areas suffered from acute deprivation, whilst other areas in the north and east were much more rural in nature.

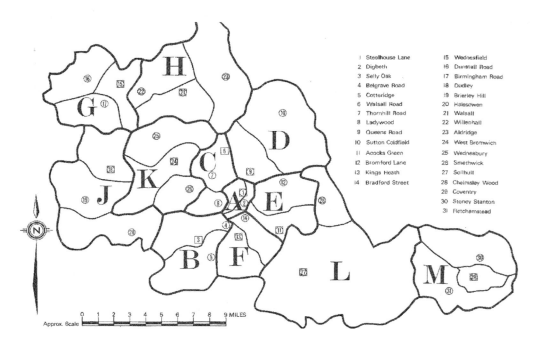

1	Steelhouse Lane	15	Wednesfield
2	Digbeth	16	Dunstall Road
3	Selly Oak	17	Birmingham Road
4	Belgrave Road	18	Dudley
5	Cotteridge	19	Brierley Hill
6	Walsall Road	20	Halesowen
7	Thornhill Road	21	Walsall
8	Ladywood	22	Willenhall
9	Queens Road	23	Aldridge
10	Sutton Coldfield	24	West Bromwich
11	Acocks Green	25	Wednesbury
12	Bromford Lane	26	Smethwick
13	Kings Heath	27	Solihull
14	Bradford Street	28	Chelmsley Wood
		29	Coventry
		30	Stoney Stanton
		31	Fletchamstead

Figure 6 Map of Territorial Divisions of West Midlands Police in 1974, courtesy of M Layton

***

In compiling this book the authors have made every effort to remain factually accurate. It would of course be an impossible task to list each and every incident, or person of note and significance, during such a long period in the history of the Force. Equally it was, and still is, made up of scores of Departments and Divisions many of which have been mentioned in the text.

That said, the authors, and many other retired officers, have provided personal recollections which seek to add some depth to a cross-section of some of those incidents and Departments, in an effort to provide a rich picture of the Force's impressive history through a period of enormous organisational change and operational challenges.

We have endeavoured unsuccesfully to obtain photographs of all the deceased officers mentioned in this book. The lack of a photograph does not mean that they are valued any less than those whose images do appear. R.I.P

1974

The Birmingham Pub Bombings

Retired officer Graham Cassidy recalls some significant events in his late father's police career and sets the scene for what was to come in 1974:

'My dad John (nickname Jock) Cassidy, joined the Birmingham City Police on transfer from the Stirling and Clackmannanshire Police in 1960. He served throughout the city, and retired from the West Midlands Police in 1975 as a shift Inspector at Ladywood.

During the early 1970's, Birmingham was in the grip of a terrible campaign of bombing by the Provisional IRA.

On the 20th August 1973, three incendiary devices were placed in shops in New Street, Birmingham City Centre.

On the 30th August, two bombs detonated in Solihull town-centre.

On the 2nd September, two more devices were discovered in Edgbaston.

On the 17th September 1973, Dad and his team were coming towards the end of a night-shift at Ladywood, when a milkman phoned in to report a suspicious package which had been seen at the rear of commercial premises on Highfield Road, just off the main Hagley Road in Edgbaston.

Dad and others deployed to the scene and put on an outer-cordon. A team of Army Bomb Disposal experts had been housed on standby to deal with the growing number of such incidents. They were based at the Police Training Centre 'Tally Ho', so were just a short distance away.

Captain Ronald Wilkinson, aged thirty years, from the Royal Army Ordnance Corps soon arrived at the scene.

He was due to go on holiday with his wife later on that day.

He went over to inspect the device which looked like a canister of some kind.

Then, as Dad and others looked on in horror, the device exploded in a massive fireball, which engulfed the officer.

Captain Wilkinson died six days later, in Birmingham Accident Hospital, as a result of his injuries.

Dad was left to manage the murder-scene until reinforcements arrived.

Just over a year later, on 21st November 1974, Dad was again on nights at Ladywood when the pub-bombings occurred in the city centre. He didn't return home from duty for over twenty-four hours.

Of course there were no counselling services available in those days. I was eighteen years-old at the time, but it was not until 1982, after I had become a police officer myself, that Dad spoke about both incidents.

It is fair to say that much as he loved the job, those events stayed with him throughout the remainder of his service and after he retired in 1975.

He passed away in 2016.'

Figure 7 John Cassidy as a Police Constable, courtesy of G Cassidy

***

On the evening of Saturday the 6th April 1974, the Force Control Room received a call claiming that 3 bombs had been planted in Birmingham City Centre.

As police officers began to evacuate the city centre, the first bomb exploded at the Lloyds Bank, in the Rotunda Building in New Street, whilst a second exploded outside the British Rail Signal Box adjacent to Hill Street.

Extensive damage was caused at both locations but no-one was seriously injured.

A third device, which failed to detonate, was found at 6am the following morning, under a pile of rubbish in Stephenson Street.

On Sunday 14th July 1974, 5 bombs went off in quick succession in Birmingham.

The Rotunda was again attacked, causing extensive damage but no injuries.

There was also an explosion at Nechells Power Station which plunged part of the City into darkness, whilst other bombs failed to explode.

***

On the 26th July 1974, PC David Robert Brown, aged 31 years, was killed in a road traffic accident whilst on motorcycle patrol.

Retired officer Ken Rowley recalls:

'I was a PC at West Bromwich at the time of the accident and had got to know Dave during his visits to the station. As a traffic motorcyclist it was quite normal for them to get about and visit various police stations. As I recall he was tall but quiet and unassuming, and very well-liked with a reputation for being a good police officer.'

***

On the 11th November 1974, Mr Sydney Grayland, the Sub-Postmaster at Langley Sub-Post Office, near Oldbury in the Black Country, was shot and killed during a robbery. His wife Margaret Grayland was also brutally attacked.

An Incident Room was set up at Oldbury Police Station, and the murder was eventually linked to two similar attacks, one in February 1974 at Harrogate, and the second in Accrington in September 1974. In both cases the postmasters were also shot and killed.

A reward of £25,000 was later offered for information leading to the arrest and conviction of the killer(s).

The man who committed these murders was in fact Donald Neilson, otherwise known as the *'Black Panther'*.

He remained 'on the run' for several months before two police officers, in Mansfield in Nottinghamshire, saw him acting suspiciously, and despite being threatened with a double-barrelled shotgun managed to overpower and arrest him with assistance from several members of the public.

Neilson was given 5 life-sentences in prison in 1976 for murdering 5 people, who included the above-named, and Lesley Whittle, a 17 year-old from Shropshire who was kidnapped in 1975. She was subsequently found dead in a drainage shaft in Staffordshire, 7 weeks later. Another case involved that of a security guard at Dudley Freightliner terminal, who died from injuries within a year after being shot by Neilson during another attempted robbery.

In 2008 a High Court Judge ruled that he should never be released.

Neilson died in prison in 2011 at the age of 75 years.

***

On the 5th November 1974, an IRA activist named James McDade planted a bomb at the Conservative Party Offices in Edmund Street, and an incendiary device at the firm of *'Guidex Ltd'* in Constitution Hill, Birmingham.

On the 14th November 1974 another incendiary device was planted at a plywood firm in Ladywood, Birmingham, whilst elsewhere James McDade blew himself up whilst trying to arm a bomb which went off prematurely in Coventry.

McDade's remains were released for burial by HM Coroner at Coventry on Thursday 21st November 1974. His coffin was eventually taken to Elmdon Airport in Birmingham whilst negotiations took place as to where his remains would be taken to by plane.

At 8.18pm and 8.20pm on that night bombs exploded in the *'Mulberry Bush'* and *'The Tavern in the Town'* Public Houses in Birmingham City Centre.

21 people were killed, and 168 injured in the explosions.

This incident led to the first operation in the Midlands of a Casualty Bureau.

Within days a number of individuals were arrested and charged in connection with the latter attacks and later convicted of 21 counts of murder following a Crown Court trial.

(Postscript: The 6 men convicted subsequently had their convictions overturned on Appeal and were released from prison on the 14th March 1991.

The so-called *'Birmingham Six'* walked free from jail after their convictions for the murder of 21 people in the two pubs were quashed by the Court of Appeal.

Paddy Joe Hill, Hugh Callaghan, Richard McIlkenny, Gerry Hunter, Billy Power and Johnny Walker, were released onto the streets outside the Old Bailey in London at 16.05 GMT.

The families of those who lost their lives continue their quest for the truth and justice to this day.)

One of the co-authors, Michael Layton, remembers the night of the *'Birmingham Bombings'* as they became known:

'I was a young PC working at Ladywood Police Station and a number of officers, including myself, were sent to Elmdon Airport to assist in guarding the coffin of James McDade. There were fears that the IRA might attempt some form of 'publicity stunt' to honour him.

There were lots of officers sat in the old Fire Station waiting for a decision to be made as to what plane his coffin would be put on, and to where. We had no personal mobile phones then but I remember an officer approaching our Superintendent and speaking to him with a sense of urgency. It didn't take long for the word to go round – bombs had gone off in Birmingham.

I was soon chosen to return to Birmingham, and a number of us were put on a Midland Red bus – we didn't have the luxury of lots of police vans then. As we drove into Birmingham you could feel the tension in the air. As we passed Digbeth Police Station I saw a column of police officers in files of three abreast marching up the road towards the Rotunda. It was black and eerie – like something I would imagine out of the 'Blitz'.

We got back to Ladywood and I was one of a few officers told to go home to get a few hours' sleep before coming back on duty to cover normal policing duties on the sub-division. The remainder were sent to man cordons in the City.'

Figure 8 Courtesy of the Express & Star newspaper

Figure 9 Courtesy of the Express & Star newspaper

The Chief Constable subsequently wrote in his Annual Report, *'Crimes of a violent nature gave most cause for concern, in particular those committed by the politically-motivated terrorist, whose vicious and indiscriminate actions brought destruction and misery. Additional problems associated with suspect letters and packages, hoax calls, and the vast number of enquiries following such incidents placed a considerable burden upon police resources.*

The tragedy in New Street, Birmingham, on the evening of Thursday 21st November, when explosions occurred at two licensed premises, killing twenty-one people and injuring one hundred and sixty-eight more, appalled the whole of the country. The grief and sorrow suffered by relatives and friends of those involved was shared by us all.'

Figure 10 Memorial to the victims of the Birmingham Pub Bombings in the grounds of Birmingham Cathedral, courtesy of B Crowley

Retired officer Grahame Davies recalls just one of the frequent calls relating to bomb hoaxes and suspicious packages during this period:

'We had a 'bomb call' to Smallbrook Queensway at Holloway Circus, to the underground cinema. It was a Friday and we were on night duty. I was sent with PC Colin Murphy, a Probationer at the time, to search the premises and to notify the night manager.

The cinema was closed to the public at the time, but was due to re-open at midnight for the Chinese community. In the gents toilet a false ceiling tile had been removed and balanced across the tie bar and on the next tile was a white plastic bag. I touched the bag and it had some weight - so I retreated and radioed in my find from outside in the street. This was standard practice at the time.

The result was that the Queensway and the Holloway Head roundabout were closed to all traffic. The whole shift attended - utilising all of our cars to close off and set up a perimeter. The Fire Brigade and ambulances arrived plus extra officers from Steelhouse Lane and Belgrave Rd.

Army Bomb Disposal officers arrived on the scene and when their guys got there the officer was kitting up when he realised that their robot could not negotiate the stairs and access to the male toilet. He was then dressed in full protective gear and was shoving a cricketers 'box' down his trousers which he said was a present from his wife!

This brave man then went down the two flights of stairs to check out my suspicious parcel. Twenty long minutes later he re-emerged with a load of white paper and the contents of the bag - not a bomb but a steak and kidney pie and chips!

The officer was brilliant - no derogatory comments at all and said I was right to call it in but you can only image the 'stick' I got off the rest of the shift!'

***

As of the 31st December 1974, the Force had an actual strength of 5,282 officers with 1,189 vacancies.

The Force was made up of 4,973 male officers and just 309 female officers, with support from 1,022 members of the West Midlands Police Special Constabulary.

In order to address the shortage of police recruits, the Force took on a professional advertising agency, McCann-Erikson Advertising Ltd, with offices in London, as well as conducting recruitment displays at Bingley Hall, the Bull Ring Shopping Centre, and during the Force Open Day which took place at *'Tally Ho'* Police Training Centre in September 1974.

Of the 304 recruits who were actually taken on between April and December, just 6 applicants were in possession of university degrees, with no applicants forthcoming for the Graduate Entry Scheme, and nearly one third having no educational qualifications recorded at all.

Taking into account wastage as a result of retirements and resignations, the Force only grew by 56 officers.

A large percentage of the total intake for new recruits came in fact from West Midlands Police Cadets, the strength of which stood at some 326 by the end of the year. The situation in relation to police support staff was similar – by the end of 1974 the Force had an establishment of 1,876 employees in manual and non-manual posts, but was carrying 367 vacancies.

ESTABLISHMENT – REGULAR FORCE

The following table shows the authorised establishment of the Force, together with the actual working strength, on 31 December, 1974.

RANK	Authorised Establishment		Actual Strength 31.12.74		Vacancies	
	Men	Women	Men	Women	Men	Women
Chief Constable	1		1			
Assistant Chief Constables	6		7		+1	
Chief Superintendents	20	1	20	1		
Superintendents	76	1	78	1	+2	
Chief Inspectors	93	3	93	2		1
Inspectors	333	13	316	12	17	1
Sergeants	980	56	902	31	78	25
Constables	4596	292	3556	262	1040	30
TOTALS	6105	366	4973	309	1132	57

Total Establishment men and women	Actual Strength	Vacancies
6471	5282	1189

Figure 11 Force establishment as at 31.12.1974, courtesy of M Layton

SECONDED OFFICERS

The following officers are seconded from the Force and are not included in the establishment figures.

	MEN						WOMEN			
	Chief Superintendents	Superintendents	Chief Inspectors	Inspectors	Sergeants	Constables	Total	Inspectors	Sergeants	Constables	Total
Central Service										
Police College	1		1				2			
Central Planning Unit		1		2			3			
H.O. Crime Prevention Centre	1						1			
H.M.I. Staff Officer	2						2			
H.M.I. Driver						1	1			
H.O. Research Unit	1						1			
Training Centres		1		5	13	2	21			
Inter Force Units										
M.I.D.C.R.O. Fingerprints		1	2	2	7	18	30			
Forensic Science Laboratory			1		1		2			
Dog Training School, Stafford					1		1			
Regional Crime Squad	1		3	1	21	22	48		2	1	3
Universities				7	1	1	9	2			2
Total Officers on Secondment	6	3	7	17	44	44	121	2	2	1	5

Figure 12 Seconded officers as at 31.12.1974, courtesy of M Layton

***

Between the 1st April and 31st December 1974, a total of 83,386 indictable crimes were recorded in the new Force Area. Of these crimes 30,191 were detected, which resulted in a detection rate of 36%.

35 cases of murder were investigated, and of these 13 were classed as detected with criminal proceedings still ongoing in respect of a number of other cases.

In relation to violent crime, 424 offences of serious wounding were recorded, with 239 detected, but these figures included the 168 persons injured as a result of the explosions in Birmingham in November.

By the end of the year the Force had responded to, and investigated, 40 separate incidents where explosives and incendiary devices were used.

***

In order to assist with traffic policing, 4 'VASCAR' (Visual Average Speed Computer and Recorder) were purchased for the Force. The device consisted of a miniature computer, together with an accurate clock and distance recorder, fitted to the inside of a police vehicle. The police operator fed in a time and distance and the computer indicated an average speed of the offending vehicle. Most importantly this removed the necessity for a police vehicle to travel at the same high speed as the offender.

A total of 8,028 street accidents of all types were reported to the police during the 9 month period ending December.

Seriously injured casualties totalled 2,400, slightly injured were 7,609 and 172 persons were killed.

Just short of 50,000 people were prosecuted for a variety of motoring offences during this period with just over 11,000 receiving official police cautions.

***

From the 1st April, control of Force vehicles equipped with V.H.F. radios, and the receipt and dissemination of '999' calls, and burglar alarms, was carried out at 3 Control Rooms for Divisions, at Newton Street in Birmingham, at Brierley Hill and in Coventry, with a fourth servicing the Motorway.

The total number of emergency calls for the new area for 9 months was 118,218, with half of the calls coming from Birmingham.

With 4,683 premises within the Force area licensed for the sale of intoxicants, officers were kept busy dealing with offences relating to drunkenness, dealing with no less than 5,537 offences on the streets and 1,791 persons being prosecuted for drink and drive offences.

The need for an increase in the use of technology was identified at an early stage and a Birmingham Command and Control project, set up prior to amalgamation continued, and the Police National Computer was installed in a number of stations.

***

Within the Chief Constable's report for this period, the work of the Special Patrol Group, the Serious Crime Squad, the Force Drug Squad, and many other facets of police work were also highlighted.

It is interesting to note that that the recorded number of addicts on prescription for heroin in the West Midlands on the 31st December 1974 was just 23– how times were to change!

Officers also dealt with 21,613 items of lost property and 9,072 stray-dogs as well as 5,663 missing person reports, of which 327 were still missing at the end of the year.

1975

The Murder of PC David Green

On the 30th June 1975, Sir Derrick Capper retired as Chief Constable to Shrewsbury, where he was among other things, president of Shrewsbury Rugby Football Club.

He died, aged 65 years, following two operations.

***

PC David Christopher Green joined the former Birmingham City Police as a Police Cadet in 1971, and became a Constable in January 1974.

Figure 13 Police Cadet David Green, courtesy of A Bryant

In just 18 months, David Green was awarded 3 commendations for good police work, one of which involved the rescue of a mentally-disturbed man from the 6th floor of a city centre building.

PC Green, then aged 20 years, was a member of the *'A'* Division and at about 11pm on the 17th July 1975, he was on patrol in High Street, Birmingham when he saw a group of youths outside the *'Rainbow Suite'*, a dance venue, shortly after an event had finished. One of this group was seen to remove a knife from his pocket and place it into the waistband of his trousers.

The officer approached this individual who then pushed him and attempted to run off, only to be detained by PC Green a short distance away. The offender was arrested, and the knife removed from him, but shortly afterwards other members of the group surrounded the officer in an effort to free the prisoner.

PC Green was punched and kicked, during which attack the prisoner managed to break free. However, the officer managed to detain one of his attackers who then produced his own knife and stabbed PC Green fatally in the heart, before running off.

Despite his injury the officer bravely tried to continue the chase before collapsing on the pavement.

An ambulance was quickly on the scene but despite frantic attempts to save his life, David Green died in hospital.

An initial search for the murder weapon proved fruitless; however, the following day further searches were conducted resulting in the recovery of a carving knife, which was found buried in a flowerbed near to *'Rackhams'* Department Store.

Desmond Arnas Wilson, aged 20 years, of Nineveh Road, Handsworth, was later arrested, convicted, and, on the 19th January 1976, sentenced to life imprisonment at Birmingham Crown Court for the murder of the officer. Two other youths were also convicted of assaulting him with intent to prevent, or resist, the arrest of the first person detained.

During the trial a number of witnesses were classed as 'hostile' by the Crown on the basis that the witness statements made by them during the course of the investigation were fundamentally different to their accounts given on oath in Court.

Passing sentence, trial Judge Mr. Justice Cobb told Wilson, *'You were brutal, selfish and callous. He was a brave, gallant officer...'*

At the time the media reported that Wilson was a member of a gang known as the *'Shortie Boys'* from the Handsworth area. They reported that Wilson gave a clenched fist salute to the public gallery as he was led away after sentence.

Retired officer Richard (Rich) Pearshouse reflects:

'Dave Green and I had been Police Cadets together, went to Ryton on the same initial course together, and ended up on the same shift on 'A' Unit at Steelhouse Lane. Our Inspectors at the time were Pete Butterworth (Office Inspector) and a little Welsh guy, Jones, I can't remember his first name; our Sergeants were Jack Haig, Maurice Walsh and Phil Walker.

On Wednesday 17th July 1975, we were both on duty working nights. I had been posted to driving 'Alpha Mike 5', the car covering the Newtown area. Dave had been posted as a walker on the one of the city centre beats. After parade, as was usual, we all had a quick 'cuppa' before heading out. I arranged to meet Dave at 11pm in Lower Bull Street and give him a ride round for a while, as was the unwritten norm between walkers and drivers on the shift.

It was about 10.45pm and I was making my way into the city to meet up with Dave but as I was driving round St. Chad's Circus a car came out of Shadwell St without stopping, or slowing down, and straight into the path of my car. He bounced off the kerb of the centre island in front of me and back in front of me again - how he missed me I'll never know. His driving was all over the place.

I followed him up to where the bus stops were alongside Lloyd House, and managed to pull him over. When the driver finally got out he could hardly stand he was that 'pissed'. I had no other option but to 'bag him' and lock him up, it later transpired that he was a member of a well-known criminal family.

Because of all the messing about with this I never made it to meet Dave as I had promised, then shortly after 11pm I heard that Dave had been stabbed and had died. It transpired that Dave had stopped a group of lads who were coming out of the Rainbow Suite, the usual 'argy bargy' took place, then for whatever reason, one of the youths decided to make a run for it, Dave gave chase and caught him somewhere in Union Street. Dave then started to walk him back down towards High Street at which point he was confronted by the other youths, and a scuffle broke out resulting in Dave being fatally stabbed in the chest.

I have never forgiven myself for letting Dave down that night and still often wonder, if I had been a couple of minutes earlier, or later, driving up from Newtown I wouldn't have come across that car and his driving and maybe, just maybe Dave would still be alive today.

It's a guilt I will carry with me for the rest of my life.'

(Postscript: On the 10th anniversary of PC Green's death, the Lord Mayor of Birmingham, Councillor Frank Carter, unveiled a commemorative plaque at Steelhouse Lane Police Station.

In July 2010 another plaque, and a tree, were dedicated to PC Green, at the National Memorial Arboretum, at Alrewas, near Lichfield, by his sister Angela Bryant and his mother Mary Green. They were placed in an area known as *'The Beat'* on the site. The occasion took place during an annual *'Care of Police Survivors'* service of remembrance, which helps to support the families of officers lost in the line of duty.)

Figure 14 PC Green 1975, courtesy of D Menzel

Figure 15 David's plaque, National Memorial Arboretum, courtesy of M Layton

Figure 16 Plaque in grounds of 'The Beat', courtesy of M Layton

Retired officer Rick Scott has some poignant memories of the officer in his early days:

'As many police officers will remember, in the days of the 'yellow-peril', when a police officer had details of a crime, they had to seek the assistance of a detective officer to confirm that it was okay to complete a crime report. In doing that, the detective officer was also gaining some ownership in further enquiries at some stage, if the crime warranted it.

Invariably the uniform officer had to enter the CID office to make that contact. The CID office at Steelhouse Lane was a rather large office with many desks. On occasions, a good few of the desks would be occupied by a detective officer, especially during the early part of the day.

As a few of the detectives had fairly heavy case-loads, they did not want to attract even more possible work and as such if a uniform officer walked into the room their heads went down so that they would appear to be engrossed in some important issue. I could remember from my early days, the atmosphere never seemed to be welcoming!

Dave Green was in the very early stages of his training when he came into the CID office to seek to report his first crime. As usual heads went down. Sometime previously, I had decided that would not be my policy. Seeing that I was looking at him, Dave came over and asked if I would authorise his report. I seem to remember that it was the usual probationary Constable's first shoplifter.

I had no problem in accepting and later had an overview of the subsequent prisoner interview, the full interview, being carried out by the experienced officer who was training Dave.

What came of that first encounter was that every time Dave wanted to have a crime authorised, if I was in the CID office, he always came to me.

I considered Dave a good example of what I believe a police officer should look like, being smart and having a very friendly attitude. In short he looked like the archetypal image associated with TV and film images that were often portrayed.

Whilst I never really got to know him well, his attitude and demeanour appeared well-suited to the role, even if he did seem a little quieter than some of his compatriots.

I later moved to West Bromwich on promotion and never saw Dave again.

I can remember the night that he was killed. My unit had completed a 2 x 10 shift. Most of the unit were in the bar at West Bromwich Police club when the sad news came through of an officer being killed in the city centre. I made a phone call and discovered that it was Dave.

I relayed the news to my unit and also my knowledge of Dave. Everyone present wanted to see if they were needed to go to Steelhouse Lane to help with the enquiry. I am certain this was a genuine request to assist, but clearly one that could not be allowed. Had such need been identified, a request would already have been received.

I feel that David Green would have progressed in the Force and that if he had later gone on to become a detective I am convinced that 'his head would never have gone down'

***

On the 1st August 1975, Mr Philip Knights, the Chief Constable of South Yorkshire Police, returned to Birmingham as the second Chief Constable of the West Midlands Police. He was to serve for ten years in that position. He was knighted in 1980 and later raised to the peerage in 1987, the first police officer to be awarded such recognition, taking the title of, 'Lord Knights of Edgbaston'.

He was later to be described as the *'true architect'* of the new Force in bringing it together as one cohesive organisation, whereas before some had previously referred to it in humorous terms as *'the Force of a thousand macs'* due to the variety and styles of uniform worn.

***

This was a good year for recruitment, resulting in a net gain of 285 officers, due mainly to large-scale redundancies in industry. In addition, the minimum age qualification to join the police was lowered to eighteen and a half years, which meant that many Police Cadets were eligible to join as regular officers.

This however, still left the Force with 903 officer vacancies to fill, and the Secretary of State finally approved a special 'under-manning' allowance in recognition of the problems that the Force faced in recruiting sufficient numbers.

At the end of the year, the Sex Discrimination Act 1975 came into force, leading to the abolition of dedicated Policewomen's Departments and female officers thus performing similar duties to their male colleagues for the same rates of pay.

Retired officer Sue Dorrian (Sue Jones), joined Birmingham City Police as a Police Cadet in October 1970, at the age of 17. She met her future husband Bryan in the cadets, but it was to be 4 years before they started going out together.

She recalls:

'I joined the regulars in Birmingham City Police in October 1972 and, after initial training, was posted to the 'C' Division Policewomen's Department at Ladywood, as P.W. '142'. The Inspector was Val Howard and the Sergeant was Chris Coutts. I can't remember all of the other officers but there was Anna Saunders, Barbara Donovan and Anne Senter. We were a specialised department and dealt with women, children and young persons. We were kept busy dealing with people missing from homes, shoplifters, indecent assaults, and rapes and did our own patrols in pairs. We developed great friendships and even now I still see some of my former colleagues.

When Bryan and I started going out I was moved to Thornhill Road Police Station. They had strict rules on relationships in those days, and routinely separated officers who worked at the same stations.

In 1975 I became Constable '8942' with the figure eight signifying that I was a female officer, and in 1975 I was posted to 'D' Unit at Thornhill Road after the Policewomen's Departments were scrapped.

Bryan and I got married in May 1976 at St Lawrence's C of E Church in Northfield, and as we left the church after the ceremony, we had a 'Guard of Honour' from 'D' Unit officers at Ladywood holding their truncheons in the air. They included Gordon Cooper and John Lamb.

I left the Force in 1978 to begin a family.'

Figure 17 Sue Dorrian, courtesy of S Dorrian

Figure 18 'Guard of Honour', wedding of Sue & Bryan Dorrian, courtesy of S Dorrian

Retired officer Julie Maley (Julie Whild), recalls:

'As a cadet on 'A' Division in 1975 I hated being in the Policewomen's Department. I found it so limited and boring and wanted to be out on the streets. I loved my time on beat patrol at Steelhouse Lane before being posted to Digbeth, after my initial course at Ryton on Dunsmore District Training Centre. When I had a year's service, Frank Brehany and myself were the 'stars' of a BBC programme and were followed around the city centre on a quiet night. They were looking at how policewomen working on the beat compared to being in the Policewomen's Departments. I had to work three times harder than male colleagues, in the early days, to be accepted, but once they saw that some of us were very capable and got 'stuck in', things settled down and were fine. I really enjoyed my time on the front-line at the best station with the best colleagues.'

Figure 19 Julie Maley nee Whild, courtesy of J Maley

Retired officer Norman Langford recalls:

'At that time I was involved with recruit-training at Ryton on Dunsmore and the impact of equality legislation and poor pay was amazing. The salary at that time for police officers was insufficient for a married officer with children, but great for a single person.
The impact of this was that in a class of twenty-four officers, it was not unusual for twenty of the officers to be female.'

Retired officer Barry John Rudge recalls:

'I was a Sergeant at Dudley at the time and we were losing male officers who found it difficult to support their families and were returning to 'civvie street' for better pay. We had one chap who returned to his old job. Consequently we were getting an imbalance of female officers. I much preferred having the female officers on the shift rather than in the Policewomen's Department where they were quite often underemployed.'

Retired officer Sharon Spriggs provides a powerful recollection:

'One of the first places all officers report for duty is, of course, the 'Stores' to pick up your uniform. Whatever else you are given; it is the uniform that symbolises who and what you are. It's the uniform that gives you the respect and is imbued with the powers handed down to all police officers, and it was with a fair amount of excitement and awe that I stood in line at Bourneville Stores with my fellow new recruits that chilly October morning in 1986.

In front of me was the typical police officer 'to be', twenty-two years of age, 6 feet tall, male, lean, broad-shouldered. Next to him was me, 5'4", and medium build, aged twenty-six, and size 4 feet. But it was okay, we were both there to be equipped to do the same job. We were equals. I knew this because I had been told so many times during the interviews and training - West Midlands Police were a modern police force going forward.

As we shuffled along the counter, we were each handed the accoutrements to do our job. Handcuffs, handcuff pouch, torch, epaulettes, collar numbers, '8830' in my case, and then we got to the actual uniform. I remember my heart beating faster in excitement and anticipation as the young man in front was asked his name and then handed two pairs of trousers. He shuffled along. I was asked my name and handed two skirts.

In front of me, my fellow 'colleague to be' was handed two blue jumpers and his pristine jacket. He held it up with pride, a big grin on his face. I held my arms out eagerly for mine, smaller of course and, I quickly noticed no pockets. I glanced back at the other jacket. It had two side-pockets, at least one breast pocket from what I could see, lots of room to put his pens, note-book, keys, and handkerchief. I quickly picked up my skirt, no pockets there either.

I turned in time to see the man next to me handed a thick leather belt to go around his long, warm, user-friendly trousers, which would undoubtedly be used to hang his handcuffs, torch, first-aid kit etc. on. Suddenly, the ugliest thing I had ever seen was thrust in my direction – a stiff, black, heavy leather handbag.

The line had started to move along and I caught up just as the man in front was holding out both his hands. Palms facing upwards, he stood there expectantly, and patiently, until a 16" piece of beautifully carved shiny wood was placed ceremoniously in his hands - his truncheon. He turned it this way and that, slipping his hand through the soft leather handle, swinging it gently, testing it out for balance. This was a police officer's only form of protection and I understood it deserved a certain amount of reverence and respect. I watched as he carefully placed it on top of his clothes. The man behind the counter stepped away momentarily and returned with an encouraging smile on his face. 'There you go love'. I quickly looked up to see if he was 'taking the piss' but no, he'd already moved on to the next in line and was holding another 'adult sized' truncheon in his hand.

I stared at the 10" piece of wood in my own hand, turning it over to check if there was somewhere to put batteries in as this was clearly a joke, and the only chance I would ever have of protecting myself with this would be if, when taking it out of my handbag, the person in front of me died of laughter!

I quickly shuffled along the counter and watched as my fellow colleague, my peer, my equal in all manner was handed his police helmet. It seemed huge. Another big grin as the recipient admired the shiny silver badge on the front, tested the strap for strength and stability then rapped it hard with his knuckles. It was solid. He tried it in on for size and I watched as his face clouded over. I knew he was imagining himself standing on the front-line, bottles and bricks flying overhead, confident in the knowledge his head would be safely protected. He subconsciously pulled his shoulders back and pushed his chest out, standing tall.

I looked down. There on top of my folded-skirts, jumpers and jacket was a round piece of white plastic. For several moments I glanced back and forth at the two pieces of headgear. I placed my forefinger on the top in the centre and pressed gently down and watched as a dent quickly formed in the middle. I picked it up by its shiny black plastic peak and noticed underneath a paper envelope. Inside there was a small metal badge to clip on the front of the hat. And that's what it was, a hat. Not a helmet. Not a piece of protective headgear. It was a hat.

For a moment my face also clouded over as I imagined myself chasing after my first burglar. Restricted by my skirt as I tried to clamber over a fence, encumbered by the heavy bulky bag slung over my shoulder, conveniently placed should anyone want to use it to strangle me, and my white shiny hat languishing in a puddle having been blown off by that strong gust of wind, and then, having caught the aforementioned burglar, having to ask him if he'd just hold still a moment while I rummaged through my bag for my handcuffs.

I glanced across and saw the young man next to me staring. He was also looking back and forth between the two pieces of headwear. He didn't say anything. He didn't need to. He just shrugged his shoulders and moved along.

Yes, we were the same, but different. Some would always be more equal than others. Nothing needed to be spoken, nothing overt in nature but in all its subtly it was there, plain to see.'

In time the uniforms worn by female officers improved....

Figure 20 Sharon Spriggs circa 1987/8 (old style hat), courtesy of S Spriggs

Figure 21 Sharon Spriggs circa 1990/1 (reinforced 'bowler' hat), courtesy of S Spriggs

***

During the year, 493 members of the Force were assaulted on duty.

***

In 1975, a total of 122,189 crimes were recorded as offences involving violence, and house burglaries increased, with a third of all crime relating to thefts of or from motor vehicles. Set against this, the detection rate overall was 38%.

A total of 30 offences of murder were recorded, and 5 offences of manslaughter, with 31 persons being prosecuted for a large proportion of these offences and only 2 murders remaining unsolved.

In road-safety terms, 228 persons were killed and 12,767 injured in accidents, with rush hour periods, and between 11pm and midnight, being high-risk times.

A total of 2,536 persons were dealt with for drink/drive offences on the roads, whilst 6,436 persons committed offences of drunkenness on the streets.

Overall, the Force dealt with a total of 167,787 emergency *'999'* calls for assistance, impounded 10,799 vehicles, took possession of 1,395 lost pedal cycles, and 6,781 stray-dogs.

***

In 1975, the Special Patrol Group, the Force's full-time reserve for public-order related incidents, made 1,194 arrests including 485 for disorderly conduct, 190 for theft and 144 for drunkenness.

The strength of the Special Constabulary at that time was 1,105, which included 134 female officers, and just 35 officers from ethnic minority groups. Mr. H. E. Price MBE, the Force Commandant, retired after nearly 50 years of service.

The Underwater Search Unit comprised 12 officers and provided regional support with almost half of their 65 searches being conducted for 3 other Midlands Forces. A total of 17 bodies were recovered during the year.

54 officers were seconded to the Regional Crime Squad, who had offices at Birmingham, Bilston and Coventry. They were tasked with the investigation of the activities of 'professional' criminals and the curtailment of the growth of organised crime.

Retired officer Tony Everett recalls his days on the Regional Crime Squad looking at one particular aspect of the work they undertook:

'I joined the job in 1969, and worked on the 'C' Division at Ladywood. I subsequently became a Grade I advanced driver as well as an advanced motorcyclist.

After the activities of the so-called 'Black Panther' in the early Seventies, a lot of meetings took place which were aimed at learning lessons as to how different Forces worked jointly on major cross-border investigations. In the case of the 'Black Panther' there were at least three police forces and the Regional Crime Squad involved, which meant four different radio systems and four different communication processes, to give just one example of the challenges that were faced.

It was agreed that improvements needed to be made and the RCS started looking at what systems were in place in the Metropolitan Police, who had in turn spent time researching the work of American police forces that had developed a surveillance system for use in kidnap, blackmail and 'adulteration of food' cases.

With a special focus on communications, an advert was put out by No 4 Regional Crime Squad for officers with advanced driving skills who would be responsible for the upkeep and use of a new dedicated communications vehicle, deployed to support surveillance operations.

I applied, together with 24 other people, and, together with a colleague Dave Carding, was successful. I transferred to the RCS on the 1st December 1975 on a 3 year attachment, and stayed for 10 years!

We went down to London ourselves in the early days to understand the scale of the task we were facing, and then awaited the arrival of a new 'Luton Body' Transit van which came in 1976.

It was empty upon delivery, and Dave and I set about creating a radio communications area in the front part and a kitchen area in the back, with a dividing wall between. It was a really complex piece of work which involved lining the roof with metal, as it had a fibre-glass body which was not appropriate for using a radio system.

The body was modified by fitting aluminium sheets to the roof area to enable the six aerials for the radio systems to be fitted properly, and a 'slipstream' panel fitted to the flat fronted area over the cab, that was a very cost-efficient modification.

I focused on the radio work, whilst Dave sorted the internal structure out. He was a 'dab-hand' with carpentry and as a team we got on really well together. Sadly he is no longer with us but I have very fond memories of working with him. In ten years we never exchanged a cross-word.

One problem that we identified early-on was that the people in the back could not speak to the people in the front. I don't recall how we found out about it but we finished up finding a piece of sophisticated intercom equipment that had been used on the 'Pope Mobile' on a visit to the UK, and recovered it from a research establishment before installing it in the van, which was given the name 'Enterprise'.

As well as the radio equipment we also had access to the earliest form of radio telephone which was called the 'Midland Radio Telephone Service'. It had just eight channels for the whole of Birmingham.

There were also three tape-recording systems inside so that every word and instruction given was recorded for potential evidential purposes. There were two separate charging systems, one for the vehicle electrics and one for the radios.

Once most of the kit had been installed we started doing a lot of training exercises aimed at making sure that mobile surveillance operatives could talk to each other over distances. We then tested it in a live environment on a case in Liverpool where an individual finished up being arrested for blackmail.

We also used to try and identify high-points, using Ordnance Survey maps, so that if needed, we knew where to deploy in advance in order to get the maximum ranges for radio reception. The furthest we ever managed was to link two RCS offices situated over one hundred miles away from each other, whilst we were parked at the top of the Wrekin Hills.

On one occasion we were on a pub car park in the Malvern Hills, doing some testing, when the pub landlord came to the vehicle and demanded to know what we were doing. We didn't quite tell him the whole truth and he told us to leave. At that precise moment two RAF jets flew very low overhead. Quick thinking, Dave looked up at them and said words to the effect of, "We'd better tell them we have to move." The landlord clearly thought that we were with the Forces, told us to stay, and shortly afterwards delivered two 'Full-English' breakfasts to the van!

The only problem with the van was that it had only a two litre engine, and with all the equipment on board it had a maximum speed of 65 mph going downhill and needed refuelling every two hundred miles. We drove very carefully because anyone sitting in the back was prone to bouts of nausea and sickness as it swayed from side to side. The idea was to have a driver, radio operator and supervisor, normally a Detective Inspector, on board, but this wasn't always the case.

In due course we received a new three-litre van and the body of the old one was literally unbolted and fitted onto the new one, saving a lot of time, effort and cost.

I manned the van single-crewed in January 1977 for seven days full surveillance during a murder enquiry in the West Mercia Force area. Dave had chosen to go to Cyprus for a winter-break. It was no fun working out of a Hereford three-star hotel, being 'on plot' from 8am until the target was 'put to bed'.

Good intelligence was obtained though, and a conviction followed later in the year.

The vehicle was also used for non-surveillance roles, such as on the 21st September 1978, when the van became the mobile HQ of 'No 4 RCS' as the Squad was seconded to the Carl Bridgwater murder enquiry. Dave and I established the vehicle in the yard of Womborne Police Station adjacent to the Incident Room. We were there for about three weeks altogether with no days off and working twelve hour shifts. We handled over 1,000 messages and calls which were all faithfully recorded on paper logs and tapes. At the end of the secondment, the Head of Staffordshire CID, Chief Superintendent ' Jock' Stewart, commended Dave and me for the professional and diligent way we had run that part of the operation.

Over the nearly 10 years I spent with the RCS it was in the main a very enjoyable and rewarding experience but there were some occasions when I thought that there must be a better way of earning a living, especially being out in the cold and wet on the Regional Crime Squad bike, a very risky operation sometimes on an 'unmarked' 1000cc machine taking calculated risks to hold a challenging surveillance operation together!

The van has long since gone, but in those days, it was a forerunner of the technological advances to come.'

Figure 22 Tony Everett & Dave Carding with 'Enterprise', late 70's, courtesy of T Everett

Figure 23 The radio room on 'Enterprise', courtesy of T Everett

Figure 24 'Enterprise' 'on tour' demonstrating to other RCS groups, courtesy of T Everett

Figure 25 The Carl Bridgewater murder enquiry, September 1978, courtesy of T Everett

1976

The Rise of The National Front

In January 1976, Her Majesty the Queen opened the National Exhibition Centre adjacent to Birmingham Airport. During the year there were 9 visits to the Force area by members of the Royal family.

Figure 26 Her Majesty and building worker Walter Denny at the NEC opening, courtesy of the Express & Star

***

On the 15th February 1976, the former offices of the Central Electricity Generating Board in Bournville, which had been acquired the previous year and renovated, were opened as the new *'B'* Division Headquarters.

***

On the 1st May 1976, the Force became responsible for the policing of Birmingham Airport, and officers selected to work there attended a bespoke one-week course at *'Tally Ho'* Police Training Centre to acquaint themselves with airport procedures.

Retired officer Tom Kenny recalls:

'Lima 3 – it was also known as the 'punishment battalion', was part of 'L2' sub-division so was staffed from there and 'L1'. I did 9 months there in 1979. The police station was a two-storey pre-fab quite near to the main terminal building. For a young man it was very boring in policing terms - the only action I can remember is dealing with fights at 'Arrivals' over the toy donkeys arriving back from Benidorm!

I remember one of the Sergeants, Jack Hague, was a really nice bloke coming to the end of his service.

The bar at the Airport was called the 'One Eleven Club' on Hanger Way and the licensee was a bloke called 'Robbo'.

We had use of a Land Rover for patrols and I remember in the Chief Inspector's office, who was Bob Lamb at the time I was there, was a lovely leather lounger.'

Retired officer Ken Marlow recalls:

'I was there, post-probation, so, August 1980 to January 1981. The other name for the Airport came from its radio call-sign – 'Echo Alpha'!

The highlight for me was the arrival of Concorde. I looked at the posting sheet for that date and discovered, to my horror, that I had been allocated 'Security of Car Park 'C', which was the big car park adjacent to the A45, just prior to the old airport entrance at Damson Lane – which is now Damson Parkway. I was talking later that day, with a much-respected colleague, who said that she had been allocated 'Security of Concorde'. She wasn't a keen photographer, and had no interest in aeroplanes, so I asked if she would mind swapping posts. She readily agreed so I rushed upstairs and saw 'The Boss', Chief Inspector Beresford, who agreed to the swap.

On the day in question, I turned up, camera and kit, in hand, and took up my posting. Later that day, I was invited on board, and had a tour of the aircraft, including the flight-deck – I was one very happy man!'

Retired officer Dave Mangan recalls:

'I was there for a six-month attachment from February to August 1983, and other than dealing with a fraudulent bus-pass, nothing happened. For a twenty-year old keen officer just out of his probation it was the posting from hell! The highlight of nights was if a delayed or diverted flight came in. The entire shift would attend arrivals and assist the baggage-handlers just for something to do and to have human contact! I too remember there being just as many toy donkeys as there were suitcases on the Spanish flights.'

***

Also in May 1976, the then Home Secretary officially opened the new Sub-Divisional Headquarters building in Stechford.

***

On the 8th May 1976, placard-waving demonstrators maintained a noisy vigil outside Winson Green Prison, as race-campaigner Robert Relf began a hunger-strike in his cell. Relf had been jailed for contempt of court for ignoring a court order to remove the *'For Sale'* sign he had erected outside his house in Cowdray Close, Leamington Spa, Warwickshire. The sign had originally read, *'Viewing. To avoid animosity, all round, positively no coloureds'*, before Relf amended it to read, *'For sale to an English family only.'*

Aged 51years, he was the first person jailed under the new Race Relations Act, and was sentenced to a year and a day for defying a court-order to remove the offending sign. He had instantly become a *'cause celebre'* that right-wing groups had seized upon to mobilise their supporters onto the streets.

On the 15th May 1976, rival demonstrations took place outside Winson Green Prison over the jailing of Relf. In the end the police charged, and quelled the *'Battle of Winson Green'*, by throwing themselves between National Front demonstrators and left-wing protestors organized by the Anti-Fascist Committee.

12 officers were taken to Dudley Road Hospital and several had stitches put in wounds whilst many injured police officers refused hospital treatment. A girl was also taken to hospital, and police made 28 arrests. Prisoners were taken to Handsworth, Ladywood and Smethwick Police Stations and all were charged and later bailed. One of those arrested was a leading member of the International Socialist Movement.

Police trying to prevent the Winson Green flare-up, at first faced hundreds of National Front demonstrators demanding the release of Relf. Left-wing protestors, more than 1000 strong, then weaved their way towards the prison from the opposite direction.

Police tried to divert the left-wingers onto a demolition site but were caught out when the marchers continued straight on. They were only halted when a police cordon five-deep trapped the demonstrators in a side-street.

The frustrated left-wingers, who had been screaming, *'Death to the National Front'*, began throwing stones, bottles and bricks in a barrage against police ranks. The main battle was in Franklin Street and Foundry Road, and police ranks bulged until a baton-charge by mounted police officers forced the mob back.

When the police horses failed to clear the street completely, a number of police motorcyclists began a *'motorized cavalry charge'*, sweeping protesters before them along the pavements.

An ambulance trying to reach an injured policeman in Franklin Street came under attack, and house windows were smashed, as police officers ran to the rear of homes to collect dustbin lids to use as shields. 3 police motorcyclists escorted a car from the street as one family made their break to safety.

More than 50 windows were smashed by house bricks and lumps of concrete, and it was some time before the lines of police managed to disperse the demonstrators and restore an uneasy peace to the streets. A large number of the Anti-Fascist demonstrators then re-formed and marched back along its original route to the Handsworth area.

A lot of the injured were police officers from the Walsall area who had caught the brunt of the brick barrage, and several left the hospital heavily bandaged. In all, 69 police officers were injured, 16 of whom subsequently reported sick, 2 police horses injured and 4 police vehicles damaged. There was a report of another civilian injury when an innocent passer-by had his car damaged, and his collarbone broken. The operation in Winson Green was completed by 4.30pm.

Whilst the *'Battle of Winson Green'* raged, Robert Relf had been moved from Winson Green to Stafford Prison on the orders of Home Secretary Roy Jenkins, a few hours before the demonstrations began.

On their way back to Manchester from Winson Green 50 National Front supporters demonstrated for three quarters of an hour outside Stafford Prison.

Figure 27 Courtesy of the Express & Star

***

On the 2nd July 1976, PC Colin Clive Nicholls, aged thirty-eight years, died as a result of serious injuries when involved in a road traffic accident.

***

On the 31st July 1976, PC Michael George Hewitt, aged thirty-seven years, was fatally injured in a motorcycle accident while travelling to work.

Figure 28 Michael Hewitt, courtesy of his daughter, Lesley Hewitt

***

On Saturday 25th September 1976, two rallies were planned in Walsall by the National Front and the International Socialist Party, in the run-up to the election campaign to contest the disgraced MP John Stonehouse's parliamentary seat. The National Front march was timed to commence at 3pm, and its route took in the outskirts of the town, terminating at T. P. Riley School, in Lichfield Road, Bloxwich, for a meeting.

The International Socialists rally, attended by up to 1,000 supporters, was originally timed to commence at 1.30pm with the apparent intention of leaving Walsall Town Centre in time to disrupt the National Front event, which attracted some 1,500 supporters.

Although police were successful in changing the time of the second rally, with a view to avoiding a confrontation, over 100 demonstrators left the International Socialist event early to make their way to Bloxwich.

A total of 962 officers were deployed to police both events.

Throughout no persons were injured, and no damage occurred to property, however 20 persons were arrested for obstruction, or disorderly conduct, from the International Socialists' group, as they tried to break through police cordons which had been put in place to keep the two groups apart.

The Chief Constable Philip Knights took personal charge of the officers on the ground, while his Deputy Maurice Buck commanded a 'Special Operations Room' on the top floor of Walsall Police Divisional Headquarters in Green Lane. He confirmed that it had been the biggest operation carried out by the Force since the *'Birmingham Pub Bombings'*.

In order to carry out the operation, bus-loads of officers were ferried along the respective routes shadowing the demonstrators, ready to be deployed in the event of trouble, whilst 20 officers had been deployed to occupy the school on the Friday afternoon after pupils had left. Officers remained in situ overnight.

Police guard rival marches

Hundreds of National Front members and their left-wing opponents were in Walsall today for rival marches and demonstrations.

International Socialists marched through Walsall's main immigrant areas in a demonstration against racialism.

At the same time the National Front assembled two miles away for an anti-immigration rally.

Police were out in force to supervise both marches, but the routes had been planned to avoid a direct confrontation between the rival groups.

About 1,000 International Socialists met at the gates of Palfrey Park.

Centre

Later they marched through the Caldmore area, with its high immigrant population, into Walsall town centre.

But a splinter group of more than 100 left the main march to hold a counter demonstration near the National Front assembly point.

The National Front with support from its branches all over the country gathered at Wolverhampton Road near the Bentley motorway interchange.

Its march was not into Walsall town centre, but through the Beechdale housing estate to Bloxwich where a rally was being held at T. P. Riley School in Lichfield Road to adopt Mr Charles Parker as the National Front's prospective candidate for the Walsall North by-election.

The International Socialists also plan to have a candidate in the election, expected later this year, to fill the vacancy caused by the resignation of John Stonehouse.

Figure 29 Courtesy of the Express & Star

March rivals kept at long arm's length

A massive police operation defused what one officer described as "a bomb with a very short fuse" when rival groups of political extremists held marches in Walsall. Twenty people were arrested and charged with assault and obstruction.

Rallies had been arranged at the same time by the National Front and the International Socialist — and 1,300 police moved into the town.

The arrests were made on Saturday afternoon at the National Front anti immigration march wound its way through Bloxwich and on to a rally at the T. P. Riley School.

Those arrested have been bailed and will appear this week before Walsall magistrates.

Earlier, there had been an incident free march by about 1,000 International Socialist and other left-wing group through Walsall.

Flanked by hundreds of police officers, the procession made its way to Blue Lane chanting incessantly "Smash the National Front."

SCUFFLE

Trouble started when a splinter group of about 100 ran off to Bloxwich Lane where about 2,000 National Front supporters were assembling.

A strong police patrol met them before they got there and there was a brief scuffle as the first few arrests were made.

At the T. P. Riley School almost all the police available ringed the complex of buildings, and a double line of officers, supported by mounted police and dog handlers, guarded the entrance.

They kept out about 200 left wingers who had made their way from Walsall after the meeting had broken up. They had been addressed by the prospective Socialist Worker candidate, Mr Jimmy McCullum.

After about an hour chanting outside the school, police ordered them to disperse and Mr McCullum was seen to tell them to leave peacefully.

The National Front meeting adopted Mr Charlie Parker prospective candidate for Walsall North seat, vacated by Mr John Stonehouse.

Special branch officers filmed incidents through both marches.

Figure 30 Courtesy of Express & Star

***

In 1976 there was an increase in the authorised establishment of the Force of 38, making a total of 6,509 officers, to take account of the policing of Birmingham Airport. Although 604 men and women joined the Force, the level of wastage was high, with many officers reaching pensionable age after 30 years' service, accelerated by added service in HM Forces, and 411 officers left.

Just one officer joined the Force on the Graduate Entry Scheme, whilst 8 university graduates joined the Force as ordinary entrants.

The strength of female officers in the Force rose by 30%, from a low base the previous year, to a total of 440 women.

During the year assaults on police officers increased to 565.

A total of 125,148 crimes were recorded in 1976, which was an increase of 2.4% on the previous year, whilst the detection rate was 38.5%.

Yet again, a third of all crime related to vehicles, and the Force Stolen Vehicle Squad targeted the top end of the criminal market as 151 arrests were made and 82 stolen vehicles recovered by the dedicated team, which also provided a vehicle examination service to Divisions. This led to the identification of a further 123 stolen vehicles.

During the course of the year, a total of 26,706 scenes of crime, and motor vehicles, were examined for fingerprints and forensic evidence by the Scenes of Crime Department, whilst the Fingerprint Department made 1,181 identifications from submissions made, and the Photographic Department produced 128,100 photographic prints for court purposes, as well as responding to 4,412 requests for assistance from Divisions and Departments.

Peter Hancox started work at the Birmingham City Police Fingerprint Bureau at Lloyd House in February 1971. From 1974 it became known as the West Midlands Police Fingerprint Bureau. He eventually retired in March 2015, so his working career in fingerprints spanned 44 years. This is his recollection:

'During that time I saw some profound changes, one of the main ones being all police officers leaving the department by the late eighties/early nineties.

The biggest change however, came in about 1992 with the advent of the 'NAFIS' system (National Automated Fingerprint Identification System). The previous manual system of fingerprint identification was by its very nature time-consuming, costly and difficult to maintain i.e. the single fingerprint collections and the two-hand collections.

Life in the Bureau – 1974 – 1995; police officers and civilians both working in the same department, was not a perfect scenario in my experience. Most of the time we got on okay, but sometimes if the spectre of pay and conditions came up there could, to put it mildly, be differences of opinion. It was felt by many that police officers were far better off financially due to their pay and conditions, and yet they were doing the same job as civilians within the Bureau.

Socially there was a better atmosphere – football matches between the 'Good Guys' (cops) and the 'Bad Guys' (the civvies), took place and were much appreciated.

Figure 31 Flyer for a football game, courtesy of P Hancox

During lunch-breaks, great card games including 'Niggle' were played by a mixture of staff, and darts tournaments were also a favourite lunch-time entertainment. Even carpet-bowls happened now and then.

Looking back most of the police officers in the Bureau were great but there were some who did not like civilians.

The Fingerprint Bureau was on the third floor at Lloyd House Police Headquarters, and later moved to another floor in the building.

Whilst on the third floor, it was adjacent to MIDCRO (Midland Regional Criminal Record Office) Back in the 'Seventies', before P.N.C. was widely used, all criminal records for the region, (Birmingham, Staffordshire, Warwickshire, West Mercia, Leicestershire, Northamptonshire and Shropshire), were kept at MIDCRO in big A4-sized tins.

MIDCRO was staffed again by a mixture of civilians and police officers and a Superintendent was in charge, I think Colin Powell was in post at one stage.

In the Fingerprint Bureau a Chief Inspector was in charge and in the 'Seventies' it was 'Johnny' Johnson.

After the police left the Bureau the top job was civilianized, with Ray Broadstock being in charge for many years.

MIDCRO was eventually replaced at County level, when every police force set up their own Fingerprint Bureaus, and the P.N.C. became the main source of criminal record information, not bits of paper in metal boxes.

Civilian life in the Bureau was at times dominated by 'Establishment Reviews', which sometimes took up to two years to complete. The point of interest for us 'civvies' was the possibility of being re-graded. At one time the Birmingham Bureau rates of pay were among the worst in the country. This was a cause of great concern with some staff leaving to take up new careers and others transferring to other bureaus, such as two who went to work at West Mercia.

Figure 32 Card for staff that left for West Mercia Fingerprint Bureau, courtesy of P Hancox

Another great change, though a gradual one in the Bureau, was the influx of female staff. Back in 1971 there was only one female – a typist. Gradually a few female police officers joined the fingerprint staff, followed by more female civilians. By the time I retired in 2015, half of the Bureau staff were female, and many of them had trained and qualified as Fingerprint experts.'

Anya Small nee Layton reflects on her experiences in the department:

'I joined the West Midlands Police Fingerprint Bureau in 1994, and trained as a Fingerprint Classifier. In those days we searched fingerprint collections manually in large filing cabinets before computerised matching systems were introduced. I have great memories of training courses at the National Training Centre in Durham and 'nail-biting' practical examinations sifting through piles of inked fingerprints in preparation for the real work. We also had gruelling cross-examinations to prepare us for giving court evidence, which I only did once in my career in fingerprints of ten years, during which time I became a Fingerprint Expert and then went into management. I eventually became the Digital Forensics Manager for the Force.'

Figure 33 Anya Small nee Layton on Initial Fingerprint course 4/1994, courtesy of A Small

Peter Cox continues:

'During the 'Seventies', we were involved in a number of crimes which hit the headlines nationally. Our job in the Fingerprint Bureau was to help to solve crimes and I recall Chief Inspector Johnson once telling me 'the purpose and job of the Fingerprint Bureau is to identify finger, thumb, and palm impressions found at the scene of crimes, to assist the CID in their investigations.'

In the years of manual searching methods, (SFP + 2H collections), a serious crime fingerprint mark would take priority, and this meant that normal work in connection with less serious matters was delayed, with work often piling up.

One time-consuming job was the hunt for the so-called 'Black Panther' – Donald Neilson. This sticks out in my memory because I spent seven months in 1974/75 working on fingerprint work connected to the case, which initially surrounded the killing of three Sub Post-Office Managers, and then moved onto the kidnapping of Lesley Whittle.

Following the discovery of her body at Bathpool Park, in a large drainage shaft, certain items which had been left by Neilson were forensically recovered. One of these was a small 'Woolworths' note-pad, and a fingerprint on the pad was developed through the use of a chemical – probably ninhydrin. It was not a brilliant mark but it was searchable and the work of manually going through thousands and thousands of fingerprints on record was a mammoth task.

Then 'out of the blue' Neilson was arrested by two police officers in Nottinghamshire.

All of the Bureaus, if I remember correctly, had copies of the same mark from the 'Woolworths' pad and when it was compared with his fingerprints at the Nottinghamshire Fingerprint Bureau it matched with Neilson's.

We held our breath for fear that somehow we might have missed identifying him however it turned out that he was not on our fingerprint records at all, having previously only come to notice for a minor traffic offence.

Other serious jobs involving fingerprints included the Carl Bridgewater murder at Yew Tree Farm in 1978.

Talking about pressure, another part of the job for Fingerprint Experts was to prepare and give evidence in court. I did so on more than twenty occasions during my career. One day you could be in the 'cosy' Bureau searching, with no-one bothering you, and next day you could be at court in the witness box.

When this did happen the 'pressure was on' as you were totally on your own. If it was at Crown Court you had at least twenty eyes looking at you, and you had to be in a position to know exactly what you were talking about. The elated feeling after finally being discharged from 'the box' was great!

Enlargements or 'charts' were taken to court by Fingerprint Experts in many cases. The photographic work involved added pressure and was very time consuming. Fortunately by 1981 they were no longer required unless requested by a Judge.

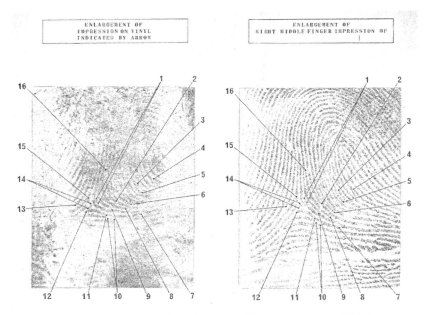

| ENLARGEMENT OF IMPRESSION ON VINYL INDICATED BY ARROW | ENLARGEMENT OF RIGHT MIDDLE FINGER IMPRESSION OF |

Figure 34 Fingerprint Identification Chart, courtesy of P Hancox

Working as a Fingerprint Expert was an unusual job, but a job which held my attention and interest for a huge part of my life.

Apart from work in the Bureau, I had for a while, an additional voluntary duty. I produced 'forensic art' – as a 'Police Artist'. It was a difficult job involving interviewing victims or witnesses to serious crimes, and drawing 'offenders' faces for TV, newspapers etc.....that's another story!'

Figure 35 Peter Hancox in more recent times, courtesy of P.Hancox

The Fingerprint Bureau did indeed produce many opportunities for civilian staff, later to become known as police staff, to develop and prosper. One such individual who commenced working for the West Midlands Police Fingerprint Bureau on the 16th November 1987, was Richard Small, who started as a Fingerprint Assistant before moving on to become a Fingerprint Expert in 1994.

(Postscript: Richard Small ultimately progressed into supervisory and management roles from 2001 and became Head of Bureau in 2007. In 2010 he was appointed A/Head of Forensic Services, overseeing all forensic disciplines and made permanent in that role in 2014)

Figure 36 Advert for WMP Fingerprint Assistant in August 1987, courtesy of R Small

Figure 37 Richard Small on Advanced Fingerprint Course 4/94, courtesy of R.Small

The number of persons killed on the roads in 1976 increased to 239, as 66,307 offenders were prosecuted during the year for motoring offences committed on the 3,782 miles of road within the Force area, which included 42 miles of motorway.

31 cases of homicide were recorded, of which 30 were classified as murder and one as manslaughter. Just two such cases remained unsolved by the end of the year.

One of the frustrations encountered by police officers at that time related to false alarm calls. During the year, 1,512 new burglar alarms were installed bringing the total to 14,180 in the Force area. Police responses to alarm activations resulted in 548 persons being arrested, but regrettably, there were 35,602 false alarm calls which led to a lot of wasted police time. This resulted in a new policy being formulated towards the end of year which led to the withdrawal of a policing response should faults not be rectified.

Another big drain on manpower was the number of persons reported missing to the police, each case of which required the filing of reports and investigation. A total of 8,748 persons were reported missing during the year by the end of which 290 people remained unaccounted for.

In 1976, the development of a fully staffed Prosecuting Solicitors Department took place, a service provided by the West Midlands County Council. During the year, 26,536 cases were referred to the service by the police as officers started to withdraw from the process of presenting their own cases in court.

1977

The 'Ladywood Riots'

During 1977, Her Majesty the Queen, accompanied by Prince Philip, paid a Jubilee visit to the West Midlands. Starting at Wolverhampton she visited all 7 Metropolitan Districts and concluded with a banquet at the National Exhibition Centre. Some 1,900 officers were deployed to the operation during the course of the day. 8 other visits were conducted in the West Midlands by members of the Royal Family during the year.

***

In April a Force 'Robbery Squad' was formed, as a temporary measure, to try to stem an increase in this type of offence. Whilst the team did enjoy an element of success, the number of offences still increased by the end of the year by 30%, with more than 1,000 offences committed.

The team worked closely with the Regional Crime Squad and Serious Crime Squad and arrested 27 persons, clearing 43 offences of robbery.

***

On the 22nd July 1977, PC Bernard Henry Church, aged forty-five years, collapsed at a police station.

Retired officer Alan Taylor recalls:

'Bernard was known as 'Bunnie' in the job and was an ex- Royal Navy diver. This led him to becoming a member of Force Underwater Search Unit. At the time of his death he was a police motorcyclist on Western Traffic based at Walsall Police Station, where I was also working, although not on the same shift.

I went into work on the day of his death and saw him sat at a desk in our office before I went off to sort some things out elsewhere in the building. I heard sirens and then when I went back to the office it transpired that Bernard had collapsed suddenly and been taken by ambulance to hospital.

Unfortunately, Bernard died of a heart attack and it came as a great shock to us. He lived and worked in Walsall so was very much one of the locals – a very quiet man but someone who was very easy to get on with. A great shame to go at such an early age.'

***

On the 5th August, the Home Secretary opened the new sub-divisional police station at Wednesbury.

***

On the 15th August 1977, a political meeting was held by the National Front at Boulton Road School in connection with a by-election which was to be held for the Ladywood constituency 3 days later. This time their opponents were the Socialist Workers Party.

When the National Front supporters bypassed the demonstrators by using a back door into the school, the counter-demonstrators attacked police lines with a variety of weapons. Of the 400 officers on duty, 58 were injured, 6 of them seriously.

Up to 300 people attempted to storm Thornhill Road Police Station in Handsworth, where ten people had been detained after being arrested following public order incidents and 'looting' in the Ladywood area. Police used riot shields for the first time in the Force area when they came under a barrage of bricks and other missiles. One officer, Sergeant Sue Bailey, was hailed as a heroine when she turned herself into a 'human shield' to protect an injured colleague, PC Selwyn Bowen, from missiles.

Figure 38 Courtesy of the Express & Star

***

On the 28th August 1977, Sergeant Peter James Brett, aged thirty-two years, died after being fatally injured in a road traffic collision whilst on duty.

***

On the 23rd December 1977, Sergeant Louis Henry Bennett, aged fifty-seven years, died as a result of injuries sustained in a road traffic accident on his way to work.

***

The Force suffered a net loss of 22 officers during the year, although general unemployment was at it its highest level, and despite recruiting a total of 465 new recruits. Poor pay and conditions, compared to other forms of employment, was blamed in part for the recruitment difficulties.

51 of the 988 police officers assaulted during the course of the year were female officers.

Of these 367 were classed as serious assaults, including one for attempt murder and 28 for inflicting grievous bodily harm.

During 1997, 7 demonstrations had to be policed to prevent possible political confrontation. 3 marches were organised by the National Front, with the remainder by those opposed to their politics. In addition students, trade unions and other protesters held a number of marches which posed the potential for public order problems and as such still required the deployment of considerable police resources.

Also, during the year, the first national strike was called by the National Union of Firemen which, whilst orderly throughout, placed even more demand on stretched police services.

Finally, a total of 232 football matches had to receive special policing attention, with 5 First Division clubs situated in the Force area. All this was at a time when the age-profile of the Force was rapidly changing and many of the resources available were probationer Constables with less than two years' service.

During the year, with assistance from the *'Barrow and Geraldine S Cadbury Trust'*, a report titled *'Shades of Grey'* was prepared by John Brown of the Cranfield Institute of Technology, which examined the relationship between the police and the community in Handsworth.

***

57

In 1977, the number of crimes recorded rose to an unprecedented 154,141 offences, an increase of 29,000 crimes or 23.2% compared to the previous year. A total of 51,231 offences were detected, giving an overall Force rate of 33.2%. Nearly 30% of the detected offences were committed by juveniles.

25 cases of murder were recorded with all bar one shown as detected, plus 3 cases of manslaughter which were detected.

There were no incidents of terrorism recorded in the year, but despite this, officers from the Explosives and Firearms Department attended 287 incidents where suspect objects were found as the Force remained on high alert.

The Force's Special Plain Clothes Department was dedicated to dealing with aspects of more serious vice and provided advice to Divisions.

A total of 733 prostitutes were cautioned and 495 prosecuted. In addition 26 persons were prosecuted for keeping brothels, 29 for living off immoral earnings and 15 in connection with the publication of obscene articles.

A total of 239 people lost their lives in road accidents, whilst 13,721 were injured.

During the course of the year, the Summons & Warrants Departments operating within the Force oversaw the execution of 57,335 warrants, which included 9,971 warrants executed on behalf of other Forces. Monies collected by the Warrants Departments totalled nearly £700,000 in unpaid fines.

George Layton, the late father of co-author Michael Layton was appointed as the first civilian Enforcement Officer/Process Server working within the Department. He served initially with the Birmingham City Police from the 1st April 1972, and retired from West Midlands Police as a Senior Enforcement Officer on the 15th March 1991. Sadly he is no longer with us.

Sharon Layton, his daughter, recalls:

'I was working in the general administration at Victoria Law Courts and sometimes went out with my father during the evenings to collect fines or execute warrants. He had a very good rapport with people and treated them with respect. He once went to an address in Showell Green Lane to execute a warrant and got more than he bargained for when he found the occupant dead in the house! He also used to go out a lot to execute warrants with a police dog-handler called George McDonald, who would always go to the back of the address with the dog whilst dad knocked on the front door.

George would frequently emerge from the back with the prisoner after they had unsuccessfully tried to escape. On one occasion they had a particularly violent prisoner who finished up occupying the spare cage in the dog van with the Alsatian in the cage next to him!

I recently spoke to two former colleagues from the Fines & Fees Department, Lynn Selby and Carol Hill, about Dad and they described him as a 'gentleman, approachable, who had common-sense, was likeable and down-to-earth'.

Figure 39 Civilian Warrant Officer George Layton in Summons & Warrants Office, circa 1970's, courtesy of S Layton

Figure 40 Staff of Summons & Warrants Office in Steelhouse Lane, late 1980's / early 1990's, courtesy of S Layton

The Force was serviced by 9 Coroners who dealt with 9,454 reported deaths during the course of the year. Post-mortem examinations were carried out in 7,114 cases, and 1,342 inquests were held. H.M. Coroners were supported by dedicated Coroners officers.

In a twelve-month period the Force's fleet of 1,016 vehicles travelled a total of 16,760,000 miles during which they were involved in 1,552 accidents, of which in 453 cases the police driver was found to be blameworthy. In addition, 139 vehicles were the subject of criminal damage, 31 of which occurred in one day on the occasion of large-scale disorder at a public meeting.

Plans were finalised for a completely new VHF radio system, as a project gathered pace in relation to a new Command and Control system, as the Force responded to 199,902 emergency calls during 1977.

1978

The 'Battle of Digbeth'

On 18th February 1978, a meeting of the Young National Front took place at Digbeth Civic Hall, near to Birmingham City Centre. Up to 5000 anti-National Front demonstrators tried to breach police cordons at the Civic Hall as they broke away from a pre-arranged march route around the venue. A group of up to 300 subsequently attacked police officers and caused damage to buildings and motor vehicles.

Police officers forming part of the cordons outside the Civic Hall came under a sustained barrage of missiles which included pieces of broken slabs. 11 police officers were hurt and the windows of an ambulance were smashed as the vehicle tried to get to the injured officers. Despite the ferocity of the attacks the police lines held firm.

Over 2,200 officers were on duty, including many from surrounding Forces on Mutual Aid from West Mercia, Staffordshire and Warwickshire Police. For the first time a helicopter was deployed, fitted with closed circuit television used for evidence gathering, and it was necessary to deploy protective shields.

Retired officer Chris Rowe recalls:

'I was on the Special Patrol Group at the time. It was the first time that the long shields were used, and on the Thursday, myself, Sgt Eddie Isaacs and Phil Allan, toured local timber merchants asking for surplus off-cuts that could be used for training purposes. The following day, Friday, the whole of the WMP Special Patrol Group gathered in the rear yard of Shirley Police Station and underwent training with the use of the brand-new shields. I'm so glad that we had that training day because we were spread across the dual carriageway in our teams of five or six, carrying three shields to the front. The demonstrators were ripping up concrete flag stones from the central reservation, breaking them up and together with bricks, hurling them at the police cordon. With minimal personal protection there were quite a few minor injuries but PC Eddie Alden received a fractured skull after being hit by one of the missiles.'

Retired officer Pete Keys recalls:

'John Swain and I were on duty at Digbeth earlier that day, and not part of the police operation, but we went for a look around to see what was going on. It was not far from Rea Street when a lot of the demonstrators all ran down Bradford Street. As John Swain walked round a corner he was hit in the mouth by a brick knocking some teeth out which were subsequently replaced with a set of false ones.

His 'party trick' used to be to drop the plate in your beer if you were not watching!' We did get a 'telling off' for being there when we were not meant to be though!'

Retired officer Julie Maley reflects on a human aspect of the day:

'I remember that day very well. It was the Saturday before I got married. The policewomen on the section were posted to side-roads on traffic duties to avoid the demonstration. Things got quite 'hairy' and I was called in to man the front-office by Inspector Roger Conway, to prevent any injury so close to the wedding. As things got worse, he called in other important wedding guests too. He was a well-respected 'gaffer'. Although I was keen to stay out, I did appreciate his concern for us.'

Retired officer Derek Rowe recalls:

I remember the 'Battle of Digbeth' well. I believe it was the first time we ever used shields in 'battle'. The mob was throwing engineering bricks at us, dug up from the central reservation. PC John Caves 3266 was next to me and got one on the head. His police helmet saved his life.'

Retired officer Lyndon Whitehouse also recalls:

'I had just completed the first week of my local procedure course at Walsall. All leave was cancelled and this turned out to be my first deployment on the streets. Not fully-trained, I had the second week to complete! I remember quite a lot about it. Philip Knights was there. We were issued with plastic visors and told not to use them unless we had acid sprayed at us. I'm sure the SPG were deployed with shields for the first time. Ivan Geffen, a well-known solicitor from Walsall was walking up and down the police lines, being quite polite. I was in a cordon outside the town hall and we were subjected to missile attacks.'

A subsequent editorial in the 'Birmingham Post' reflected, 'police stood up stoically to the barrage of abuse and missiles and did nothing to feed the febrile minds of those who would have loved to have accused them of brutality.'

500 rioters fail to break cordon
Police blame 'hard core' for rally clashes

Officers rush to help a colleague hit by a brick.

Police today blamed a hard core of militants for the fury that erupted during Saturday's anti-National Front demonstration in Birmingham, in which 19 policemen were injured.

A breakaway group of about 500 demonstrators charged a police line in a bid to lay siege to Digbeth Civic Hall where the Front was holding its first youth rally.

The rioters hurled bricks, bottles, cans, fireworks and lumps of concrete at police armed with plastic shields.

Two officers — Constables Edward Alden and Peter Burrell — were still in hospital today with head wounds. At least three civilians were injured.

Violence flared when the militants mainly teenagers, broke away from a protest

Singing fans kicked out

A dozen singing teenagers were ordered from the rally by the Front's national organiser Martin

Police face the bricks behind riot shields.

Foster | Prince

Figure 41 Courtesy of the Express & Star

***

On the 1st April 1978, the Birmingham Divisions were restructured and the number of Divisions was reduced from 6 to 5, with the sub-divisions being increased from 12 to 14. The Central Division of the Force ceased to be known as the *'A'* Division after 135 years, and became the *'F'* Division.

Across the Force the number of territorial Divisions was thus reduced from 12 to 11, and the number of Sub-Divisions increased from 29 to 31.

This restructuring process also saw the introduction on each sub-division of either one, or two, double-crewed *'First Response Vehicles'* which became commonly known as *'Zulu'* cars due to their call-signs - some 40 vehicles in total.

Their drivers were trained to advanced standards and the vehicles equipped with a VHF radio to allow the Force Control Room to direct them if necessary.

Retired officer Derek Rowe recalls:

'When the Area car, (First Response), system was 'bolted' on to the Unit Beat/Panda system I was 'in on the ground floor' as it were, having just successfully completed an advanced during course. I was posted to 'D' unit at Steelhouse Lane and was working with PC 2271 Jeffrey Barley, a partnership that endured until June 1980 when I went onto the Central Motorway Patrol Group. We were a great team, got on from day one and were very productive in terms of work/prisoners.'

Figure 42 Derek Rowe with 'Zulu' car, 1978, courtesy of D Rowe

Derek Rowe continues:

'One night in 1979, we were sent to a fire-brigade turnout on the top-floor of a tower block in Newtown. The occupant was preventing fire-fighters from entering the burning flat by waving a large machete about. Jeff and I arrived on scene to find a young, very agitated guy waving a big knife. We managed to take it off him, without getting decapitated, arrested him, and left the brigade members to fight the fire.

He was taken to Steelhouse Lane where he was very thoroughly searched again - woe betide any officer who didn't do this properly! He was placed in a cell and I went off to type the report. A few minutes later, I was greeted by the Lock-Up Duty Inspector who showed me to the cell occupied by our prisoner, who was sitting on the bed shivering and thoroughly wet, with charring to the legs of the jeans he was wearing.

It appeared he had set himself on fire and quick-acting staff had 'put him out' before he sustained any injury. I was told he had secreted a number of matches up his anus. Even Lock-Up staff hadn't found them.

The lad was committed under The Mental Health Act and we later transported him to Highcroft Mental Hospital.'

***

On the 1st April 1978, approximately 50 senior Special Constables were compulsorily retired and a new rank structure introduced. In some cases officers had served from the early 1930s. The majority saw service during the Second World War and were a valued asset when areas were subjected to nightly air-attacks.

During the year, Special Constables adopted their new grade insignia, together with shoulder-flashes and diced cap bands, providing a clear distinction between the uniform worn by regular officers and that of Special Constables.

The strength of the Special Constabulary by the end of the year was 745, which included 100 female officers.

In April, a Technical Support Unit was established, with Home Office approval, to provide expertise and equipment of a technical nature to police forces in No 3 Region. Based at West Midlands Police HQ, it was staffed by a professional Technical Officer, seconded from the Home Office, and 4 other members of staff.

***

On the 21st May 1978, PC Brian Lawrence Phillips, aged thirty-five years, was fatally injured when his patrol car was struck by another police car as they were responding to a call.

Brian was a member of 'C' Unit at Stechford Police Station, who were devastated by his death. At his subsequent funeral at Yardley Crematorium there was a mass turn-out of officers from the Division to pay their respects, including Superintendent Derek Owen who was known to many as simply *'D.O'*.

Retired officer Paul Hooton recalls:

'Brian was a popular 'Geordie', a good practical police officer, who died in a tragic accident with another police car.'

Figure 43 Brian Phillips, courtesy of Debbie Menzel

***

On the 10th June, an Anti-Racist march was held in Wolverhampton.

***

On the 10th August 1978, PC Phillip Mark Sanderson, aged twenty years, died in a patrol car crash while responding to an assistance call.

PC Sanderson had been in the Force for just 9 months, when the car he was in hit a tree in Holbrook Lane, Coventry. Officers were responding to a call that 3 youths had been seen acting suspiciously in Holbrook Lane itself.

At the time the media reported that he had been described by colleagues as one of the most popular at Stoney Stanton Road Police Station, where he was based.

Retired officer Tom Duffin recalls:

'Phil Sanderson was born in Coventry. He went to Cauldon Castle school and was so pleased to join the police and thoroughly enjoyed his career. He was a Probationary officer and working as the observer in a 'First Response' vehicle when they received an urgent 999 call. The vehicle skidded on a wet road surface and tragically Phil lost his life. (R.I.P.) I saw Phil socially just before he died. It was his passion for the job that confirmed to me that I had made the right decision to apply to join the police.

He was a friend, a strong young man with a thirst for life and a passion for helping others.'

(Postscript: On the 3rd October 2004, a service was held at St Pauls Cathedral in London to remember up to 200 officers who had died on duty, including PC Sanderson. The event was part of a National Police Memorial event.)

***

On the 11th August 1978, a medical photographer who worked at the University of Birmingham Medical School, by the name of Janet Parker, fell ill. She died a month later and became the last known person on record to die of smallpox in the UK. On the day of her funeral the hearse was escorted by police cars in case of an accident, such was the fear that the disease created.

One theory put forward was that she had most likely been accidentally exposed to a strain of the smallpox virus that had been grown in a research laboratory on the floor below her workplace. This was later disputed in a court case under the Health and Safety Act.

Eventually over 500 people were placed in quarantine in their homes for two weeks as a precautionary measure.

Retired officer Adrian (Ada) Howles recalls:

'I remember the smallpox scare in Birmingham well. On one occasion the whole of 'D' Unit in the city centre, who were working a set of nights, were awoken at about 11am and told to attend the Public Health Department in town, to be vaccinated. When I got there virtually the whole of my shift was also there, and it was all down to a stolen car we had stopped during the previous night duty. We arrested the occupants, one of whom should have been in quarantine because of the smallpox.

Sometime after the death of the member of staff at the Medical School, one of the individuals involved in the research committed suicide. When the scare blew over, the Minister of Health deemed that the Medical School's provisions for storing the smallpox virus should be transported to a hospital in London. Together with a Traffic officer I had the job of transferring it from Birmingham to London.'

Birmingham was officially declared free of smallpox in October, and two years later the World Health Organisation declared that smallpox had been eradicated globally.

***

On the 2nd September an Anti-Nazi League march was held in Handsworth.

***

October 1978 saw the publication of the first edition of the *'Beacon'*, the new Force newspaper, which the Chief Constable hoped would play a part in *'further welding together of all the components which go to make up the West Midlands Police'*.

On the 4th October, the Castle Vale project commenced. It consisted of a Sergeant and 5 Constables being dedicated to work on the estate, which had an estimated population in excess of 20,000, many of whom were living in high-rise flats. The estate had a reputation for high levels of crime and vandalism, some of which were committed by lifestyle criminals who lived within the communities there.

The officers initially worked from an empty ground-floor flat in one of the blocks, with the emphasis being on high-profile foot patrols in the area.

Retired officer, Rod *'Smudger'* Smith, was the epitome of the 'local community beat bobby' in the area, and this is his story:

'Castle Vale estate was created in the 1950s and 60s. I remember some of the flats being built and in time there were more than 30 tower blocks and 6 pubs on the estate, which wasn't much more than a square mile, with 26,000 residents living in a warren of alleyways and cul-de-sacs.

I joined Birmingham City Police in 1960 as a seventeen year-old Police Cadet and served predominantly on the 'D' Division, with postings at Aston, Erdington, Sutton Coldfield and Castle Vale, where, on and off, I served more than seventeen years of my service.

In the 1970's, I used to drive there from Erdington Police Station to walk the beat.

I knew most of the local criminals on 'first name' terms, which was a big help, although it didn't stop the odd violent confrontation.

When the original full-time beat team was first created under Sergeant John Jennings in 1978, I wasn't one of the original members, but joined it later.

The original police accommodation was in Cranwell Tower. The door was made of reinforced steel with iron bars on the windows! Later on we moved to other accommodation on the estate.

In May 1987, the Birmingham Evening Mail Crime Reporter Nick Parker did an article on 'one of the City's toughest beats'. I was interviewed at the then age of forty-five years, with twelve years' of pacing the Castle Vale Estate under my belt.

I was quoted as saying, 'From our point of view the design of the estate is a nightmare. It's like a rabbit warren and offers so many avenues of escape that it is virtually unpoliceable. But it has its consolations, and the vast majority of people on the estate support the police and are as keen to stamp out the unruly elements as we are.'

The previous week to the article being published, a police car was ambushed on the estate and had stones and petrol bombs thrown at it.

Also in the article one of my colleagues PC John Wilkes, a former British Leyland maintenance fitter, described how he had lost count of the number of times the blue light had been stolen from the top of his police car, whilst patrolling on his own on the estate. He was nicknamed 'Stumpy' by local youths because he was just 5'8" tall.

Another officer, who was relatively new to the team at the time, was PC Neil Creed who was nicknamed 'Chinky' by some of the locals, and despite being beaten up by a gang on one occasion and hospitalised for a few days, enjoyed the work there.

In 1995, I was awarded the MBE in the Queen's Honours List for distinguished police service. By that time I had spent thirty-five years in uniform and found that good communication and gaining peoples trust helped me to do my job effectively. I retired in the same year.

Today there are just a couple of tower blocks left and no pubs. To this day I still have close friends on the estate and visit the area frequently.'

Figure 44 Rod 'Smudger' Smith at Buckingham Palace in 1995, courtesy of R Smith

***

On the 18th November 1978, a visit by Mrs Indira Ghandi to Birmingham required significant police resources.

***

On the 17th December, terrorism returned to the West Midlands when a bomb exploded in a pedestrian area close to the centre of Coventry. The device was estimated to have contained between 3 - 5 pounds of explosives. Damage was confined to shop windows in the area, and thankfully no-one was injured. The attack formed part of a series of attacks throughout the UK in other major cities.

***

In 1978, retired officer Roger Baker joined the Force Stolen Vehicle Squad, having previously served an attachment with the team. He recalls some of its history:

'The Stolen Vehicle Squad was created in the 1960's and was part of the City Crime Squad. Detective Sergeant Norman Harris was put in charge, and it was based in Newton Street. In the beginning there was a traffic patrol officer on the team for vehicle examinations. The first was Ron Wooding, followed by Norman Hawksford. Both were later promoted to become uniform Sergeants and moved on.

In 1965, Detective Neville Mawdsley transferred in and he eventually made Detective Inspector. The Squad remained part of the Crime Squad until West Midlands Police was formed and then moved from Newton Street to Lloyd House. Norman Harris was made Detective Inspector on the then 'F' Division and Neville Mawdsley was promoted to Detective Sergeant.

The squad then had an additional Detective Sergeant - Alan Small, and later increased by two more attached-men. D.I. Harris returned to the Squad in 1974.

I had an initial attachment to the 'SVS' and, after serving with both Divisional CID and the Anti-Terrorist Squad, I transferred in 1978, my mentor being D.S. Mawdsley.

During my time on the Squad as an operational detective I was appointed Intelligence Liaison Officer, which included the gathering of intelligence on the activities of persons involved with vehicle orientated crime. That was when I first met Detective Sergeant Layton.

I was also further tasked to lecture to both probationary officers and CID courses.

The role of operational 'SVS' officers was to conduct investigations into vehicle thefts of all descriptions and 'ringing', as well as the investigation of insurance frauds, plus the examination of vehicles to establish the identity or legitimacy of a vehicle .The work was wide and varied and crossed force boundaries, which led to working together with other forces nationally as well as internationally.

I remember many interesting investigations and the following are worthy of sharing.

I was engaged on an enquiry into the theft of Porsche cars stolen in both Milan and Strasbourg and imported into the United Kingdom before being sold onto innocent purchasers. There were two Italians involved, together with a second-hand car dealer in Birmingham. It was necessary to travel to Milan to make further enquiries about the vehicles, the suspects, and the Italian nationals.

On arrival at Milan airport, and passing through customs, we were pointed out by an armed guard, and an Italian who spoke no English led us to a Fiat car. Our luggage was thrown into the boot and we were driven at speed to a hotel in the city centre where we alighted. Our luggage was dropped on the pavement and I was handed a scrap of paper with instructions as to where we should meet our Italian police officer/translator the following morning.

We duly arrived the next morning, but the contact hadn't turned up as he was returning from an overnight visit to Switzerland - a good start. We waited and when he arrived and introductions were made it transpired he had learnt his English from 'Lingaphone' records! Things were chaotic to say the least, and during the entire week he was continually late, or wanted to work afternoon and evenings.

I managed to guide him in the right direction, but as time wore on I was aware that at police stations and record-offices we were continually watched, and it was quite apparent that there were concerns. I raised the issue with him and it transpired that the two men we were looking at were known members of the Mafia and there was a certain amount of distrust.

One investigation I was involved with was the theft of Range Rovers from the Rover Compound. The vehicles were being exported to Southern Ireland and this resulted in visits to Eire where we liaised with the Garda Siochana Stolen Vehicle Squad based in Dublin.

It was a totally different experience but very enjoyable. Everyone was very helpful and I was well looked after. On one occasion we travelled to County Waterford to a small country Garda police station staffed by a Sergeant and two Constables. On arrival there was a hand written notice on the closed station door announcing, 'Closed for dinner - we are in the pub!'' Hospitality was extended, and then we got the job done.

On another occasion we travelled to County Wexford and had arranged a meeting time. On arrival, the local Sergeant and his two officers were standing outside and when we pulled up they stood to attention. When I later asked my escort what it was all about, to my embarrassment he said that he had told them he was bringing a very important officer from Birmingham.

My contacts were very laid back and very hospitable. I always arrived, as you do, in the office at Dublin Castle at about 8.45 am. I usually had a word with the two armed Gardai on duty outside the offices, and they always had a laugh and eventually told me that the usual time of arrival was about 10.0am!

It was a very successful investigation that resulted in the recovery of stolen Range Rovers, and the conviction of the villains involved in Birmingham.'

Retired police officer Alan Small recalls:

'There was a degree of misunderstanding about the role of the Stolen Vehicle Squad in the early days of criminal investigation, and many thought it was all about climbing under dirty oily motor cars looking for chassis and engine numbers. Occasionally this was the case, but the majority of my time on the Squad, as a Detective Sergeant, was spent investigating serious crime, from murder, to organised theft of motor vehicles direct from the manufacturer, and disposing of the same in the UK and abroad. The Stolen Vehicle Squad was an integral part of the Serious Crime Squad, but had its own rank structure, headed by a Detective Chief Inspector.'

***

In 1978, the Force still had an Antecedent History Department with branches at Force HQ, Brierley Hill and Coventry. They were responsible for the preparation of the antecedent history of defendants appearing before Crown Courts.

In 1978, material was prepared for 4,421 trials, 963 committals to higher court for sentence, and 975 appeals.

During the year a Central Information Unit was set up combining the HQ Administration, the Central Convictions Department and the inclusion of a Police National Computer Bureau. They began to offer a 24 hour service to officers, as they held records on all persons living in the Force area that had been arrested, reported, and convicted of a crime and other serious offences.

In 1978 alone, proceedings were initiated in the West Midlands against 108,862 persons in respect of all types of offences committed. Of these 7,073 related to drunkenness offences and 61,514 for motoring offences.

In addition to those prosecuted, a further 6,692 persons received cautions for indictable offences, including 5,574 juveniles.

For non-indictable matters, another 1,242 persons were cautioned, which included 496 juveniles.

Also, at HQ was the Midlands Criminal Records Office, (*MIDCRO*), which consisted of a Records and Fingerprint Section.

***

Football matches placed a considerable strain on police resources with arrests being made, and officers being assaulted, during most First Division matches. The West Midlands played host at the time to 5 First Division football grounds, and the Special Patrol Group alone made 338 arrests for public order offences during the year at, or in the vicinity of these grounds.

In relation to assaults on police officers in general, a total of 1,120 members of the Force were assaulted whilst on duty, of which 474 were categorised as being of a serious nature, including one case of attempted murder and 57 cases of causing grievous bodily harm. 34 of the attacks were on female officers.

***

In 1978, The Motor Show was held at the National Exhibition Centre for the first time and involved joint working with staff from the Ministry of Transport, West Midlands Passenger Transport Executive, British Rail and the Society of Motor Manufacturers and Traders.

***

In 1978, 39 cases of murder were recorded of which 36 were detected. A further 6 deaths were recorded as manslaughter, all of which were detected.

On the roads, 242 people were killed as a result of accidents, some of which occurred due to a failure to wear seat belts, and 13,467 people were injured.

During this period, responsibility for the administration, supervision, recruitment and training of School Crossing Patrols still rested with the police, whilst the County Surveyor was responsible for the authorisation of sites. A total of 1,007 such patrols were in place by the end of the year, although there were 1,154 authorised sites, and wherever possible police officers and Traffic Wardens attempted to make up the shortfall.

1979

The 'Battle of Cronehills'

The deployment of *'Zulu'* cars did not always run smoothly, as evidenced by an accident, during bad weather, at Camp Hill, near to Birmingham City Centre in January 1979.

Figure 45 Damaged 'Zulu' car, courtesy of J Richards

***

The new Force Control Room was opened at Bournville Lane Police Station on the 4th February 1979, and at the time was viewed as one of the most sophisticated communications networks in Europe.

***

In early February officers were deployed outside the British Leyland Plant at Longbridge to contain the situation, as violence was anticipated in connection with an industrial dispute. In any event the incident passed off peacefully.

***

On the 22/23rd April 1979, DC Alexander Lawson Hamilton Forrest, aged forty-five years, suffered a heart attack, whilst on duty, and subsequently died at Coventry and Warwickshire Hospital.

DC Forrest was stationed at Fletchamstead Police Station in Coventry, and was a married man.

The officer had been on duty at a Conservative Party election meeting at St. Christopher's Primary School, Allesley Old Road. He had contacted his station by radio to say that he felt unwell, but despite this he stayed at his post until relieved, before being taken to hospital.

***

In April violence flared at a National Front meeting in West Bromwich. Officers from the West Midlands were supported by officers from 7 other Forces in violent confrontations which became known as the *'Battle of Cronehills'*.

On the 28th April 1979, a National Front election meeting took place at Cronehills Primary School in West Bromwich. On the same day, Mr Enoch Powell MP gave a speech at a public meeting in Birmingham City Centre, and the *'Rock against Racism'* movement held a torchlight procession in the evening in the city centre to protest at the activities of a local nightclub.

The police operations that ensued led to the cancellation of all leave in the Force. At the West Bromwich meeting a number of missiles were thrown at police cordons surrounding the school. The meeting broke up and 27 arrests were made.

Figure 46 Courtesy of the Express & Star

2675 officers were deployed to these demonstrations, including officers on Mutual Aid from Avon and Somerset Constabulary, Gloucestershire Constabulary, Greater Manchester Police, Leicestershire Police, Staffordshire Police, West Mercia Police and Warwickshire Police.

Retired officer Chris Rowe was a member of the Special Patrol Group between 1977 and 1979, based at Bradford Street on *'F'* Serial. He recalls an occasion when he was part of a Mutual Aid request to another Force:

'We were deployed on Mutual Aid to a National Front march in Leicester in the late 70's with a number of other Forces. I remember when Greater Manchester Police turned up, they were in green police carriers and wearing the best protective kit. Dressed like quasi-military, they were well ahead of us in appearance. On the march we had to pass some advertising hoardings, which were about twenty-feet high, behind which was some waste-ground. As we passed, house-bricks started being thrown from the waste-ground, over the hoardings and on top of us. All we could do was keep going.'

***

In May 1979, David Millichamp, who was then a Sergeant, was credited with promoting a significant change in the way the Force tackled serious crime by recommending in a report to senior CID management that the Force set up a dedicated surveillance unit.

He reflected, *'It had long been accepted that there was a need for some form of sophisticated surveillance, to be operated at Force level, in order to combat the increase in serious crimes such as blackmail, robbery and terrorism.*

A good number of officers in the Force had already completed secondments to 'No 4 Regional Crime Squad' with several of them having experience of instruction on RCS surveillance courses.

My proposal was to provide sufficient resources and technical equipment to be able to cover a sixteen-hour period of duty.

I recommended the establishment of an independent control room and the purchase of 'Pye' and 'Motorola' radios for both mobile and foot surveillance.

Based on past experience, I advised the purchase of a number of four-door saloon cars having engines of not less than 1800 cc, some of which could be three to four years old and then mechanically refurbished. In terms of a motorcycle I advised something not less than 750cc and potentially one of the popular Japanese makes.

In relation to manpower I proposed that the operational head should be a Detective Chief Inspector, who would manage two teams of surveillance operatives, and that it was important to have a mix of male and female officers.

I took the view that the Unit needed to be accommodated away from police stations to minimise the risk of operatives and vehicles being exposed, and that for the same reason they needed to be employed on a full-time basis.

My report acted as a catalyst for this type of approach and in the fullness of time the Force developed a Unit which attained national recognition for its professionalism and approach.'

Retired officer Roy Shotton recalls:

'Having received approval to proceed with putting a dedicated surveillance unit together I was approached by Dave Millichamp in 1979 whilst I was on traffic. I was an experienced motorcyclist and he asked me if I would be interested in working on the new Unit.

It sounded like an exciting challenge and I wanted to be part of it. Initially we had limited access to vehicles and even used our own, for which we were given an allowance. They were fitted with Force radios and so our first three cars were a VW Beetle, an Austin Maxi, and a Renault 4. I remember that my car was somewhat limited in terms of speed and even struggled one day to keep up with a builder's skip-lorry that we were following on the motorway!

For some time we had only one operational team but we worked hard in training to develop expertise in both foot and mobile surveillance. The team was made up of a mixture of officers who had come from Traffic, the Force Robbery Squad, ex-Crime Squad officers, Divisional staff, Regional Crime Squad, and both CID and officers who had previously worked in uniform – it was a real mix, and included two female officers.

At that time the Force was also trying to cover all eventualities and it was decided that we should receive firearms training in the use of revolvers. I passed the course to carry firearms although I don't recall actually deploying on a surveillance operation with a firearm.

We did however have to do regular re-assessments in the use of firearms and I got to know the Firearms Instructors very well.

I left the surveillance unit in 1981 due to its intensity and the effect it was having on my family-life, but did return on a number of occasions to support the Unit when they were heavily committed with particular jobs.'

Figure 47 Roy Shotton on surveillance motorcycle circa 1980, courtesy of R Shotton

***

In June 1979, terrorism returned to the West Midlands in the form of letter-bombs as 13 devices either exploded or were defused at Post Offices in the Birmingham area. This necessitated police officers checking every individual item of mail at the Central Post Office Sorting Depot in Royal Mail Street.

Retired police officer John Richards recalls this incident and also what it was like to work on the busy city centre sub-divisions:

'I was in the CID for twenty-two years from 1979 to 2001 and worked mainly from Digbeth and Steelhouse Lane Stations, on what was the 'A' Division, later to be renamed the 'F' Division. There are some things that you do forget over the years but others where the memories stay with you as if they had happened yesterday.

I had previously served at Digbeth since early 1972, working as a uniformed officer and in plain clothes, on various squads. I had early experience in 1974 of the horror and tragedy of police work with the 'Birmingham Pub Bombings'. I was one of four officers who had to sort out all the property and clothing that was recovered from the pubs. It was an extremely difficult, sad and sensitive task.

Looking back today, although items were meticulously examined and methodically listed, there were no computers, specialist equipment or even protective gloves for us to use.

Later in 1979, I was again one of a small group of officers involved in searching mailbags at the Royal Mail Sorting office, following a number of letter-bomb explosions. Again there was no specialist equipment for us to use other than a boiler suit to wear. Health and Safety was not a requirement then, indeed our directive was to search mail-bags, conveyor belts etc. and should we find anything amongst the thousands and thousands of letters that we thought suspicious, we were to alert the dog handler. He would then bring his 'expert sniffer' dog to determine if there was any explosive substance present!

In terms of major incidents you got used to expecting the unexpected. I was involved in investigating the taxi driver murder outside the 'Locarno' night-club in Hurst Street, when loads of people were arrested following a large-scale disturbance. It was so difficult because many of the witness statements described similarly dressed 'bikers' who had been involved in the fighting.

Initial interviews were carried out with all those arrested, but there was no positive evidence to implicate anyone as being the actual murderer. The suspects were released on bail whilst enquiries continued.

I can remember the chart in the Incident Room that Mike Layton, who was a Detective Sergeant at the time, had prepared with more accurate descriptions etc. I and another officer went to one suspect's house to ask him if he had a knife. He sketched his knife which matched the one that had already been recovered and identified as being the murder weapon.

The suspect, who was a member of one of the hardened and violent motorcycle-gangs involved in the incident, then showed us where he had thrown it, and on being taken to Steelhouse Lane Police Station confessed to being the murderer and then thanked us for being so decent!

In another murder case a man came into Digbeth Police Station one Saturday afternoon to report his two year-old daughter missing in the Rag Market. There was an extensive search for the child but there was no trace of her.

It transpired that he had killed her and the body was buried in Clent Hills. I think Davindra Jisra was amongst the officers who went to recover her body.

The person who reported her missing eventually admitted the murder and I took his statement in which he described in detail what he did to the child, causing her to choke to death. All because the child, his daughter, wouldn't use the potty!

I and Bruce Gilbert were working Bradford Street area one night and were called to Sergeant Geoff Mander being stabbed in Sparkhill.

We found the three offenders and chased them for ages on foot, as well as in the 'Zulu' car. Bruce chased and caught one in a railyard I think.

Sometime later as it got light, two others were seen hiding in some grass near Camp Hill. Another foot chase resulted in us managing to capture them – I've never been so 'knackered' in my life!

Another case in which I was involved was where a man decided to celebrate his 21st birthday with acts of violence. He drove to Small Heath, fired a crossbow through an Asian man's neck, and then kidnapped a motorist and got him to drive to London.

He memorised his victim's name, address etc. and threatened that his home and family would be destroyed if he informed the police. That victim did not report the matter because of that threat.

When interviewed following his arrest the offender was able to recall all the victim's details and it was only following this that the victim was traced, interviewed and gave details of the incident.

Having been driven to London, the offender then booked into a hotel waiting for things to settle down before he returned to Birmingham. After a few days he kidnapped another victim, a woman, to get back.

When he got to Coleshill he put her into the boot of her car, bought a can of petrol, and drove to Digbeth intending to set fire to the Socialist Book Shop. Unfortunately he spilt the petrol in the car and it set alight. He ran off but was detained and taken Bradford Street.

I went up to interview him with another officer. When we spoke to him, he asked if the woman was alright – this was the first that anyone had known she was there. We contacted officers and the Fire Service at the scene, but tragically she was still in the boot – dead.

In another incident an elderly man who resided in hostel accommodation off Bradford Street had been drinking in a local pub. He met a much younger homeless man and invited him back to the hostel.

Exactly what occurred in the hostel in the elderly man's room will never been known, but he was attacked and almost had his head cut off. His room was literally a blood bath! These are the just some things that you don't forget.'

Figure 48 John Richards mid 1980's, courtesy of J.Richards

***

On the 17th October 1979, a rugby match took place at Coundon Road, Coventry between the South African Barbarians Touring Team and Coventry Rugby Football Club. Groups opposed to the tour by the South Africans had threatened to disrupt the game and 2,000 police officers were deployed to prevent disorder, including officers from 3 other Forces on Mutual Aid.

1000 anti-apartheid supporters were present outside the ground to protest and to march into Coventry City Centre. The heavy police presence prevented disorder and only two arrests were made, as a police helicopter was used to monitor crowd movements.

***

In November, police officers were again deployed outside British Leyland in Longbridge, as a dispute arose following the dismissal of a trade-union official, but again no arrests were made.

***

On the 24th December 1979, PC John Nicholson Pacey, aged thirty years, died when his police car skidded on ice on a bend and crashed.

Retired officer Ken Rowley recalls:

'John was a 'First Response' 'Zulu' driver at Birmingham Road, Wolverhampton. I was a Sergeant on another Unit there and as such didn't know him very well, but I do know that he was really well-liked with a good work reputation.'

***

Police recruitment and retention reached record levels during this period, due in no small part to the implementation of the 'Report on Police Pay and Conditions' by Lord Edmund-Davies, and record levels of unemployment. A total of 648 officers were recruited into the Force during the year which, after wastage, led to an improved manning level of 299 officers, albeit the Force was still short of 349 officers.

***

A total of 210 people died following road traffic accidents during the course of the year.

Speed was identified as a constituent factor in many accidents, and during the year, 6 hand-held KUSTOM HR4 speed detection devices were purchased by the Force, leading to 2,215 motorists being reported in a 3 month period leading up to the end of December.

During 1979, 43 cases of homicide were reported, of which 39 were recorded as murder and 4 as manslaughter. All except two of the murders were shown as detected and all the manslaughters.

In 1979, the Force Commercial Branch continued to investigate allegations of fraud committed by persons connected with business and public bodies. At the beginning of the year 35 active investigations were underway, and a further 110 new complaints were received during the course of the year. The value of enquiries subject of investigation was about £2,000,000, and 46 arrests were made.

Retired officer Derek Rowe recalls one aspect of fraud that some years later was incorporated as a separate section within the Commercial Branch:

'In the late 70's, a growing number of stolen cheques were being used fraudulently in Birmingham City Centre. Cheque books and cheque cards would be stolen at burglaries, robberies or from unattended motor cars, not always in the Birmingham area or even the Midlands. The use of these cheques was classed as crimes committed in Birmingham, and mostly in the city centre. A small number of DC's and a DS from 'A1' and 'A2' were seconded to form a fledgling Cheque Squad. Handwriting and fingerprints were used to investigate, and forgers were identified. Handwriting samples were taken and examined by forensic scientists to determine guilt.

As the amount of cheque-fraud grew, and more crime was committed on the outer Birmingham Divisions, those Divisions supplied PC's for a six-month attachment on a rolling programme. Coventry CID also had a small Cheque Squad.

In early 1986, West Midlands Police decided to form a force-wide Cheque Squad to incorporate the Birmingham and Coventry squads, to be based in Birmingham under the umbrella of the Commercial Branch, which investigated company fraud. Both entities operated separately within the newly named Fraud Squad. The new cheque squad included a Detective Inspector, two Detective Sergeants and nine Detective Constables.

Five DC's and a female DS from the original squad were incorporated, as their accrued experience and expertise were vital.

We were led by a very energetic and keen Inspector, Guy Johnson, whose nickname was 'Skippy'. The squad went from strength to strength. The amount of crimes detected was phenomenal; and credit is due to the civilian infrastructure put in place to deal with the cheques and identify suspects'.

Figure 49 Derek Rowe at Cheque Squad garden party in 1986, courtesy of D Rowe

Figure 50 Derek Rowe in Cheque Squad late 1980's, courtesy of D Rowe

***

For the greater part of the year a number of Robbery Squad officers were seconded to the Metropolitan Police to work on an investigation relating to a group of armed robbers who became infamous as the *'Thursday Gang'* due to their propensity to carry out armed robberies on a Thursday throughout the country. This ultimately resulted in the arrest of 47 persons, and all of the robberies recorded in the West Midlands committed by them going back as far as 1973 were cleared.

1980

The Gail Kinchin Shooting

In January a march to commemorate *'Bloody Sunday'* commenced at Sparkhill Park and terminated in Birmingham City Centre at the Bull Ring. Up to 1,500 people took part and 800 police officers were deployed to public-order duties given the potential for opposition groups to gather. In the event there were only minor outbreaks of violence with just 17 arrests being made.

***

On the 11th June 1980, 16 year-old Gail Kinchin was fatally shot by police officers attempting to rescue her from David Pagett, who was holding her as a human-shield, whilst keeping officers at bay with a shotgun for 2 hours.

Retired officer Mick Foster was involved in a post-incident investigation in relation to this tragic incident and reflects:

'On the evening of 11th June 1980, after first visiting the home of his ex-girlfriend Gail Kinchin, who was pregnant with his child, David Keith Pagett armed himself with a shotgun which he discharged at the family home, then proceeded to the address of one of Gail's friends where he abducted Gail at gunpoint.

With the police now in pursuit, a siege situation then developed at a three-story block of flats in Deelands Road, Rubery, Birmingham with Pagett holding Gail in one of them, whilst armed police officers surrounded the flats to prevent his escape.

It was after midnight, and pitch-black in the stairways of the flats. After a number of pleas for him to surrender, two armed officers, who were on the top floor, were fired at by Pagett. They returned fire, but unknown to them, in the darkness Pagett was holding Gail as a shield. He fired a second shot at the officers with his twelve-bore shotgun, whilst Gail was hit three times by bullets fired by the officers.

She was taken to hospital, but sadly medical staff were unable to save her unborn child, whilst Gail died from her injuries four weeks later.

Pagett survived to face numerous charges.

A clear case where the bravery of the two officers, who narrowly escaped death themselves after the shots fired at them were deflected off a stair bannister, soon became a real tragedy.'

Pagett was later sentenced to 12 years imprisonment after being convicted of manslaughter, attempted murder, two counts of kidnapping and possessing a firearm with intent to endanger life. He was freed from prison after 8 years.

Figure 51 Michael Foster QPM, courtesy of M Foster

***

In August 1980 The National Front gave notice of an intended march and Rally at West Bromwich which attracted considerable attention from opposition groups. The Chief Constable, fearing serious public order issues, applied to Sandwell District Council for an order prohibiting public processions. The order was later formally approved by the Home Secretary.

Undeterred by the ban, 3 days prior to the intended march, Martin Webster of the National Front sent a letter giving formal notice of marches to take place in Wolverhampton, Walsall, Dudley, Birmingham and Coventry. Further bans were sought and approved and nearly 3000 officers were deployed, involving Mutual Aid from 5 other police forces.

On the day in question, Martin Webster arrived at West Bromwich as opposition groups gathered. He was not allowed to walk with a wreath and two juvenile supporters, as a breach of the peace was considered likely, and the event passed off without incident.

National Front sympathisers did however gather at Stonebridge before making their way to Nuneaton in the Warwickshire Force area to demonstrate. A total of 33 Police Support Units were re-deployed to assist Warwickshire Constabulary.

During the course of the year, the West Midlands Police also provided officers on Mutual Aid to support other Forces in connection with National Front demonstrations and an Anti-Nazi League march.

***

In September 1980, the Wallace Lawlor Centre was opened, as the *'Lozells Project'* was fully implemented in the community. The Youth Club Section was organised by two Police Constables and became well-established.

***

In October a dispute by officers from the Prison Service resulted in prisoners being kept in police stations throughout the Force area, and at the Central Lock-Up in Steelhouse Lane.

The action lasted until the end of the year and placed a great strain on the Force as additional officers were deployed to deal with custody, feeding, welfare and escorting prisoners.

Retired officer Malcolm *'Doc'* Halliday recalls some more human aspects of the dispute:

'I did a day in the Central Lock-Up in 1980 during the dispute. I recall that one prisoner who was in custody in connection with a serious shooting, never stopped banging the cell door, or shouting, for the whole twelve hours I was in there!

At Bradford Street we had three cells and the corridor was also used during the dispute. There was one chap in there who had been arrested after a police vehicle pursuit who was a big time fraudster. He was very personable and became the 'head' of the other prisoners, negotiating with us regarding their needs and doing a rota for their visits from family.

He did such a good job that the Superintendent authorised him to have access to the front-office telephone to organize the times for visits, requests etc.

He then gave us a promise not to try and escape and was left in there to get on with it. He supervised it very well and I still smile when I think of hearing him answering the telephone with, 'Good morning, Bradford St Police Station, Prisoner Smith speaking.'

He also requested showers for the prisoners and the Superintendent had us taking them to the single-men's quarters in the station to shower - the single officers played 'merry hell' over that!

The Superintendent was a very compassionate man and it did upset him but he had to make other arrangements.

When the Chief Inspector came back off leave and saw this bloke working in the front-office, and when he found out he was a prisoner on remand he went ballistic!! Anyway, he never did try to escape. He turned out to be a great organizer and the families saw us as being human too and brought us cakes and chocolates.

After this particular prisoner was transferred to the Central Lock-Up I did pay another visit one day to take some other remand prisoners in and saw our 'trustee' again. There he was, organizing everything and doing his bit for the others. He said to me that most of the prisoners there needed help more than locking up. I don't think he was far wrong with some of them!'

Retired police officer Mark Simmonite recalls:

'The marmalade sandwiches will forever remind me of the Lock-Up. Many hours spent on overtime during the prison officer disputes on nights, showing officer's from outer Divisions the passage through to the court cells, and going out through the doors where prisoner vans came in for a 'breath of fresh air'. The majority of those prisoners were well behaved in the police cells, possibly looked after better than inside the prisons.'

Figure 52 Inside 'Lock-Up', courtesy of S Burrows

***

Also in October, a *'Motoring Spectacular'* event was held in Birmingham which attracted 80,000 people, due in part to the fine weather, but required the deployment of 556 uniformed officers for safety and security, at a cost of over £17,000.

***

On the 24th December 1980, PC David Cameron, aged forty-nine years, died as a result of injuries sustained in a road traffic collision.

***

During 1980, the Force recruited 694 new officers, and after taking wastage into account, manning levels improved by 375, meaning that it had finally achieved its authorised establishment level. In addition to this a further 129 officers were seconded to various specialist posts, and not included in the establishment figures.

A total of 1,104 police officers were assaulted in 1980, a substantial increase on the year before, with 558 classed as being serious. These included 2 cases of attempt murder and 87 cases of wounding. Female officers were assaulted on 76 occasions.

During the year, 30 West Midlands Police officers, along with another 50 officers from across the country, were sent on attachment to Rhodesia (Zimbabwe) to supervise the elections.

Retired officer Julie Maley recalls:

'I remember when the request came out for officers to go to Rhodesia, we all thought it would be great to be able to go to Africa, so I think nearly all of our Unit put in for it, along with most other Units. The response was reported as being overwhelming and the decision was made to only allow those who were firearms-trained to go.'

***

Overall crime increased by 12.5% compared with the previous year, with a total of 166,031 crimes being recorded and a Force detection rate of 32.5%.

36 murders and 3 manslaughter/infanticide cases were recorded during the year, all of which were detected.

A total of 193 persons lost their lives in road accidents, and 12,935 suffered injuries.

Due to the advent of hand-held devices, 1980 saw the highest number of drivers ever detected for speeding by the Traffic Division, with 25,862 persons being reported, half of which came from the use of hand-held radar.

At this time there were 12 Petty Sessional areas within the Force, at Aldridge, Birmingham, Coventry, Dudley, Halesowen, Solihull, Stourbridge, Sutton Coldfield, Walsall, Warley, West Bromwich and Wolverhampton. Prosecution Departments were established on each of the territorial Divisions to service these areas apart from Birmingham where a Central Summons and Warrants Department dealt with these two issues.

A total of 153,481 summonses were served within the Force area during the year, and 49,469 warrants executed.

The establishment of the Traffic Wardens Department was set at 688, whereas the actual strength was just 229. Nevertheless they issued 122,666 Fixed Penalty Notices between them.

1981

The Women Hold the Line

In late January the Prison Officers dispute was resolved.

***

In February, the authorised establishment of the Force was increased by 175 officers, giving a new figure of 6,684.

***

In March 1981, notification of intention to march in Wolverhampton was given by the 'New National Front'. An order prohibiting the march was successfully obtained, and supporters of the group gathered in the Force area and then went to Burton-on-Trent where a demonstration passed off peacefully.

***

In April members of the Campaign for Nuclear Disarmament marched through the Force area without incident.

***

On the 30th April 1981, PC Paul Kenneth Worth, aged thirty-four years, was hit by a lorry and fatally injured while assisting a motorist on the motorway.

Figure 53 PC Worth, courtesy of Mavis Worth

***

In May there was a recurrence of the Prison Officers dispute leading to industrial action, which led to prisoners from the Magistrates Courts again being held in police cells for ten days.

Also in May, the *'Peoples March for Jobs 1981'* crossed the Force area and although only 300 people completed the full march, numbers swelled considerably as they passed through.

On the 23rd May 1981, the *'Coventry Committee Against Racism'* held a march and a rally in Coventry City Centre. It was necessary to deploy 962 officers as counter-demonstrations were expected. An estimated 7,000 people took part, and in Cathedral Square there were incidents of disorder as opposing factions clashed. Over 70 arrests were made during the course of the afternoon.

***

During July, nationwide outbreaks of disorder took place, and it was necessary for the Force to call upon Mutual Aid from 11 other Forces on a number of occasions, with up to 400 such officers at any one time fed and accommodated within the Force area.

Except for some driving courses, all training was suspended for two weeks in order that personnel could be deployed to support public-order efforts. The training school at *'Tally Ho'* was used to accommodate some of the officers from other Forces.

Retired officer Norman Langford recalls a unique aspect of policing at this time:

'Six years after the Equality legislation, and the demise of the Policewomen's Department, I was a Shift Inspector at Acocks Green.

In July of 1981 rioting occurred in Handsworth. To deal with this, all of the male officers from my shift were seconded to police this problem.

This left me to police the Acocks Green Sub-Division with a much depleted shift comprised solely of policewomen.

It is fair to say this left me feeling initially very concerned. However, for over a week the policewomen provided cover for the whole area brilliantly. There was not a single issue that they did not cope with admirably. They were able to deal with potentially violent situations calmly without problems, and impart professional policing to the whole area.

In the end it became very clear to me that day-to-day policing could be carried out by women officers as effectively and efficiently as it had been when male officers were present. I wouldn't previously have thought this possible.

Call me sexist if you like, but in that week, where I never thought this could happen, and that there would be several issues where a male presence was really missed, it never once happened.

Those policewomen policed the Acocks Green Sub-Division as effectively and efficiently as it ever had been policed previously and I recall feeling very proud of them all!'

***

Bob Smalley was promoted to Chief Inspector, (Western Traffic), at the Bevan in 1976, before moving to Duke Street, until a vacancy for Superintendent (Head of the Driving School) came about. Bob attended an Advanced Driving Course at Stafford following which he took up the post at the Driving School between 1980 and 1982.

***

On 4 occasions during 1981 the Force provided Mutual Aid to other Forces to assist in dealing with large-scale demonstrations, and at one event in Liverpool a number of West Midlands officers were injured in violent confrontations.

***

In September, the Labour Party gave notice of their intention to hold a national march and rally in Birmingham. An estimated 5,000 marchers completed the route and the rally was attended by prominent politicians.

***

During the year, 383 new officers were recruited into the Force. Taking into account wastage and the new authorised establishment, the Force was fully up to strength by the end of the year. This was a milestone in the history of the West Midlands Police, as for the first time in many years a waiting list of accepted officer candidates was established.

At the end of the year police pensions were being paid to 1,837 retired officers, with 767 widows of police officers, or ex-officers, also receiving a pension.

A total of 793 officers were assaulted on duty and a grand total of 1,270 officers suffered some form of injury on duty, which included 118 who suffered from slips or trips and 23 who were bitten by dogs!

***

For many years the West Midlands Police ran a very successful Police Cadet Scheme with many of them going on to join as Regular officers.

In January 1981, 19 new cadets of an older age were enrolled and underwent an initial training course at 'Tally Ho' Police Training Centre. In August a further intake of 68 cadets followed. After their induction they were enrolled at Matthew Boulton Technical College to continue their education with a view to obtaining BEC General Awards and Diplomas, as well as additional GCE 'O' level and 'A' level passes.

During the senior stage of training, Cadets went to Divisions and Departments as well as completing one month's 'Adventure Training'. During term breaks from college they also engaged in community projects, many of which involved children and vulnerable members of the community.

In the summer months, most cadets attended the West Midlands Cadet Adventure Training Camp at Elan Valley in Wales, whilst a small number went to other Outward Bound Schools. In 1981, 3 cadets even went on various ships for sail training.

Two teams of cadets, one male and one female, took part in the annual walk on Dartmoor known as the *'Ten Tors Expedition'*.

During the year, a total of 89 cadets also qualified in First Aid, and 2 female cadets obtained Gold Awards on the *'Duke of Edinburgh'* scheme.

West Midlands Police Cadets also fielded teams in various Divisions in sports such as football, rugby, athletics, cross-country, swimming, cricket, and hockey. Great emphasis was placed on swimming, with those unable to swim on joining being taught to do so, and with 72 cadets passing the Royal Life Saving Society Bronze Medallion Award.

Paul McElhinney was one of those cadets who joined in August 1981 and went on to become a regular officer. He recalls:

'My journey to Secondary school involved catching two buses, the number 63 from Rednal to Northfield, and the number 18 from Northfield to Bartley Green. On the top deck of the buses, beside the lights for the 'upper saloon', there was a space for companies to advertise their product or service. Circa 1980 there was an advertisement for West Midlands Police. It was a photo of a bobby watching a burglary suspect. The tagline was 'Can you act quicker than most people can think?' Well this egotistical fifteen-year-old mentally answered in the affirmative and the seed was sown. Add to that a generous dash of 'Jack Regan' in 'The Sweeney', and my joining the police service was a foregone conclusion.

I discovered that one had to be 18 years and 6 months old in order to join the job as a Constable. I had worked very hard for my 'O' levels and had achieved nine passes with very good grades. I suppose I was becoming bored of academia, so in August 1981 I became Cadet '102' with West Midlands Police.

An entire school year would join the cadet corps every summer. Some were September birthday's, some were August of the following year. Hence some people spent about 18 months in cadet training, and others two and a half years.

The Cadet Training department was based at the police training centre at 'Tally Ho', Edgbaston. The department shared the facility with various other training schools including CID Training, the Mounted Branch, and Force Training.

Our initial induction course was a fortnight at Birmingham University. I collected my uniform from the uniform stores at Bournville Lane. It was an identical uniform to police officers except our cap bands were blue and we had a cloth 'Police Cadet' badge on our tunic shoulder. We were taught to press our uniform and 'bull our boots'. Back in those days there was still a very strong emphasis on military-type discipline and uniform presentation. We also spent a lot of time doing what Monty Python's Michael Palin would call 'Marching up and down the square.' Members of the training staff had been on courses with the military and were competent drill instructors. For a fortnight we were marched around the university campus, we were 'beasted' on runs and we were 'beasted' in the gym. A few people dropped out and those that remained repaired to 'Tally Ho' to continue their training.

I should add at this point that the Department drew cadets from all over the country. Local recruits lived at home with parents, whilst recruits from Wales, Scotland and other regions were accommodated in single-quarters with police officers. The female cadets 'hostel' was called Burgess House in Moseley. Male cadets lived at Bordesley Green 'nick' and Soho House in Handsworth, the former home of industrial giant Matthew Boulton and now a museum dedicated to him.

Why a cadet training department? Well I am led to believe that in the days before what old time 'bobbies' called 'The Edmund Davies Report', police pay was relatively poor. The job struggled to recruit sufficient officers and they therefore decided to try to recruit sixteen-year-olds then transfer them into the regular job at eighteen. The aim of cadet training was to turn teenagers into smart, fit, conscientious eighteen-year old's ready for training as a Constable.

From what I can recall, a typical week was as follows. We had been recruited onto a college course at Matthew Boulton College in Highgate. It was a BEC National in public administration. We did that three and a half days a week. On Wednesday afternoons we had force sport, I represented the Cadet Department at rugby. On Thursdays we had a Training Day at 'Tally Ho'. This would entail parading in full uniform at roughly 8am on the parade square at 'Tally Ho'. Sadly this is now a carpark, the first carpark on the left as you enter the service road from the Pershore Road. We had to be perfect; sharp creases in both trousers and tunic sleeves. Boots had to be 'bulled' military style. We'd be inspected by the Chief Inspector who in my day was Graham Heeley. We'd then fall out. During the course of the day we'd have a swimming lesson, a gym lesson in the gym doing calisthenics and then a four mile run. We'd also have a drill lesson, an hour of drill practice. We all got very fit as training days were very tough. A couple of the lads in my intake could get round the 3.7 mile 'Dogpool Run' in 19/20 minutes.

As a fifty-three year old man I can now reflect on my cadet service and say that some of the instructors like Sgt Ian Darnell were excellent. He was a mature man who sought to get the best out of the lads in his charge and turn them into mature police officer candidates.

One cannot talk about Birmingham City and West Midlands Police Cadets without mentioning 'camp'. Birmingham has a special relationship with the Elan Valley which began during the first decade of the 20th century. Birmingham's water supply comes from reservoirs in the valley which were built by the Birmingham Corporation. Every summer, Police Cadets would go to Elan Village where they slept for four weeks in ten-man ex-army tents and completed a very arduous outward bound course. The instructors slept in wooden dormitory huts on the site. The camp commandant was an Inspector, and there was a Sergeant, then various PC instructors drawn from around the force. There were was a rock-climbing trip to North Wales, canoeing on the reservoirs and River Wye, and the dreaded PT&A days, PT and assault course. The assault course had been built just behind the camp on the steep banks of the river. The aim of PT&A days was to leave you completely exhausted. The instructors certainly achieved that aim.

During the course of the four weeks the various squads of eight cadets had to complete the three-day and four-day treks. This entailed walking a prescribed route in the Elan Valley and the Brecon Beacons, stopping for the night at prearranged locations.

Everything you needed was in your Bergen, and you slept in small two-person tents. My lasting memory of these treks is waking at 6am in a warm dry tent, taking off my dry tracksuit, putting it in a carrier bag and tying the neck then putting on my soaking wet clothes from the day before which had spent the night in the bell end of the tent - a most unpleasant experience.

The Cadet Training Department is long since gone and quite rightly so. There is no shortage of applicants these days for police service jobs so the original concept no longer exists. However I consider myself very fortunate to have been part of it. Almost everyone who I speak to who was in the Cadet Corps says the same.

Whilst on camp, if an individual was struggling on runs and was deemed not to be trying hard enough the training staff would tell the rest of the squad that if that 'lazy b...ard' didn't buck his ideas up and pick up the pace the whole squad would be doing the run again that evening. I remember this scenario with a popular cadet who was trying his best; the lads rallied round him and encouraged him to get through it.

I'll sign off with an anecdote. Graham Heeley was a much-feared Chief Inspector, a 'no nonsense' kind of 'gaffer'. One training day we decided to see how many cadets we could get in the lift at 'Tally Ho', which said 'Maximum 6 Persons'. We got about ten in standing then a further six female cadets and smaller male cadets hopped up on our shoulders. We were trying to break some sort of record set by the cadets of the previous year, the 'seniors'. Someone with a free hand pressed the button for floor 1 and off we went. A few seconds later 'clunk', the lift died! We probably shouted and people became aware that people were trapped in the lift. The fire service attended and we were winched back down to the ground floor.

Nick James said, "Shhh, I can hear Heeley." We all fell silent; we were rather hoping that he might not be around. "We'll have you out soon" he said, "How many of you are in there?" I said, "Err, sixteen." His response was "You had better be joking Mr. McElhinney". When the 'squirters' jemmied open the doors Heeley nearly had a fit.

Needless to say the 'Birmingham Lift 16' spent several evenings after college running around Cannon Hill Park.'

Figure 54 Police Cadet McElhinney 1981/2, courtesy of P McElhinney

Figure 55 Elan Valley Cadet Camp 1981/2, courtesy of P McElhinney

Figure 56 Police Cadet McElhinney (L), courtesy of P McElhinney

***

A total of 188,230 crimes were recorded during the year as crime continued to increase. The Force detection rate was 31.6%.

30 offences were classified as murder and 5 as manslaughter, with all but one offence of murder being cleared.

A total of 179 people lost their lives in road traffic accidents.

During this period the Traffic Division normally deployed 16 double-crewed vehicles throughout the Force area in a 24 hour period. In addition 2 motor-cyclists were allocated to each car patrol area between the hours of 7am and 11pm. The motorways were patrolled by 7 double-crewed vehicles during the day with a reduced number on duty at night.

Retired officer Roy Shotton recalls:

'After serving in the Force Surveillance Unit I returned to Force Traffic in 1981 and remained there for seven years, where I was also a member of the police motorcyclist display team.

Because of my background I also became a member of a special team of officers who operated on a firearms call-out rota. There was about sixteen of us in all, including Nev Hayes and Dave Millichamp. We did more training in the use of revolvers and pump- action shotguns.'

Figure 57 Police Motorcycle Display Team, circa 1982, Roy Shotton second right, courtesy of R Shotton

Figure 58 Police escort of European Cup Winners Aston Villa, Birmingham City Centre 1982. (Peter Withe, winning goal-scorer). Roy Shotton far right. Courtesy of R Shotton

Figure 59 Roy Shotton with traffic car, late 1980's, courtesy of R Shotton

***

The Dogs Act of 1906 placed upon the police the responsibility of feeding and retaining stray dogs. Such animals were usually kept in kennels at police stations for a short period, before being transferred to animal welfare organisations if not claimed by their owners.

In 1981 a total of 11,753 stray dogs were processed by the police at an administrative cost of nearly £80,000 over a twelve month period.

Street robberies in 1981 rose by 22 per cent compared with the previous year, bringing the following response from the Chief Constable, *'Many attempts have been made over the years to analyse the reasons for the continual rise in crime. I remain convinced that the reduced moral standards prevailing within the community today, affording a greater tolerance of anti-social behaviour, remain the main reason, and that crime will continue to rise until society as a whole decides to do something about it.'*

1982

Down in The Crypt

On the 2nd January 1982, a terrorist device exploded at the rear of Ariel House, Coventry Road, Sheldon. Responsibility was claimed by the *'Welsh Army of Workers for the Revolution'*.

Following an order banning a National Front march in Coventry, the organisers gave notice that they would march in Solihull, Birmingham, Walsall, Wolverhampton, Sandwell and Dudley on the 31st January 1982. The organiser of the National Front march was subsequently prosecuted for offences under the West Midlands County Council Act 1980.

On this date, 2,000 supporters of Sinn Fein also held a march and rally through Birmingham to commemorate *'Bloody Sunday'*, and a large policing operation was put in place to prevent disorder.

***

On the 18th May, a First Division football match took place at The Hawthorns Football Ground between West Bromwich Albion and Leeds United. It was a crucial game for the clubs and there was advance intelligence to suggest that there would be up to 5000 visiting supporters.

A policing operation was put in place and at the end of the game there was serious disorder and significant damage caused to property in and around the stadium. 28 police officers and 33 supporters were injured, primarily as a result of being struck by missiles. A total of 46 arrests were made.

***

His Holiness Pope John Paul II visited Baginton Airport, in Warwickshire on the 30th May, where he celebrated Mass before an estimated crowd of 200,000. A special Papal Visit Team was created to co-ordinate Mutual Aid.

Figure 60 The Pope at Bagington, courtesy of the Express & Star

***

Retired officer Ken Rowley recalls taking up a new post on the 7th June 1982, working with local youths in Wolverhampton to try and divert them away from crime.

'The origins of the 'Crypt', which was situated at Darlington Street Methodist Church, in Wolverhampton, go back to the early 60's, when a snooker hall was created in the basement. It eventually became a youth centre after several years.

This centre was managed for the church by one Geoff Parsons who attracted youths , who were mainly of Afro-Caribbean descent, and eventually became a centre employing kids on the Youth Opportunities Scheme, which was government funded.

The importance of this work came to the notice of local politicians who oversaw its progress.

During the late 1970's, tension grew between the police and the 'locals' and it was decided by the 'G' Division senior officers and Geoff Parsons to second an officer to 'build bridges' with the community. There had already been trouble in the town involving a number of local youths.

In 1982 I became the third officer to be seconded to the centre, having worked from 'G3' sub-division at Birmingham Road. I was also a native of Wolverhampton, born and bred as they say.

My involvement centred on sporting activities for which I had a particular expertise. I introduced Karate, set up a weight-training and power-lifting gym, and also organised football and cricket matches, I was an ex-county football player and divisional cricket representative. Matches were played against 'G' Division police officers, and presentations made by the then Chief Superintendent, Roy Massey.

Sir Philip Knights was a regular visitor, as was occasionally Sir Lawrence Byford, then HMI. High-profile politicians also dropped in, including David Mellor, then a Minister in Government, and Neil Kinnock. On one occasion Princess Diana also came to visit.

While all this was going on we did have riots in the town-centre during my stay. Because of the riots, tension in the centre could at times be quite high, but by this time everybody had come to know me and I was accepted to a degree - I became simply 'Ken', from the 'Crypt'.

In 1985, Geoffrey Dear came to the centre, having not long arrived as Chief Constable. With him came a member of the Police Committee, so they saw the importance of our role down there.

For a brief period, I returned to uniform duties at 'G3', only to be summoned back after problems with my replacement who had to quickly leave for his own safety. I remained there until 1986 when I was posted to 'H2' Willenhall - it had been a long haul!'

Figure 61 Ken Rowley with members of 'The Crypt Club', mid 1980's, courtesy of K.Rowley

***

In July, the Lion Alcolmeter breath testing device was introduced to the Force, designed to replace the Alcotest R80 breathalyser tube and bag which up to that point had been the sole method of determining breath samples since 1967. The device was welcomed by operational officers who saw it as a much more accurate and easier piece of kit to use.

As detections for drink-driving started to rise, efforts continued to address speeding motorists, with 18,000 individuals being reported during the course of the year.

***

In September, the Motorcycle Action Group held a demonstration and rally in Birmingham attended by some 3,000 motorcyclists who travelled at an average speed of 20 mph between Rednal and Sandwell Valley Car Park.

***

On the 14th November 1982, PC Joseph Anthony O'Brien, aged forty-eight years, was fatally struck by a car while directing traffic in a road -race. He was a highly-respected community officer, and following a request from his former colleagues, Mercia Housing Association later named a close after him within a housing complex opposite Chase Avenue Police Station, in Coventry.

The driver who knocked the officer down was subsequently cleared of criminal charges but later ordered to pay his widow damages after another judge apportioned responsibility to the person driving.

PC O'Brien joined Coventry City Police in 1962 and transferred to West Midlands Police in 1974. For ten years, up to the time of his death, the officer was a local beat officer in Ernesford Grange and Binley, in Coventry.

He was an accomplished athlete, being a member of the *'Coventry Godiva Harriers'* for 20 years and was the Midlands Police record-holder for the 1,500-metre walk.

Coventry Olympian David Moorcroft, a friend of the officer, had been talking to him just before the incident in which he died.

(Postscript: A former colleague, PC Dave Watson, set up an annual event in the officer's memory named the *'PC Joe O'Brien Memorial Run'* which was sponsored by a local firm, *'D & J Henry'*. The last such event took place on Saturday 1st July 2017, to raise funds for *'COPS – Care of Police Survivors'*.)

***

In 1982 the Force managed to sustain sufficient recruitment levels to maintain the position of being at its authorised establishment level by year-end, with a waiting list of successful applicants, as the police service continued to enjoy a period where it was seen as being an attractive profession to join.

During the year, 922 officers were assaulted whilst on duty with 420 assaults classified as serious. There were 58 assaults on female officers.

A total of 210,688 crimes were reported during the year, representing an increase on the previous year. The Force detection rate was 33.1%.

Of these, 39 deaths were recorded as murder and 6 as manslaughter, with all of them being recorded as detected.

***

The Force still maintained a Home Defence Department under the control of a Superintendent, who was the Staff Officer to the Chief Constable in his capacity as Regional Police Commander (Designate). He had the support of an Inspector, a Sergeant and a typist. In addition to Regional Police War Duties Courses, officers visited the Home Defence College, and 3 Inspectors did Air Reconnaissance Training. There were still 277 air raid sirens and 224 carrier broadcast receivers situated within the Force area, controlled from 5 'Carrier Control Points' at police stations within the County, that also served 148 similar installations in 3 neighbouring Forces.

Testing of the siren equipment was carried out on a quarterly basis by the Department and the carrier receivers on a yearly basis.

***

The establishment of the Communications Department was 1 Chief Superintendent, 2 Superintendents, 6 Chief Inspectors, 6 Inspectors, 10 Sergeants and 30 Constables. In addition, 156 civilians were employed as Control Room operators, PNC Operators, Radio Operators and Telephone Operators, and on other administrative functions.

The Force Control Room was originally set up in February 1979, and its primary functions had changed very little. In 1982 the FCR handled 308,871 calls, compared to a Force total of 694,643 calls.

The Force VHF and UHF radio schemes continued unchanged.

1983

'Passing Out'

This was not an easy year for the Force, as demand increased against a backcloth of reduced resources. Although recorded crime showed a slight decrease there was an increase in serious crime, notably in the categories of robbery, assaults and burglary. Emergency calls increased by 13.85% whilst the budget set for the Force in real terms was 3% less than the previous year. Whilst the Force managed to maintain police officer levels, this was at the expense of retaining police staff vacancies.

To combat these challenges the Force embarked on detailed analysis which was designed to identify further opportunities for civilianization as the role of police support staff achieved greater importance. It also aimed to release police officers who were involved in non-operational duties back into operational roles.

One of the officers who did join as a recruit in 1983 was co-author Stephen Burrows who, like most West Midlands Police colleagues, attended Ryton On Dunsmore District Police Training Centre in order to complete his initial training course on Intake 9/83.

In those days a lot of emphasis was placed on uniform turn-out and regular parade- ground drill exercises, as well as the ability to quote law definitions verbatim!

He recollects:

'I was twenty-five years-old and had been working at various jobs for several years. In those days, an application was followed by a 'home visit' from an Inspector, purportedly to check one came from a 'good family' and didn't live above a brothel, or in a pub. I can remember my Mom, who was pretty 'straight-laced', being embarrassed when the Inspector called because I was away with my girlfriend, and not married,. Mom must have made a good impression on my behalf, because I was subsequently asked for interview on the 'mezzanine' floor at Lloyd House, Police Headquarters where I was successful. It took nearly twelve months from application to beginning training as a police officer.

Little did I know it, but it was going to be a culture shock.

The first couple of weeks, the 'Induction Course', were fine. A gentle introduction to the police, led by Sergeant Mick Ferris, a very experienced and pleasant man that I became good friends with in subsequent years.

We were based at 'Tally Ho' Training Centre, and received inputs from the Police Federation, and on the structure, culture and values of the Police and Force. To this day I recall a Superintendent speaker who gave a talk on integrity and good behaviour saying, 'don't do anything you wouldn't want your Mom to know about, or see on the front page of the Daily Mail along with your photo'.

We began in 'civvy' clothes, but were 'fitted' with uniform at Bournville Lane during induction. This was hilarious, as a lot of the stuff only roughly matched body size and shape. Too large, and you were promised that you'd 'bulk up to fill it' due to the meals and physical training, too small, and you were told you'd 'slim down a bit in training'. I still recall being told I needed to 'get a few curries down my neck', by the storeman.

We had to take the uniform home in a huge cardboard box and then start wearing it once we had sorted it out. The first time I tried it on it felt like 'fancy dress', but you started to get used to it after a few days. I always felt that my helmet was too big and about to fall off, and for a while catching my reflection in a window was a strange experience.

Then we were off for Initial Training. Fourteen weeks at a District Centre with new recruits from other local Forces. I went to Ryton-On-Dunsmore in Warwickshire.

I had no idea what to expect. I was twenty-five, an older recruit in those days, and I met a militaristic regime that treated everybody as teenagers.

I arrived on a Sunday evening, nervous and unsure. There was a queue to register, be allocated a room and class, and to meet the two Sergeants who would be the class tutors. I approached the desk, but during the conversation I called one of them 'Sarge'. 'I'm not Sarge, I'm Sergeant to you!', (swear words removed), was my introduction to Ryton.

We marched between classes, stood up when we answered a question in class and saluted senior officers. There was a 'parade' every morning, when uniform would be scrutinised and punishment details handed out for every blemish, no matter how minor. We all got really good at 'bulling' boots, spending hours perfecting a shine like a mirror. Every so often disaster would strike, a deep scratch, peeling of polish or even the whole toecap of polish coming off. I was hopeless at marching, a failing that remained with me during numerous Remembrance Day Parades as a senior officer.

Lessons comprised learning crime definitions off by heart, exploring the legal nuances, and being tested by fiendish multiple-choice questions. Those who regularly failed were given extra tuition and nicknamed 'The Woodentops'.

Then there were 'practicals'. Learning how to direct traffic correctly, stopping and searching vehicles, licensed premises 'raids', arresting drunks, (play-acted with vigour by directing staff). We were taught life-saving skills in the pool, and physically tortured in the gym, especially during 'self-defence' lessons, if you were the unfortunate one selected by the instructor to demonstrate the amount of pain that could be inflicted with various 'holds'.

Our fitness levels were improved by the swimming, cross-country runs and gym-work. There were regular fitness tests that had to passed, including push-ups, sit-ups, a timed run and the dreaded 'pull-ups' on the bar.We bonded, helped by evenings in the bar, but there was a curfew, policed by staff members, to keep the sexes apart.

It was regimented, strict, militaristic, full of rules and regulations. Some liked it, but I hated it. I still sometimes return to Ryton, but it is very different now - the old ways are gone, the parade ground now a car park.' I'm still in touch with some of my class members at Ryton, thirty-five years later

Figure 62 'Boot bulling' at Ryton, courtesy of S Burrows

Figure 63 In the Bar at Ryton, courtesy of S Burrows

Figure 64 Passing out Parade, 1983, courtesy of S Burrows

Figure 65 Passing Out Parade 1983, courtesy of S Burrows

Figure 66 Passing Out Parade 1983, courtesy of S Burrows

Figure 67 Class of 9/83, courtesy of S Burrows

***

On the 25th March 1983, an exercise was held at Birmingham Airport to test the contingency plans for all emergency services in relation to major incidents and terrorist activities.

***

On the 1st May, Sinn Fein held a march and rally in Birmingham to commemorate the deaths of several hunger strikers. The event passed off without incident.

Also, in May, Intoximeter evidential breath-testing' machines were brought in for use in police stations, and the introduction of seat-belt legislation was seen as a major step forward in terms of improving road safety.

***

A total of 210,051 crimes were recorded for the year, which represented a slight decrease on the previous year. The Force detection rate was 35.8%.

42cases of homicide were recorded, of which 40 were recorded as murder and 2 as manslaughter with just 1 case of murder remaining unsolved.

A total of 199 offences of domestic violence involving assault on a spouse or co-habitee were recorded during the year. The figure included 10 deaths, 17 serious wounding's and 172 less serious assaults. In a sign of increasing awareness, it was accepted that a number of assaults would not have been reported to the police.

Offences of robbery increased by 10%, whilst another emerging pattern of concern was the movement of organised crime into so-called 'white collar' crime.

The huge impact of burglary dwelling offences was revealed when it was announced that from a total of more than £12,000,000 worth of property stolen, less than £500,000 was recovered.

1984

The Demise of Duke Street

On the 3rd January 1984, the Central Traffic Sub-Division, Central Garage Workshop, Home Office Radio Workshop and the Headquarters of the Mounted Branch moved from their Duke Street base to what was to become known as the Central Traffic Unit, built in Park Lane, Aston, Birmingham. The move ended a 132 year link with Duke Street, which was the first purpose-built police station built in Birmingham in 1852.

At the same time, mounted branch stables at Duke Street, Bordesley Green, Kings Heath and Ladywood were closed, and the horses and officers transferred to Park Lane.

Figure 68 Closure of Duke St, 1984, courtesy of B Smalley

***

The introduction of the Police and Criminal Evidence Act in 1984, which required prisoner reception locations to be designated and to meet a minimum standard, caused the Force to carry out a review of all of its custody facilities.

The same Act also created huge challenges for the Force Training Department as the implications of the new legislation hit home.

Training as a whole continued to be fragmented throughout the Force. Staff at *'Tally Ho'* ran a variety of courses including National CID training and cadet training courses. The centre housed the Law Research Unit and CCTV Unit. Probationer training was carried out at Training wings at Bournville and Walsall Police Stations, whilst the Force Driving School was at Halesowen.

Ron Cornwell, now aged 92 years, joined the Birmingham City Police on the 4th March.1950, and served on the Force Driving School for 30 years between 1956 up to his retirement as an Inspector in 1984. On his last day of service, he completed a final test and when he got back was greeted with a surprise 'farewell banner'.

Figure 69 Ron Cornwell's last day of service, 1984, courtesy of R Cornwell

Figure 70 Ron Cornwell 2017, Tally Ho reunion, courtesy of R Cornwell

Another colleague and close-friend of Ron's was Bertram 'Leo' Harris who joined the police in 1953 and went on to have a long career both as a traffic officer, predominantly as a 'biker', and later as a driving instructor on bikes and cars.

Figure 71 Leo Harris (front right), Instructors Course 1970's, courtesy of L Harris

Figure 72 Leo Harris (centre), Driving Course 1979, courtesy of L Harris

Figure 73 Leo Harris wearing 'Duke Street Traffic' tie, 2017, Tally Ho reunion, courtesy of L Harris

***

In 1984, the Stores Department continued to provide a service from the stores at Bournville Lane Police Station and two mobile clothing-stores.

This year saw the introduction of a lightweight nylon car coat, designed to replace the heavier gabardine coats which had been in use for some years. The Police Authority also approved the adoption of the 'hostess' style hats for female police officers, cadets and traffic wardens.

***

During 1984, the Force's Police Cadet scheme saw a reduction in numbers as recruitment was halted. In the same year several 16-year-old school leavers completed 12 months on a Youth Training Scheme. The aim was to offer unemployed young people the chance to become more employable.

In 1990, Anya Small nee Layton joined the West Midlands Police Youth Training Scheme and recalls:

'My first placement was at Rose Road Police Station Sub-Divisional Administration, and I spent one day a week at Handsworth College completing a diploma in Business Administration. We were given training in the phonetic alphabet, which is still useful over the phone today, telephone techniques and memo and fax writing – no emails in those days to contend with! It was a great start to a 23 year career with the service and a really good way to introduce young people to the world of work. I have fond memories of working in a busy police station with an array of 'characters', both police and support staff. It was a bit of a shock to the system for a 16 year-old from Harborne who came straight from a girl's school!

In 1992, a group of us on the YTS scheme did 5 day 'outward bound' course at the Cadet Camp in Elan Valley in Wales. We were all aged 17 or 18 at the time.

Some had never been away from home before so it was a bit of a 'culture shock'.

Our first task when we arrived was to set up 3 tents in a large open field whilst the rain came pouring down.

The camp 'commandant' was Sergeant Phil Wright who made it clear that discipline was the order of the day. Things didn't start off too well when we were ordered out in the dark to do some orienteering after a basic lesson in map and compass reading.

During the week we did rock-climbing and water sports on the reservoir, which included a challenge on how to make a raft, when we were split up into 2 groups. One stayed fairly dry – the other did not! We also did some canoeing.

Our next challenge was completing the assault course under the supervision of PC Chris Price and PTI Andy Symonds, who were the Instructors for the week.

The whole week was co-ordinated by the YTS training manager Dee King and it went by very quickly.

I think that they classed the experience as 'character building', but overall it was good fun.

Figure 74 Anya Small nee Layton, first day of YTS scheme 1990, outside Tally Ho Training Centre, courtesy of A Small

Figure 75 Anya Small nee Layton on 'Outward Bound' course 1992, courtesy of A Small

***

On the 3rd February 1984, Ravindre Mhatre, an Indian diplomat, was kidnapped. His body was found two days later in Leicestershire. The whole of the Serious Crime Squad were engaged in the investigation and a number of Kashmiris were arrested and charged with murder and abduction.

***

On the 4th February 1984, PC Andrew Stephen Le Comte, aged twenty-one years, was killed in a fall while searching for suspects on a shop roof at night.

On that night PC Le Comte, a probationary Constable working on the *'D'* Division at Erdington Police Station, with thirteen months service, was on duty in High Street, Erdington.

Retired officer Colin Tansley recalls the tragic events leading up to Andrew's death:

'It was Friday 3rd of February 1984 when we paraded for duty at Erdington Police Station. 'A' Unit were expecting the usual frantic Friday night-shift and although it was February all the local public-houses were full of weekend revellers. For me it was extra special as I had just learnt that I had passed by promotion exams to Sergeant and on the coming day it was my birthday.

I was posted to Area Car 'Delta Zulu 7' with PC Phil Cowley, and our good friend, and colleague, Andy Le Comte, was posted to walk Erdington High Street. Andy was still a probationer and was learning his trade-craft by walking a tough beat on his own although the mobile units were never that far away. Andy had been posted to that beat all week and unfortunately for him a large, three-storey tall, General Store on the High Street, known as 'Grandfare' had been broken into twice that week through the roof. Andy was furious and determined to catch those responsible.

The night began in a lively fashion but by midnight the jobs had begun to slow, which allowed Phil and I to cruise along the High Street to catch up with Andy. Just as we thought, Andy was standing outside the store in question. He walked over to our vehicle and we asked him if he was ok, making sure he hadn't encountered anything too worrying. The plan was that we would keep close by to bring him in for his refreshment break at 1am barring any tasking from our controller.

Andy decided he would go and check the rear of the premises and walked off into the dark courtyard area where deliveries would be made to the store. Phil and I stayed close by, watching Andy disappear in to the dark. Shortly afterwards our radios crackled into life with Andy's hushed voice. He said, "There is someone on the roof, they are on the roof now". Phil and I ran from the vehicle to Andy - it was now 00.18hrs on the 4th February 1984.

Andy and I stood by a metal fire escape that led up on to the roof. Although there was a tall protective fence around the base it was easy to climb over it onto the stairs. Andy and I ran as fast as we could up onto the roof. It was pitch black with street lights silhouetting the outline of the building curtilages. The building in question was shaped like a square 'C'.

Where Andy and I were standing we could see over onto the other roof, on the top of which was a lift-housing, and on top of that we could just make out the shape of two bodies lying face-down, trying to hide.

I instinctively moved towards the other roof area using the side of the building illuminated by the street lights. I last saw Andy running, crouched down into the pitch-black night. I heard a loud 'smack' as though someone had landed flat-footed having jumped down from a height.

It was then that PC Lynn Ford who had arrived as back-up, radioed in saying, "There is someone on the roof they have just thrown concrete down". It was then that my blood ran cold, I knew what had happened, I knew Andy had fallen.

How badly he had fallen I didn't know. As I ran towards the suspects they were now standing up on the lift-housing, they too had realised that something dreadful had happened. As I pulled myself up to their level, I saw two figures jump from the roof onto an adjoining roof and disappear into the dark night.

I couldn't get to Andy quick enough, so I hung from the roof edge and dropped down to him, in doing so I damaged both ankles.

I limped over to Andy on my hands and knees, he was lying face down on the hard service-yard ground. Phil had joined me by this time and we both turned Andy over and we began to render CPR. I tried and tried to breathe life into his still body, but it was too late.

Andy was dead, twenty-one years of age, and I genuinely feel it was my fault - I was there to look after him as he was the probationer. Despite what everyone said that night and subsequently thereafter I have carried this guilt for so, so long.

Andy died trying to protect his community. The two suspects were detained by other officers and taxi drivers, and I believe that they each received a twelve-month custodial sentence.'

A plaque in the police station, to his memory, is inscribed as follows:

'We his fellow officers who were so fortunate to serve with our young colleague, pay tribute to his 'policeman-ship' and erect this plaque for our respect and love of a fine young man. His memory remains an example and inspiration to us all.'

Figure 76 PC Le Comte, circa 1983, courtesy of D Menzel

Figure 77 Plaque at National Memorial Arboretum, courtesy of M Layton

Figure 78 'The Beat', National Memorial Arboretum, courtesy of M Layton

***

Between Wednesday 14th March 1984, and March 1985, West Midlands Police were heavily involved in providing substantial Mutual Aid to other Forces as a result of the Miners' dispute.

Mutual Aid was provided to the following Forces: Cleveland, Derbyshire, Durham, Humberside, Leicestershire, North Yorkshire, Nottinghamshire, South Yorkshire, Staffordshire, Warwickshire, and West Yorkshire. Over 73,000 days were dedicated to Mutual Aid during this period, all the activities of which were coordinated by the Force's Uniform Operations Department. The Operational Support Group alone spent a total of 9,441 days engaged on the Miners' Dispute in 1984.

Retired officer Lyndon Whitehouse was on the OSU at the time and recalls:

'I was on the OSU throughout the dispute. We paraded at Tipton at 2am and travelled to Orgreave on a daily basis. We used to get back around 7pm and were back on duty at 2!

On one occasion I suffered a sprained ankle, and was taken to Rotherham General Hospital which was packed with police officers and miners!'

Figure 79 Lyndon Whitehouse (centre), courtesy of L Whitehouse

Retired officer Bob Moon recalls:

'I was on the OSU, and like most of my colleagues spent a week away, a week in-Force, a week away etc. At Orgreave I caught a brick on my ankle, which cracked it, and I got a very nice personal letter from the Chief Constable of South Yorkshire Police. All in all they were happy days. We were well-trained and equipped and it was good to put all that training to use.'

Retired officer Paul Dobbinson recalls:

'I went up to Orgreave the day after the 'battle' with a 'C' Division serial, leaving at 0200hrs from Ladywood. We had breakfast at 0600hrs, the first and last time, I have ever had hot pork-pie with chips, peas and gravy for breakfast, horrible, but when you are hungry, I guess anything will do!'

A total of 92 West Midlands Police officers sustained injuries during the year whilst deployed to the dispute.

A quote from retired officer Tony Price sums up the enormity of the operation to move thousands of police officers around the country:

'It was a 0300hrs start at Wednesfield, for a 'day-trip out'. Off we set on a coach. I woke up two hours later somewhere on the M1 motorway. I looked behind and saw police vehicles in convoy as far as the eye could see.'

Retired officer Peter Keys recalls:

'I was at a pit in Yorkshire where there was the usual pushing and shoving. A striker once blew a whistle because a police officer had fallen over. Everyone stopped until he got up. The whistle blew and it started again – crazy! My impression was that the men didn't want to strike but if they didn't block the pit entrance, they wouldn't get strike-money. We used to give them our packed-lunches to eat.'

Retired officer Steve Smith has similar memories:

'I remember my first mutual-aid at a pit in Nottingham. We formed a line to protect the few miners that went into work.

The miners on strike were pushing and shoving us whilst calling the workers 'scabs'. As soon as they were safely in the pit, one protester just said to the police, right lads it's time for breakfast. Then the police officers and miners sat down for breakfast together - very strange!'

Retired officer Dave Mangan recalls:

'I remember being on the 'L' serial on the first week of Mutual Aid, staying at a mothballed army base called Proteus in Nottinghamshire. Our day started at about 5am with a disgusting breakfast, then a full day at Mansfield pit, returning exhausted at about 5pm. A Chief Inspector told us we were not allowed off camp in case we were needed to respond to any event, e.g. 'flying pickets'.

Our Sergeant was a Federation Representative who advised the Chief Inspector that this restriction placed us on 'stand-by', which meant we were on duty and therefore we would have to be paid. He wouldn't listen, but the result was we were paid 24/7 for the whole week!'

Retired officer Grahame Davies also recalls conditions at the camp:

'At the camp there was a film-crew making a feature film - they had to renovate the other barracks they were using for their filming of a 'Stalag' - ours were left with broken windows, no privacy curtains, metal bunk beds with crappy mattresses, a pot-bellied stove at one end with no fuel; and don't start me about the food. Even washing and other basics were terrible.'

One of the hundreds of West Midlands Police officers so deployed was retired officer Paul Rainey, who took some personal photographs at the time showing how officers 'survived' the experience.

Figure 80 The miners' strike 1984, courtesy of P Rainey

Figure 81 The miners' strike 1984, courtesy of P Rainey

Figure 82 The miners' strike 1984, courtesy of P Rainey

Retired officer Bob Moon recalls the impact that the miners' dispute had on ordinary people's lives and communities:

'We were billeted at a Royal Air Force base. This was luxury compared to what we had grown accustomed to. We had proper houses within the base - three-bedroomed semi-detached houses. The lounge had been turned into another bedroom so each house could contain ten men, which was one crew.

We cleaned ourselves, our kit, the vans, and then tried to decide how to relax for a couple of hours. Some guys slept, some went to the gym on the base, some phoned their partners, and some went out. I went out.

Four of us went down into the village, to a quiet-looking pub. We were dressed in jeans and sweatshirts and were just looking for a quiet couple of hours away from the mind-set of the strike.

I went to the bar and asked for four pints of ale. Not a big deal in most pubs. However the barman looked me in the eye and said nothing. I asked again, and again he just stared at me and said nothing. I wondered whether I'd got two heads, perhaps I still smelled bad, or maybe I'd said something to offend him. I again asked for four pints, but this time added, 'Look, we just want a quiet pint, OK?'

The pub by then had fallen silent and I was aware that all the customers were looking at me. I glanced at the boys, who were sat at a nearby table by the door. We always sat by the door so as to give ourselves room to fight and to drag our opponents outside, and to see who came in. It was a Birmingham thing. Ron grinned and indicated that another crew were outside.

I turned back to the barman and simply raised my eyebrows without saying a word.

Very quietly he asked, 'Are you Police?'

We never hid what we did and so I said, 'Yes, from Birmingham.'

He asked, 'Are you here because of the strike?'

I replied, 'We wouldn't be here on fucking holiday would we?'

At that he laughed and started pouring the beer.

I asked him why he was so circumspect and he explained that the pub had been visited numerous times by men dressed as us but who were 'political activists', and that they had upset the locals.

I asked him what he meant by 'upset' but he just shrugged and said that most of them now carry weapons.

I took the tray of beer over to the boys and we sat enjoying the flavour and the ambiance.

A young girl came over and sat down at the only spare chair at the table. She asked where we were from.

All four of us started talking at the same time, four young lads, an attractive girl in an unfamiliar place, and then we fell silent. I explained that we were police not RAF. She knew that, as did everyone in the pub. I kind of assumed that because we were from out of town, with strange accents, that they would believe us to be from the RAF base. They did, but they knew that the police had taken over the base.

The girl, she was only about 17, told us that she lived in the village. She'd never liked the police because she alleged that her brother had been arrested and beaten, but now her opinions were changing. Her father was a retired miner and she told us that he had visited the miner's social club the previous week and been beaten-up when he left. She had tears in her eyes which she wiped away with a nicotine-stained finger.

While she was speaking the whole pub was quiet. Everyone seemed to be watching us and we were watching them out of the corner of our eyes. I was waiting for a sign to indicate trouble, to react, but I did not see one. What I saw was a group of people who wanted to talk but couldn't - people who were scared.

The village was a 'working' village - a village where some men had refused to strike, and one of the places that had been visited by activists. The people had been intimidated, threatened and some of them had been attacked. They were honest peaceful people and all of this trouble had come as a shock. They did not want it, had not invited it and did not understand the violence. The activists were bad enough, but then there were armies of police from other parts of the country. Their whole world had been turned upside down.

She wanted to know why we were there, but it was simple – we were ordered there. She wanted to know what we were going to do – again that was simple – we'd do what we were ordered to do. She asked whether we were part of some special unit, but that was more difficult to answer. I lied and said we were just 'every day' cops.

She returned to her friends and we carried on our muted conversations. It was a small pub and so any conversation could be overheard, so we had to whisper. We were only talking about the usual bloke things – sport, birds, home, and family.

A short while later an elderly woman appeared beside our table. She had a kind, but weathered face with hazel eyes that seemed to speak sadness. The crevices in her face were deep and did not move as she spoke. She simply said, 'be careful lads and don't trust anyone'. I smiled at her and said, 'so why listen to you?' At that she gently touched my arm and said, 'don't forget you have a mother'. I didn't reply. We then left and as I placed our glasses back on the bar the barman winked and said, 'take care'.

At the barracks we slept for a few hours but were woken at about 1am by Ian, our Sergeant. 'Get the fuck up – shit's hit the fan – on the van now! 'We dived out of our sleeping bags, threw our kit on and in less than five minutes we were in the van and ready to roll.'

Figure 83 Bob Moon, courtesy of R Moon

Retired officer Roy Shotton was on Force Traffic at the time and recalls:

'As we were traffic officers we had only received basic public order training and were used mainly to man gates. During the dispute I did some Mutual Aid in North Yorkshire where the miners used to throw snow-balls at us with rocks inside. In Derbyshire however, we actually played cricket with them on the lawn outside the pit and we were even taken down the mine to be shown around. '

Figure 84 Miners' washing area, courtesy of R Shotton

***

In April 1984, Bob Moon recalls coming face-to-face with robbers armed with a cosh:

'In early April 1984 I was a Constable on the Operational Support Unit.

It was a day off, so having got myself up, and consumed copious amounts of coffee, I decided to head into Solihull to my bank on the High Street, to get some cash. I pulled on some jeans, a T-shirt, my favourite leather jacket, and headed out.

At about 11 o'clock I arrived at the ATM outside the bank. It was a few yards to the right of the bank's entrance opposite a bus-stop where there was a small queue of waiting passengers.

I'd just retrieved my bank card and cash when I heard a scream. Looking to my left, in the direction of the sound, I saw a 'Securicor' van parked outside the bank and group of men, five of them in all, beating and struggling with a security guard. They then managed to grab a cash-case from him and began to run in my direction.

Instinct kicked in and I immediately, without any thought, went to intervene. In the split second that this had taken place I saw that at least one of the men was holding a wooden 'truncheon-style' cosh in his right hand, and as they ran towards me, I made a lunge at him. Realising he was armed with the cosh I tried to grab him in a rugby-style tackle to wrap my arms around his whole body, however he managed to swing the cosh and hit me heavily across my right side of my face. I can remember letting out a shout of pain as he struck me, but carried on with my aim of grappling with him.

We then entered into a pretty vicious fight while the remaining robbers ran past. The man was trying to get away from me and hit me again as I was trying to grab him and punch the 'daylights' out of him. For a split second I thought that I recognised him. We eventually fell to the floor at the roadside with me on top and I managed to get the cosh off him. I then swung the cosh at his head trying to mark him and gain some blood evidence as I can remember expecting his mates to come to his aid which would have no doubt led to his release from me.

My thoughts were confirmed when I felt a pair of hands pulling me from behind just as a car shot round the corner from a car-park and screeched to a halt beside us. Three men jumped out and set about freeing my attacker. One of them pushed me in the face to get me off his mate while the others helped him into the car and they all then sped away.

Dazed and in pain, I felt blood pouring down my face and my right eye was almost closed, but as I turned to look behind me, I found a middle-aged man standing looking at me with fear and confusion in his expression. I told him that I was a police officer and at that he helped me up apologising profusely. He had grabbed me from behind thinking that as I had the cosh I must have been the attacker. I was after all dressed in jeans and a leather jacket as opposed to a uniform.

By then I could hear sirens in the distance but I was feeling faint and so with some other people I was helped into an estate-agents office next to the bank. I was offered a chair but asked a young lady for a pencil and some paper, saying I needed to sketch what had happened before I passed out. She kindly said that she had already done a sketch and that I should wait for the, soon to arrive, ambulance.

Police cars and an ambulance duly arrived and I was taken into the back of the ambulance. While one of the technicians was attending to me, a police officer, who I vaguely recognised, looked in at me. He visibly winced when he saw my face.

Another ambulance arrived for the stricken 'Securicor' guard.

Everything then became a blur but I remember being treated at the local hospital. In between treatment, a detective from Solihull Police visited me and we discussed what had taken place. I told him that I vaguely recognised my attacker but could not name him. He said he'd got a good idea and left.

That evening the incident was reported on local news media and I was released from hospital with many stitches to my lacerated cheek and a fully swollen and closed right eye.

The Security guard was treated for bruising and released from hospital.

On the following day I went to Solihull Police Station to make my formal statement.

I subsequently discovered that the team of bank robbers, realising that a police officer had been injured, had decided to try and head for a 'safe house' in the Republic of Ireland. Through their sources, the Garda Siochana, the Irish Police, had found out about this and obtained the names of the robbers before alerting Solihull Police. An 'All Ports Warning' was issued so that all ports of entry and exit to the UK were checked, and addresses were being searched.

The getaway car had been found and was a stolen car. So far forensic analysis had found a perfect palm print in blood on the back paintwork of it. The young lady in the estate-agents office had proved to be an excellent witness and had even provided an expertly drawn image of the man I had been fighting with.

Weeks later I was called to the Police Station to take part in a series of identity parades and managed to pick out three of the robbers from line-ups of similar looking men. I remembered that one of them had a deep scar down his left cheek and although he was by then sporting a full bushy beard I recognised him. I picked out my attacker from a photographic line-up as he had not been arrested by then.

It transpired that the robbers were a close criminal gang from Acocks Green in Birmingham, with Irish connections. Word was on the 'criminal grapevine' that they were planning a cash-in-transit robbery somewhere in the Birmingham area, but at that time it just wasn't known where.

Four men were charged with robbery and other offences but the one I was fighting with managed to escape to Ireland with the cash. The four charged were eventually sentenced to lengthy prison terms following a trial at Warwick Crown Court.

The fifth one, my attacker, was captured in Dublin following another robbery and sentenced to prison in Ireland. When he was released he was met at the prison gate by Solihull detectives and extradited to England where he pleaded guilty to robbery and received twelve years in prison.

I later attended before the Chief Constable and Police Authority where I received a Police Authority commendation for bravery - I considered that I was just doing my duty.'

Figure 85 Bob Moon as an Inspector, courtesy of R Moon

***

On the 3rd September 1984, the Criminal Intelligence Operations Unit was formed, based at Nechells Green Police Station. Its objectives were to investigate the most prevalent crime of the day, including 'on the pavement' cash-in-transit robberies, and to obtain intelligence on criminals who transcended Divisional boundaries, using crime pattern analysis. They made 35 arrests and cleared 170 offences during the year.

***

In 1984 crime again rose by 8.3% on the previous year to 227,566 offences, whilst the Force detection rate dropped to 30.2%.

There were 45 murders, all of which were detected, and 4 of manslaughter.

Offences of robbery increased by almost 30%, with a third of all such offences being committed by juveniles.

During the course of the year there were 187 fatal accidents on the roads in the West Midlands.

A total of 999 police officers were assaulted whilst on duty, of which 399 were of a serious nature, including 65 offences of wounding. A total of 62 assaults were on female officers.

1985

The 'Handsworth' Riots

Lord Philip Knights, was replaced upon retirement on the 8th April 1985 by Mr. Geoffrey James Dear, who was to be the Chief Constable for 5 years, after previously holding the post of Assistant Commissioner *'A'* in the Metropolitan Police.

Lord Knights passed away in 2014 at the age of 94 years. In his personal life he was among other things Vice-President of the Warwickshire County Cricket Club, the Birmingham County Scout Council and the Birmingham Federation of Clubs for Young People. He completed a total of 48 years policing service, having started as a Police Cadet with Lincolnshire Police.

In his first full year in office Geoffrey Dear was to put great store in the use of the word *'professionalism'* in so far as it affected the quality of service he expected his officers to apply at all times. He was acknowledged as being the architect of a number of wide-ranging changes within the Force and was once described by the broadcaster and writer Sir Robin Day as, *'the best known and most respected police officer of his generation.'*

In the 1997 New Year's Honours List he was knighted, and in 2006 made a life peer, taking the title *'Baron Dear'*.

***

On the 11th May 1985, on what was dubbed the *'blackest day'* in the Midlands, more than 100 people were arrested before, during and after a football match at the St. Andrews ground between Birmingham City FC and Leeds United, when scenes of extreme violence were witnessed at the ground and in Birmingham City Centre, all of which were viewed on national television.

At the height of the disturbances at the ground a wall collapsed, resulting in the death of one innocent young fan, with several people being injured. 145 police officers were treated for injuries as well as up to 400 other people.

More than 125 arrests were made on the day and many more retrospectively. The chair of a Committee of Inquiry set up to investigate events at Bradford, (the fire disaster), and Birmingham on that day, Mr. Justice Popplewell, commented on the disturbances at St. Andrews that it was, *'more like the Battle of Agincourt'*, than a football match.

The incident led to a reappraisal of the scale of protective clothing available to officers.

Many of the police officers who were injured on the day were taken to East Birmingham Hospital, and the Consultant in charge of the Accident and Emergency Department was later to comment, *'One of the things which impressed me most was the stoicism and the calmness of the injured policemen. Their behaviour was remarkable. They were less concerned with their damaged heads, crushed feet and other injuries than with trying to help other people, and if this is the typical British 'bobby' we have every reason to be proud.'*

Figure 86 Officers struggling on the touchline at St. Andrews, 1985 courtesy of the Express & Star

Figure 87 Birmingham City FC riot, 1985, courtesy of The Express & Star

Co-author Stephen Burrows recalls:

'I began my police career on the 3rd October 1983, at Acocks Green Police Station, on the 'E3' Sub-Division, which was one third of the 'E' Division. The other two Sub-Divisions were Bromford Lane and Stechford. The 'E' Division was responsible for hosting St. Andrews football ground, and therefore led on providing policing at 'The Blues'.

The outcome of this was that I regularly spent many hours on the touchline and terraces of St. Andrews during the first eighteen months of my service. My abiding memory is that it was the coldest I had ever been. It was said that there was nothing between St. Andrews and the Ural Mountains, and much of any match was spent taking turns warming up in the hot air from the outlet vent on the hot-dog stand.

In those days there were not many stewards and we policed both inside and outside the stadium. It was thought to be good experience for young officers to police the football and it certainly resulted in a good grounding in the handling of public order situations.

One also came to know the troublesome clubs in terms of the minority of their supporters who got involved with hooligan acts. Birmingham City FC had one of the worst groups with the 'Zulu Warriors' being at their peak in the mid-eighties. One of the others was Leeds United.

On the 11th May 1985, Leeds were due to play at St Andrews, in the old Division Two, in the final match of the season. Nothing rested upon the result other than that Birmingham would top the table if they won. The hooligans had other ideas however, and it was rumoured that the Leeds 'firm' intended to stop the match, to prevent Birmingham City going top.

One should remember that this period was at the peak of football violence, fences had gone up at the grounds, and trouble was always expected, as rival 'firms' vied for the glory of causing the most trouble, often pre–arranging fights with each other, inside or outside the ground.

I recall that a couple of days before the match I was sent to Sheldon Police Station and bumped into the Football Intelligence Officer who asked me if I was to be at the Leeds match on that Saturday. He then confirmed that there were going to be big problems and that the Leeds fans intended to attend en-masse to mark the end of the season with a massive fight.

They were however also expecting trouble at the West Bromwich Albion v Arsenal match a few miles away, and had deployed the Operational Support Unit there.

The 'OSU' were the experts in public order policing in the West Midlands Police. They were specialist units, trained in public order techniques and formed into 'serials' of one Sergeant and ten Constables per van. The 'OSU' could always be recognised by the fact that they wore their helmet chinstraps down and their black gloves in public order situations

Thus, it was, that on the 11th May I found myself sat in the Railway End Stand at St. Andrews that Saturday morning for a match briefing, looking around at what appeared to be far too few officers scattered in the seats, and thinking that this could be an interesting afternoon.

The briefing took place, after which I took up my duty post on the touch-line at the Railway End. This was where the 'Family Enclosure' was situated, thus there was no fencing at this end of the ground.

The visiting fans end had a full security fence and this is where the Leeds fans gathered.

I could sense tension after policing many matches, and as I took my place on the touchline at about 1.30pm, I could taste it, never mind sense it. As I looked around the ground the situation was not looking promising. I could see that there were already several thousand Leeds fans in the ground. It was a volatile mood and some were already throwing missiles.

I recall parts of seats flying over the fence, together with other objects, and some 'fans' then proceeded to remove the roof from the hot-dog stand, passing it down the terraces over their heads before throwing it over the fence.

The situation at my end of the ground also began to deteriorate. I had spent much of the previous eighteen months policing the Gospel Oak Estate in Acocks Green together with parts of Tyseley and Sparkhill. I had learnt to recognize by sight many of the troublemakers that would frequent the pubs of Acocks Green and 'The Gospel', often ending their drink-fuelled nights out by kicking in a few windows and fighting.

Thus, as I viewed the gathering crowd in the seats at The Railway End I started to spot familiar faces. Not excited youngsters, but a selection of those local troublemakers with whom I had regularly crossed swords, many of whom were members of the infamous 'Zulu Warriors'. Such were the numbers that it gradually dawned upon me that they had arranged to infiltrate the Railway End in numbers, where there was no fence. To this day I believe that the day's subsequent events had been orchestrated to some extent between the 'Zulu Warriors' and the Leeds fans in advance.

The match began, and for much of the first half the situation remained tense but without incident. The half-time whistle was the signal for the first pitch invasion and it came from the Railway End.

This was clearly just a scouting mission, the lull before the storm. The second invasion at the end of the match involved hundreds of youths, all Birmingham 'fans,' and all from the Railway End. Seats were ripped up and skimmed as missiles. I recall being hit on the arm by one and it was thrown from such close range I saw who did it.

We were clearly losing the battle, heavily outnumbered and in possession of no riot gear.

An irony not lost upon me, even as I fought on the pitch, was that the other end was by now policed by the OSU in full riot gear, including NATO-style crash helmets with visors and shields. They had been diverted from The Albion v Arsenal match at half-time. The OSU were in line, on the touchline, facing the fence in front of them.

Meanwhile, on the other half of the pitch, we had no riot gear, standard helmets, no shields, wooden truncheons and no fence. The battle lines between us and the pitch invaders ebbed back and forth and at one stage I was nearly in the centre tunnel, thinking that if we got backed into there, we would get a good hiding.

The day was saved by the West Midlands Police Mounted Section. Whenever I watch a historical film depicting battle with cavalry I'm reminded of that moment. I quickly appreciated the effectiveness of horses against foot soldiers. It was like the 'Charge of the Light Brigade', especially the white horse that continually rode backwards and forwards, knocking the hooligans over like 'ninepins' and was later immortalized in an oil painting by the artist John Edwards. The horses drove the mass of the invaders inexorably back towards the stand.

Encouraged by this development, we were formed into a line with truncheons drawn and mounted a ferocious foot charge and in a beautiful moment of poetic justice, I came face to face with the seat thrower who had injured me earlier.

We finally beat the pitch invaders back into the seats and I can remember a number of them being hauled up onto the upper tier by others in order to escape due process.

Their resistance and momentum broke, and they fled the ground. A kind of peace descended. I could see that the ground was clear, bar the Leeds fans penned behind their fence by the OSU, not to be released until the Birmingham fans had been dealt with and marshalled away from them, the ground and the railway station.

'Job done' I thought. Our Chief Inspector, quite rightly, had other ideas.

He formed us up on the centre-line, praised us and then told us that trouble outside the ground needed sorting out and we were the only ones available to do it.

There were about thirty of us I guess, in various states of injury and exhaustion, none of us having any riot gear as yet. We exited the ground into Garrison Lane. In those days you came out onto a road that led to a children's playground set at a much lower level than was visible from where we were standing.

About one hundred yards away I could see about forty youths milling about, and the Chief Inspector decided that another baton charge would be appropriate. We formed into a line, drew our truncheons, and with a blood curdling cry of which William Wallace would have been proud, off we went. As we got closer, the hooligans began to run, disappearing out of sight over the edge and down the drop into the playground.

As we drew closer to the playground, which was a large tarmacadam area, it began to become visible. This revealed a daunting prospect as we realized that the playground was occupied by several hundred youths busily ripping the swings out of the ground to use as weapons.

We were forced to withdraw, as our pursuers stopped to turn over a police van, which probably saved us, as reinforcements arrived in the form of a phalanx of police motorcyclists, having the advantage of crash helmets and full leathers. As luck would have it, the overturned van belonged to the OSU and was full of shields that we 'liberated' and joined our rescuers in chasing the crowd off.

Saturday afternoon at the football did not end there. Next stop after a home match for the 'Zulus,' was traditionally Birmingham City Centre, and I can remember having to walk from the ground into Birmingham, shield before me, chasing football hooligans.

When I got home I expected to have been part of big news but it was the same day as the Bradford Fire Disaster, which overshadowed an event that was probably one of the worst instances of football violence ever seen in England.

I must not conclude without mentioning the tragic death of fifteen-year-old Ian Hambridge from Nottingham, at his first ever football match, when a twelve-foot wall collapsed at St Andrews, at the height of the riot. It is believed that he was sheltering from the violence under the wall, a truly innocent victim of football hooliganism.'

Figure 88 Police officers carrying an injured supporter, St. Andrews 1985, courtesy of the Express & Star

Figure 89 Collapsed wall, St. Andrews, 1985, courtesy of the Express & Star

(Postscript: - In 1987 the West Midlands Police Federation paid John Edwards to paint the riot scene at St. Andrews involving the white horse. The Chief Constable Geoffrey Dear agreed to autograph a limited edition of 250 prints taken from the painting. The prints were sold at £35 pounds each with all proceeds going to the Police Convalescent Home charity. At the time a police spokesperson said, *'The picture shows a turning point in the history of the West Midlands Police in the new level of violence which they were expected to cope with – without any increase in manning levels or equipment'.*)

***

Retired officer Karen (Kay) Lenyk recalls her life on the Force Mounted Police Section:

'I joined the West Midlands Police on the 10th March 1980, and my collar number was 8710.

My birth name is Karen, but I have always been called Kay and my maiden name was Weale but it's now Lenyk.

I initially worked on the 'L1' Solihull Division, a large, mostly rural area, dealing mostly with burglaries and shoplifters', so moving to Park Lane was a big change!

I did my ten-week mounted riding course at 'Tally Ho' Police Training Centre from October until just before Christmas of 1984, then went back to the 'L' Division, as practically all of the male officers were sent up to Yorkshire regarding the miner's strike.

We worked twelve-hour shifts for quite some time, and surprisingly enough the 'wheel did not come off'!

In June of 1985, I transferred to the 'A' Division and was based at Park Lane as the first female officer on the Mounted Branch.

The press came and did some photos when I took up my post - my only ever 'claim to fame'! The day after they were taken they were published in the newspapers and shortly afterwards I was riding up Ladywood Middleway when a car passed and a little girl who was leaning out of the window started yelling "Hello Kay!"

Over the years I also worked from stables at West Bromwich, Chase Avenue and Tally Ho, but most of my service was at Park Lane.

The initial Mounted Course was hard work but great fun. There were four of us, myself, Steve Tolley, Simon Kirby and Mick Wakeman. The then Sergeant Fitzmaurice was our trainer.

The horses were 'Daisy', the most uncomfortable, 'Hertford' the largest, 'Javelin' the laziest and 'Jemedar' the craziest!

We had to groom the horses, learn how to 'tack up' then strip and clean all the kit, then every afternoon was class-work. We had to pass both the riding-test and the written-exam.

My first ever 'dunk' in the water trough occurred after our last ride on the course. I was chucked in so ran upstairs to change into dry clothes, leaving my wet stuff in my locker. I then rushed back down to see to my horse.

As I was then a few minutes behind the lads, they took the opportunity to ransack my locker. You can imagine my horror when I went back upstairs to find my wet underwear on full display - I was speechless with embarrassment but it was part of the banter that went on at the time.

Each horse had a stable name, a number, and an official name - alphabetically named for the year they started. They all had their own personality. At the start of each shift we would look at the board to see which horse(s) we were riding and the Division to patrol. Some days you smiled - others you didn't!

'Javelin' would NOT walk past the abattoir, 'Paragon' wanted to eat you, 'Polo' hated milk-floats, 'Hidalgo' knew every tea-stop on the patch, whether you wanted to go there or not! 'Limber Gunner' could not be stopped if his feet touched grass, 'Olympic' would have liked to kill you, 'Merlin' enjoyed a bucket of tea - they all had their peculiarities.

My first allocated horse was 389 'Hidalgo', known as 'David'. He was an ex-race horse and very small for a police horse. He had a wonderful nature and taught me a lot. He got loads of cards and presents from the public when he was injured at a violent football match.

He enjoyed the attention of being an invalid and tried to stretch it out for as long as he could. Once when he was coming back into light work he would pretend to be lame, but got caught out because he held up the wrong hoof. He was very clever!

The grey horse 428 'Polo' was very special to me and I adored her. I bought her when she was due to be retired and she lived out her retirement with me in Wales. I used to give her a bath and take her out for a nibble of grass whilst being sun-dried. The police horses were looked after very well but 'Polo' was kept in a stall so whenever the opportunity arose I took her outside so she could have a roll.

The Mounted Branch was an enormous part of my life and I have many great memories. We were kept fit as we 'mucked out', groomed the horses, unloaded and loaded hay and straw deliveries, cleaned the kit and stables etc. Gradually more civilian grooms were employed and we spent more time out on the streets. Changes were obviously afoot!

I started on the Branch just after the Blues/Leeds match, which ended in a riot, and is why I think there was so much concern. The chaps were worried that they would end up having to babysit me! That game was talked about for a long time and the fact that the young lad died when the wall collapsed upset a lot of people. I have already mentioned 'Hidalgo' recovering from injury at a match, well that was the one.

As I am sure you well know, the 'Zulu Warriors' did not just disappear. I remember the chants "Zulu, Zulu, Zulu"! I have had bricks, bottles, coins and spit aimed at me on several occasions, but thankfully was never hurt.

My first football match, at the 'Blues' St Andrews ground was highly entertaining. There used to be a lot of trouble with street fights between opposing sides.

I was crewed up with 'The Gaffer', Inspector (later to become the Chief Inspector) Des Turner. After the game there were punch-ups all around. He said "just stick with me" and off we went.

I did not have time to feel nervous, it was actually quite exhilarating! We just had to split people up and keep them moving. At one point we were chasing a group along one of the side streets off Watery Lane. I shall leave it to the imagination the names we were being called and the taunts we were receiving. One particularly obnoxious individual was being really vile, he kept looking back at us and swearing, he was so intent on trying to 'wind us up' that he didn't look where he was going and ran at full pelt into a lamppost.

I laughed so hard that I nearly fell off my horse! I decided that I was going to enjoy this job!

I attended several matches where there was bother and one was certainly at West Bromwich Albion. I remember it being a long day as we had ridden up there. There was chaos on the streets afterwards! It was a very long time ago now and my memories are all intermingled so I cannot be specific about anything but I do remember that truncheons were drawn!

We did see quite a bit of bother but were pretty good at keeping it under control. Under the leadership of Chief Constable Geoffrey Dear, a true gentleman who used to ride out with us occasionally, we obtained more horses and more kit. Many a time someone would tap my leg and say "Excuse me mate, can you tell me where so and so is" then be mortified once I opened my mouth. Until I spoke they had no idea that I was female. With my riot helmet and body armour on I was just one of the lads!

Eventually, I believe the West Midlands Police obtained a reputation as 'not to be messed with'. Fans used to tell us that if they wanted bother they would go elsewhere! Our OSU, Dog Section and Mounted branch made a fantastic team!

The job consisted of either public liaison or public order. In the summer we did school visits, carnival processions, musical rides and patrolling open spaces. In the winter it was mainly football matches.

The horses were clipped in the winter so if it was a match we stayed at during the game then our macs were left on the horses to keep them warm. I used to wear many layers of clothes to try and stay warm. I never did understand why some 'hard guys' at the matches would be wearing short sleeve tee-shirts in the snow, whilst I was wearing twenty-seven separate items of clothing - I did not think of them as tough, just stupid!

We used to do a lot of public order training. Obviously it was very important that all parties involved knew the drill. Sometimes it was the old Round Oak steelworks in the Black Country, and then later on at RAF Cosford.

We used to practise the various manoeuvres over and over again until everyone knew what they were doing. I was always glad to be on the horse approaching the line of shields rather than the other way around. I often had bruised knees from hitting the helmets of the poor souls not quick enough to move aside.

Our favourite training days were always those for the new recruits - never having attended public-order training before, they had no idea of what to expect. After running through the normal routines the best was always saved for last. They would be told that we were about to try 'The Beechers' tactic – 'The Beechers' they would ask 'Yes, Beechers' they were told. 'Just huddle together and tuck your heads in because the horses are coming over the top!'

You can imagine the colour draining out of their poor little faces as twelve enormous great horses formed a line, waited for the command "All ride, CHARGE" and then would approach at speed, before veering off at the last moment. Somehow I cannot see it being allowed to happen today - I think it was called 'character building' then!

I absolutely loved working on the Mounted Branch. I spent five years at Solihull first so it was a very different environment, but I never regretted a minute of it. Several of the lads did not appreciate the infiltration of a 'bloody woman', but I hope that I eventually won them round.

At first I think they were concerned that I would be a hindrance, but I hope that I proved them wrong. I did take a lot of stick but I tried to just keep smiling and give as 'good as I got'!

At times it was like a kindergarten. I learned to check doorways for the inevitable bucket of water before entering a room.

I was forced to leave in 1997 following a neck injury which prevented me from ever wearing a riot helmet again. I was inconsolable when the Police Surgeon informed me that after 13 years on the Branch my riding days were over. On the plus side I had already gone by the time the Branch was disbanded in 1999. To have had to watch it being taken apart would have broken my heart. I still think that it was an enormous mistake. One horse was the equivalent of 40 men on the ground, plus we had the advantage of height and speed.

I often used to say to my colleagues, "Do you realise that at this very moment people are paying a lot of money to go and ride a horse, whilst we are being paid to do it"! I do realise how lucky I was to have held such a fabulous job! It was a huge part of my life and I loved practically every minute!'

Figure 90 Kay Lenyk and Jo Dix, (second female on Mounted branch) circa 1986/7 in Aston Park pre 'hard – hats', courtesy of K Lenyk

Figure 91 Kay Lenyk during charity bike ride, late 1980's, courtesy of K Lenyk

Figure 92 Kay Lenyk and a section of 'Chestnuts', heavy horse parade, Cannon Hill Park, circa 1988, courtesy of K Lenyk

Figure 93 Kay Lenyk in ceremonial dress on 'Polo', circa 1989, courtesy of K Lenyk

Figure 94 Kay Lenyk with 'Polo', Park Lane, circa 1989, courtesy of K Lenyk

Figure 95 Kay Lenyk in football 'kit', circa 1996, courtesy of K Lenyk

***

On the 24th August 1985, police officers were engaged in an armed raid on a house in Kings Norton, Birmingham in an attempt to arrest a suspect who it was believed had earlier been involved in a robbery where a 12-bore shotgun had been used. In the course of searching the house a police revolver was discharged and a 5 year old boy, John Stonehouse, tragically died.

***

On the 9th September 1985, at about 5.15pm, a dispute arose between a police motorcyclist and a local resident over the issue of a parking ticket outside the *'Acapulco Café'* in Lozells Road. The officer called for assistance, and as other officers arrived, fighting broke out, during which 11 officers were injured.

At 7.40pm the Villa Cross Bingo Hall was set on fire, but as the Fire Brigade attended they found their way blocked by crowds.

At 7.55pm the first petrol-bombs were thrown at police, and by 9pm shops in the Lozells Road came under attack and burning barricades blocked roads.

Large-scale rioting and widespread looting then took place which resulted in premises and shops being firebombed, including a Post Office in Lozells Road where two men, Amirali and Kassamali Moledina, who had been lawfully inside their premises, were later found dead from suffocation as a result of a fire.

Such was the intensity of the firebombing that a fire officer driving through the area later described it as like, *'driving through an oven'*.

Rioting continued next day, and when Home Secretary Douglas Hurd visited, missiles were thrown at him and he was forced to make a speedy exit.

79 police officers were injured in total as well as 35 members of the public.

Damage worth over £1,000,000 was caused, relating to 83 premises and 23 private vehicles. A total of 57 police vehicles were also damaged.

Nearly 400 crimes were recorded in relation to the two days of rioting, and more than 290 arrests made.

Terror in flames of hatred

Eyewitness report
by Ken Tudor

It was just after 8.15 when I arrived in riot-wrecked Handsworth — to be met by a full-blooded police charge racing towards me with more than 20 officers screaming behind their shields. This was the Handsworth Blitz — a cruel re-run of the troubles which hit the run-down suburb of Birmingham four years ago.

But this time it was a much more serious crisis, with many more injuries and devastated properties, more terror and horror.

In the July riots of 1981 I had witnessed at first hand some incredible scenes, widespread looting, burning of cars and stone-throwing at police officers.

Last night and early today there was much, much more — firemen being bombed by Molotov cocktails, families being terrorised out of their homes, widespread muggings and businesses fire-bombed out of existence.

When I arrived at the Villa Cross on the busy Villa Road the trouble was still mainly confined to the area in which it had started. The police were lined up behind battle shields, truncheons at hand, dressed all in black and staring straight ahead as the marauding looters came menacingly forward.

Wailing

Suddenly they charged, and I was forced to run back down Barker Street as the 100-plus group — some of them not even teenagers — ran from the wailing black line of police with their blood-curdling screams.

Some were caught, some were pushed about and one black radio reporter complained bitterly about being truncheoned in the chaos. That charge was frightening — and left a bitter taste in the mouth.

But much worse was to come as the trouble spewed down the road into Lozells. Cars were overturned one after another and set on fire, people frightened out of their homes and, finally, the real looting and burning started.

It was an amazing sight to see the grilles ripped from the jewellers' windows, like cans of sardines being opened, and every last jewel, watch and ornament stolen.

Many of the Asian people were crying, sobbing openly as they saw their businesses burning, the butchers, the greengrocers, wine merchants and general dealers could not believe what was happening.

"They are all our shops that are being hit," said one. "It is always us who suffer."

Rates warning as full inquiry is promised

A full inquiry — with the outcome made public — into the rioting in Handsworth was promised today by police authority chairman, Councillor Ed Shore.

His pledge came as West Midlands ratepayers were warned that they were likely to be billed for the damage.

He vowed that people behind the disturbances would be tracked down and prosecuted.

Councillor Shore said: "It is intolerable that a relatively small minority should go on the rampage, looting shops and causing a riot, resulting in the deaths of innocent people.

"It is also intolerable that public servants in the police and fire services should be subjected to abuse and violence when carrying out their duties."

It will be left to the police authority to decide whether the disturbances constituted a riot under the Riot Damages Act, but no one was in doubt today about the likely ruling.

Property-owners would be able to claim compensation, and payments would be made out of public funds.

The 1981 riots, which were more widespread, resulted in about £250,000 being paid out. But there were fears today that last night's flare-up will bring a much bigger bill.

The scene of destruction in Lozells Road — a group of riot police stand huddled to the left while a blazing hijacked car and other street debris light up the area.

Riot police use the burned-out wreck of a van — hijacked by the thugs and set alight — as temporary cover in Lozells Road, near the junction with Finch Road.

Firemen fight the flames as buildings in Lozells Road smoulder.

The Lord Mayor of Birmingham, Councillor Frank Carter, surveys the scene.

Figure 96 Courtesy of the Express & Star

RIOT HORROR

● Flashpoint . . . the start (top right) of the blaze in which three died. The aftermath is seen above and right as the massive clearing-up operation gets underway.

Three dead–then Home Secretary pelted by gangs

Home Secretary Douglas Hurd was attacked by a mob of rioters this afternoon.

The attack happened as violence which has already claimed three lives spread to Handsworth.

on fire as the marauders took to the streets again.

A police van was overturned as a 150-strong mob surged up Heathfield Road, pelting the police line with petrol bombs.

Mr Hurd came under a hail of bricks and bottles as police tried to pull him to safety.

He was mobbed by the angry shouting crowd just seconds after he had stepped from his car to see the scene of last night's devastation.

The Minister, who was walking with a stick, was jostled against barricades.

Extra police contingents were drafted in as the Home Secretary stopped to talk to some of the shopkeepers whose homes and businesses were gutted in petrol bomb attacks only hours earlier.

But then a 300 strong crowd broke through the police lines and raced after the minister.

● Turn to Page 5

Figure 97 Courtesy of the Express & Star

Fear—in haven for drug kings

The turbulent Villa Cross area where the riot started is noted as a centre of drug dealing which has terrified people who live there.

An angry public meeting heard last week that children were being used as drug carriers. Two meeting places — the Villa Cross pub and the Acapulco café — have been branded as the main centres.

In May, 17 people were arrested for alleged drugs offences when 150 uniformed and plain-clothes officers swooped on the pub. Two months later, more than £1,500 worth of drugs were seized when 160 officers raided the cafe.

There have been several other police raids in the area since then. But at last Thursday's public meeting people were critical of the police, claiming that the softly-softly approach they adopted was ineffectual.

They were also annoyed that the city council had granted permission for the former Villa Cross cinema and bingo hall — where last night's trouble exploded — to be turned into an amusement centre.

They are fearful that the amusement centre could become another centre for drug dealers and takers. Mr Eric Faux, chairman of Handsworth Soho Residents' Association, urged the police to adopt a higher profile in the area.

He said people were too frightened to leave their homes at night or sometimes during the day because muggings and other attacks. He s: "We have a situation in which pec are having to go out in threes or fo to protect themselves."

Mr Jeff Rooker, Labour MP Perry Barr, which includes much the area where the riots erupt branded the Villa Cross pub "a c grace to the brewers who own Ansells." A spokesman for the br ery said there had been a probl with drugs, but it had been clear up.

3 die in firebombs riot

Street battles in night of shame

THREE people were burned to death in a night of violence in the Handsworth area of Birmingham as marauding gangs of petrol bombers wrecked more than 50 shops and offices.

The bodies were discovered by firemen as dawn today as they damped down the burned-out shell of the Lozells Road sub-post office.

They were so badly burned that it was impossible to tell whether they were male or female, but the sub-postmaster is feared to be one of the victims. Later there were unconfirmed reports that firemen had found a fourth body.

Geoffrey Dear – arrest not to blame for riot

West Midlands Chief Constable Geoffrey Dear today said that the best way to control the riot would have been to use rubber bullets — a weapon banned by his police committee.

The night of shame saw more than £3 million damage caused to shops, offices and homes.

For more than seven hours 500 policemen fought non-stop battles with rioters who rampaged through shopping centres bringing panic, terror and sheer lawlessness to the streets.

Police were powerless for a long time to stop the orgy of destruction and Mr Dear said that the damage to the community was worse than the infamous Brixton and Toxteth riots four years ago.

Twenty three West Midlands police officers, six firemen and two members of the public were injured in the fracas.

In the early hours Mr Dear toured the area to witness the devastation. He praised residents and shopkeepers about their night of terror.

He said afterwards: "In terms of feeling able to cope, I think West Midlands police and West Midlands fire brigade coped admirably.

"Bearing in mind that there were buildings collapsing into the road and ambushes taking place, I think they did enormously well to confine it to one area."

Mr Dear had to draft in several hundred men from Stafford, West Mercia, Warwickshire and Leicestershire to help control.

Policemen were today counting the cost of the bombing with more than 10 shops in a row totally wrecked by fire. Some collapsed into the streets as dawn broke over the city.

The rioting started soon after 7.30 last night when firemen were pelted with scores of petrol bombs as they tried to fight the first blaze of the night at the now-defunct Villa Cross bingo hall.

They were marooned in a safe back street and Station Officer Steve Halsall said: "I've never known anything like it — it was sheer hell."

West Midlands Assistant Chief Fire Officer Mr Lee Wills said: "It is the worst I have seen in 28 years. It is a horrible, disastrous situation.

"We took time moving in to tackle the fires because we had no police protection and the atmosphere was very ugly. Without a doubt we could have saved a lot of the shops if we had been allowed into the area."

His men were pelted non-stop with petrol bombs and bricks and it was only after several hours of police snatch charges that the firemen were able to get through to the blazing shops in Lozells Road.

At one stage a firebomb was hurled into a fish and chip shop as customers were being served. When emergency crews tried to deal with the blaze they met another bombardment of flaming missiles.

Another major incident was in Berners Street when a "bomb" hit a mechanics training centre for unemployed teenagers. The one-time coach depot housed propane gas cylinders which shook the terraced street as they exploded.

One of the problems facing police was the fact that the looters had so much ammunition available — bricks from building sites and a milk bottle on almost every doorstep.

When they ran out of ammunition they raided a do-it-

yourself store in Soho Road. Cars were used as "bullets" too — they were driven at speed and left to career driverless towards the police lines.

At least 20 cars were burned out on the streets and throughout the area Asian businessmen who remembered the damage of the 1981 riots called in friends and relatives to help protect their premises.

Black county councillor James Hunte today claimed that he had repeatedly warned police chiefs that serious racial problems were brewing in the multi-race Handsworth area.

He said he understood the trouble started over a parking fine near the Villa Cross pub. "The tension was there and it just needed that kind of little spark," he said.

Black community leader Mr Gus Williams laid the blame for the riots on the new Chief Constable. He said: "The impression as far as the black community is concerned is that he is determined to make his reputation on the heads of the black people.

Police looking into the reasons for the flare-up say initial inquiries had shown that there were two possible theories — the stabbing of an Asian shopkeeper and an incident with a motor cyclist making inquiries about a possible offence of driving while disqualified.

Near the post office a petrified woman and her two children cowered in the back of a grocer's shop as knife-wielding robbers attacked her husband.

They ransacked vegetable stands, smashed every window and demanded money from shopkeeper Mr Zukarman Sikander. They snatched £370 from the till and ordered 28-year-old Mr Sikander to hand over £70 from his pockets.

Police arrived as the rioters threatened to harm his family huddled in the back room. Mr Sikander was cut to the struggle with the youths.

Firemen from West Bromwich were given a police escort late last night to reach blazes raging in four shops and a church.

Mrs Thatcher today described the Birmingham riots as "utterly appalling" and called on all local community leaders to see such events never happened again.

Labour leader Neil Kinnock today said unemployment was a contributory factor to the "hysteria and horror" of the Birmingham riots.

SDP leader Dr David Owen said last night's events were "extremely tragic for the people of Birmingham".

FROM FRONT PAGE

Officers with riot shields took up positions as Mr Hurd was hurriedly bundled into a police riot van. Seconds later fires were started along the Lozells Road.

Afterwards Mr Geoffrey Dear, the West Midlands Chief Constable, who accompanied the Minister, said that Mr Hurd had insisted that he wanted to talk to the people on the street.

Mr Mirza Mohammed Zaman, aged 39, chairman of the Handsworth Muslim Community and also Asian welfare officer on the local police defence committee, has told of the death of the Asians in a sub post office.

He said: "The rioting involving several hundred youths, mainly West Indians, had been going on for some time and many shops in the road were already ablaze.

Chanting

"Sometime after 8 pm I was standing opposite the post office when a mob of chanting youths smashed open the shutters and surged inside.

"My friends the Moledina brothers were upstairs at the time. From what I could hear of their screams and cries for help they appeared to be suffering a terrible beating."

He described how the rioters then poured out of the shop. The next thing he knew, a petrol bomb was hurled through one of the windows.

Home Secretary Douglas Hurd arrives at the West Midlands Police headquarters at Lloyd House in Birmingham today.

Firemen carry a body from the burned-out sub-post office in Lozells.

Rubber bullets 'the answer'

West Midlands police chief constable Geoffrey Dear today said today that he would be prepared to use rubber bullets against rioters.

He said the weapons — banned by his police committee — would have been the only way to control the riots last night.

Mr Dear said: "The fact is that we have used them in training, and we have equipped in this force to use them.

"I've warned all other police forces in Britain so that they could

Mr Dear said last night's trouble intensified when car loads of people some from as far away as Wolverhampton, joined in the looting after news flashes on television.

He had earlier described the riot as "spontaneous action by a crowd of hooligans". And he described last night as "an orgy of thieving".

Police had arrested a man for driving while disqualified in the area — but it was three hours later that the rioting began.

Mr Jeff Rooker, Labour MP for Perry Barr, later toured the area. "There has clearly got to be an inquiry about what happened last night," he said.

"But we don't need an inquiry to tell us what is wrong with the area. It is more deprived than Brixton or Liverpool."

Mrs Imlyn Phillips, a black woman, of Crompton Road, said: "I know that this trouble could have been avoided if the police had moved earlier to stop it.

"At one stage I saw shops on fire and just one lone fireman, no police. Everybody was involved in the trouble — Asians, West Indians and whites.

But Mr Dear defended the police response to the riot. He said that there were 12 policemen on duty in Handsworth, which in fact was a rather heavy presence for an area of

that size.

Mr Mushtaq Rabbani, an Asian community leader, said there was a good relationship between Asians and West Indians in the area, but this did not extend to the police.

Mrs Thatcher today described the Birmingham riots as "utterly appalling" and called on all local community leaders to see such events never happened again.

Labour leader Neil Kinnock today said unemployment was a contributory factor to the "hysteria and horror" of the Birmingham riots.

SDP leader Dr David Owen said last night's events were "extremely tragic for the people of Birmingham.

●Message that went unheeded — Page 6.

Figure 98 Courtesy of the Express & Star

Co-author Stephen Burrows recalls:

'I was woken by the jarring sound of the telephone ringing. Not a mobile by the bed – there were no mobiles - this phone was downstairs and it was the small hours of Tuesday 10th September 1985.

"Handsworth's gone up," said the voice, "Your course is cancelled, get yourself into Acocks Green as soon as you can."

It was just four months since being involved in the riot at the Birmingham City versus Leeds match, and it seemed that disorder was stalking me. The previous day I had commenced my 'PACE' course. This was a week–long introduction to the recently enacted Police and Criminal Evidence Act which had changed every facet of prisoner handling, interviewing and evidence collection.

Every able-bodied person who should have been on the course formed a public-order 'serial' for the Handsworth riot, and thus I ended up in a Transit van with an interesting collection of characters of some service length.

Once assembled, we were sent to Thornhill Road Police Station, Handsworth, where we were hurriedly fed and sat around the yard by the van awaiting orders. We must have arrived at dawn because I can remember looking through the van window as we drove past Lozells Road and seeing the smoking ruins that looked just like pictures of the Blitz.

There had been a temporary lull in the disorder and many weary colleagues, who had been on duty since the previous evening, were going off duty, to be replaced by us. Their faces, and the devastation in the streets made me realise that this was the most serious and potentially dangerous incident I had ever been part of.

This sight did not dampen the spirits of my colleagues though. There was a line of vehicles; public-order vans, dog-vans and police cars, parked to one side of the yard at Thornhill Road, with their officer contents sat on the floor between the vehicles and the station wall. We were waiting for something to happen.

It must have been about 10am when our wait ended. We were told that trouble had started again and into the van we climbed. I can remember the Superintendent coming to the open back doors of the van and wishing us luck. I can still recall the feeling. I was going into battle.

I already knew that people had died the previous night in the Post Office that they ran, after they decided to remain in the premises to protect it from the mob. Tensions were high and there were reports that many troublemakers from outside of Handsworth were travelling to 'have a go' at the police and maybe do a spot of incidental looting.

We were deployed to Heathfield Road, in public-order attire, and had shields and what were termed 'NATO' helmets. There were people around, but mostly they seemed to be older locals, Asian and Black, upset and bemused by what had happened to their community - and all very clear and unanimous that it had not been done in their names.

The Asians in particular, who owned the vast majority of business in Handsworth, were incensed and vowing to mobilise as vigilantes to protect their livelihoods. Everyone blamed a small minority of black drug dealers and troublemakers who centred themselves around the 'Acapulco Café' in Lozells, where the trouble had started. I was on the streets of Handsworth for a week after the riots and spoke to many locals, and not a single one blamed deprivation. In fact a lot of those arrested came from outside Handsworth.

Relationships between the police and the local younger black community were not good and there were constant potential flashpoints. Ironically, the Superintendent at Thornhill Road Police Station had been diligently pursuing a campaign to improve relationships with black youths, with some positive results, but it had now literally all 'gone up in flames.'

Many officers felt that the police had become too soft and let liberties with the law be taken in an effort to improve things, but that was an understandable reaction upon seeing Handsworth burning. The community policing initiatives undertaken after the 1981 riots were seen as being very innovative and the riots caused huge disappointment. It has to be remembered that this was a period when rioting and confrontation involving black youths and the police was not uncommon across the UK, so anything with a prospect of improving relations was seen as worth pursuing.

Anyway, back to Heathfield Road. We drove around for a while but it seemed to be quiet. My best memory of the Handsworth riot occurred when I saw a black man, probably in his fifties; emerge from a house opposite the shops. He approached us.

"Do you all want tea?" he enquired politely.

We nodded enthusiastically. About ten minutes later he emerged with a huge teapot and cups and saucers on a tray and we took tea by the side of the road.

The morning passed, and we were informed that the then Home Secretary, Douglas Hurd, was attending to inspect the scene at lunchtime. We were deployed to the area. Crowds of youths began to gather on the street again and the mood changed for the worse. As a police officer you develop a sixth-sense for trouble, an ability to almost taste tension, and all my sensors were ringing.

Hurd was a tall man and I can remember seeing him approaching, surrounded by a cluster of senior officers. Suddenly bricks and colourful abuse started flying from the crowd towards Hurd, who beat a hasty retreat. Shields were swiftly gathered from the van and a shield wall formed.

A shield wall with officers behind it has an immediate effect on a disorderly crowd - they throw things at it, and this crowd did not disappoint, as bricks and bottles began to bounce off the shields.

We advanced, and I received my first and only experience of being petrol-bombed in anger, as several were lobbed from the crowd.

The crowd broke and ran, leaving a milk crate containing half-a-dozen unused petrol-bombs which we seized as evidence.

We spent the rest of the day chasing groups of youths around the Birchfield Road and Heathfield Road areas. They rampaged through Birchfield Road Shopping Centre, and the Post-Office in Rookery Road was raided.

We eventually restored order later that night, but the damage was done, and burnt buildings, burnt-out and overturned cars, bottles, bricks and makeshift barricades littered the streets. Every time I see a war film I am reminded of that day.

The next day I returned, and the plan was to flood the streets with police, but in conventional attire in a 'return to normality', that's if it's normal to have pairs of police officers every hundred yards. I was with another officer, a 'seasoned campaigner', and we made a point of speaking to everyone we saw. We made the national press - photographed with a young black boy who was wearing my helmet, a photograph that re-appeared in many subsequent articles usually with a by-line about 'community police restoring relations'.

One moment I had been in the 'riot squad', then just twelve hours later, the 'community police.....'

***

On the 14th October 1985, Birmingham closed some streets to facilitate a motorcade of racing and vintage cars, as a prelude to an Act of Parliament being drafted which would authorise a Formula 4 car race. The Act received Royal Assent the following year.

***

In 1985 the Force recruited 281 officers but taking into account wastage, by the end of the year they were 129 officers below the authorised establishment.

No new recruits were enrolled into the Cadet Corps, leaving just 6 cadets in the Force as a whole, following a suspension of recruitment in 1984. The remaining cadets no longer spent time at Matthew Boulton Technical College, and in the main were posted to 'Beat Patrol' duties with operational officers, or working with community projects, and in hospitals and schools.

Despite the low cadet numbers they entered a team in the Ten Tors competition and also the Snowdon Seven Mountain race organised by North Wales Police. The race covered nearly 15 miles and included ascents up to 9,000 feet. The West Midlands Police Cadets achieved first place.

At the end of the year a total of 1,636 civilians were employed within the Force.

During the course of the year the strength of the Force Drugs Squad was increased to 55 officers, the largest squad of its type in the country. The work of the squad saw substantial increases in the seizure of cocaine and amphetamine sulphate as a number of 'hotlines' were introduced.

Crime again rose to a total of 231,606 offences with a Force detection rate of 30%. As crime rates grew, so did the rate of 'Community Watch' schemes as the public began to engage more in contributing towards the protection of their own homes and communities.

There were 38 cases of murder of which one remained undetected by the end of the year. 4 cases of manslaughter were detected.

A total of 178 fatal accidents occurred on the roads, many of which were drink-related.

Just 207 cases of domestic violence involving assault on a spouse or co-habitee were recorded in 1985, which included 8 deaths, and 55 cases of serious wounding.

A total of 1,188 members of the Force were assaulted whilst on duty, of which 534 were classified as serious with over 100 relating to offences of wounding. A total of 236 officers were shown as receiving injuries whilst performing crowd-control during 1985, at football matches and demonstrations.

In 1985, the Force Immigration & Nationality Department recorded the presence of 3,169 registered *'Aliens'* within the Force area, consisting of 2,130 males and 1,039 females. They originated from 82 countries with the largest number coming from the Asian continent.

The Unit operated from Lloyd House Force Headquarters, an office block situated in Birmingham City Centre, and their main duties consisted of naturalisation enquiries, registration applications, and in conjunction with the Immigration service, the tracing of illegal immigrants who had overstayed their lawful stay.

Figure 99 Awards ceremony photograph outside Lloyd House, 1985, courtesy of S Burrows

During 1985 the work of the Central Plain Clothes Unit continued apace as, working with other Forces, they were responsible for seizing obscene material with a value of £9,000,000. Prosecutions under the Obscene Publications Act included an increasing number of so-called *'Video Nasties/Horror'* videos.

Throughout the year several Royal visits took place which involved detailed planning and large numbers of police resources, that invariably included highly-trained police motorcyclists.

The first photograph below was taken as officers on motorcycles lined up prior to carrying out escort duties on one such occasion.

Figure 100 Police motorcycle escort, 1985, courtesy of P Rainey

Figure 101 Neil Taylor, Eastern Traffic at Solihull, circa 1985, courtesy of N Taylor

1986

Joining the DOTS

The 1st April 1986, saw the demise of the West Midlands County Council, and the Force became answerable to a new Police Authority which was charged with *'securing the maintenance of an adequate and efficient police force for the area.'*

One third of the members of the Authority, under the Chair of Councillor P.R. Richards were unelected, whilst others were the subject of proportional political representation.

Among issues which exercised the minds of the Police Authority during the reporting year were modernising the vehicle fleet, creating opportunities for new and more efficient, and appropriate, uniforms and protective equipment, including the use of baton rounds in public order situations, as well as the introduction of a dedicated Firearms Unit. A new computerised *'Crime Information System'* was installed and a report was awaited on the viability of a Midlands Regional Air Operations Unit.

As the so-called 'war on bureaucracy' gathered pace, so too did civilianisation, and pilot schemes started in respect of Administrative Support Units (ASUs), which were designed to remove some of the burden of paperwork and administrative tasks from 'front-line' officers.

***

On the 28th April 1986, PC Anthony Thomas Edmund Hughes, aged forty-six years, was on duty at the Mounted Branch stables at Park Lane in Birmingham when he suffered a heart attack and died, just prior to going out on patrol.

Figure 102 PC Hughes, courtesy of D Menzel

On the 21st July 1986, PC Jeffrey Thomas Barnes, aged forty-three years, died in a road accident travelling to a police motorcycle refresher course.

Retired officer Steve Foster recalls:

'Jeff was on 'D' Unit Traffic. He was on his way to Halesowen Driving School on his own BMW motorcycle when the accident occurred near to the 'Black Horse' LH in Illey Lane. He was a lovely man and a great 'Bobby' who helped me and many others in our careers – sadly missed.'

***

Between the 1st January 1986, and the 31st August 1986, the *'F'* Division Shoplifting Squad, based at Steelhouse Lane Police Station, dealt with a total of 1,637 prisoners who had been detained predominantly within Birmingham City Centre, and recovered stolen property in excess of £20,000.

At the beginning of August, the Force embraced the concept of 'intelligence-led' operations and created a Detective Sergeant (Local Intelligence Officer) post on each Division, who was to work closely with newly-created 'Divisional Observations Teams' more commonly known as *'DOTS'*. Each team was provided with nondescript vehicles which were adapted for use in static observations and were highly effective in crime 'hotspots' where officers often witnessed 'crimes in action' and were able to guide arresting officers in without the offenders even being aware of their presence.

These moves were taken against a backcloth of rising crime and a relatively low detection rate.

In the period January to August 1986 more than 533 officers were assaulted, and the detection rate was just 27%, even though more than 2,000 more arrests had been made compared to the same period in 1985. The Force Drug Squad had seized cocaine and heroin worth over £1,000,000 in one 7 day period.

All this was at a time when the Chief Constable Geoffrey Dear said publicly that he needed an additional 1,000 officers, to add to the existing establishment of 6,684.

In addition, 160 officers were seconded from the Force.

There was an establishment of 1,996 civilian staff, plus 538 Traffic Wardens and 60 Police Cadets, giving an overall establishment figure of 9,438, albeit the number of staff in post was 8,476.

The Force had a staff budget of nearly £121,000,000 as well as budgets to maintain a vehicle fleet of just over 1,000 cars and motorcycles, and nearly 700 premises, which included 60 police stations and just over 600 police houses, used to house married couples.

For single officers, 8'single-quarters' were maintained across the Force area.

At the end of 1986, the Force faced a 10.3% increase in reported crime, and for the first time in its history exceeded 250,000 offences for the year.

1987

Operation 'Red Card'

At the beginning of the year HM Customs & Excise declared that the price of heroin on the streets of Birmingham had increased dramatically, following enforcement activity, and was higher than in any other city in the UK with the exception of Edinburgh. This brought the work of the 55 strong Force Drug Squad into sharp focus.

***

At 12.24 hours on Friday 9th January 1987, PC Paul Rainey was engaged as one of a number of police motorcyclists escorting the Prime Minister Margaret Thatcher, who had visited Royal Brierley Crystal, and was on her way to a luncheon appointment in Birmingham.

In Saltwells Road, Quarry Bank, his motorbike was struck by a motor car and seriously damaged. Whilst the driver was unhurt, Paul was taken to Russell's Hall Hospital and released after treatment in the afternoon, when he resumed his duties on another bike.

Paul remembers the incident well and recalls, *'I collected another bike and met up with the escort at the last-but-one venue over on the eastern side of the Force. I was approached by one of her close-protection team and told that the PM wanted to have a chat with me before she flew off back to London. So before she boarded I had a chat with her.'*

***

At about 11pm on Saturday 10th January 1987, a 25 year old off-duty West Midlands Police Constable, Harry Doyle, entered *'Boogies'* nightclub in Birmingham City Centre. He was alone, but was a tall, strapping, officer who could look after himself. On this occasion though he was entering hostile territory, as the club was frequented by members of arguably one of the most infamous football hooligan groups of the time, namely the *'Zulu Warriors'* who followed Birmingham City Football Club.

Zulu Warriors.

Pride of the MIDLANDS

Figure 103 Zulu Warrior 'calling card', circa 1987, courtesy of M Layton

Co-author Michael Layton was a Detective Sergeant working in intelligence at Steelhouse Lane Police Station at the time and recalls:

'In those days it was quite common for off-duty police officers to present their warrant cards to door-staff at nightclubs to gain entrance, so it would not have been surprising that it did not take long for his presence to be felt inside the club, and it wasn't welcome.

Some of those whose attention he attracted might have come to the conclusion that he was working undercover, but in truth he was merely looking for somewhere to have a drink. At some stage he got into a heated argument with a number of men following which he was punched, knocked to the floor and then 'glassed' in the face, sustaining injuries which required thirty-two stitches.

Three people were subsequently arrested, two of whom were considered to be prominent members of the 'Zulu Warriors'

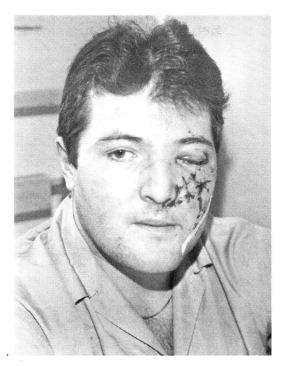

Figure 104 PC Harry Doyle, courtesy of the Express & Star

This attack on a police officer was deemed to be the 'straw that broke the 'camel's back', as senior police officers determined that something needed to be done to combat this group. They had simply gone too far and crossed a line. Pub licensees were also complaining of intimidation and it was strongly suspected that many of the group were involved in organised criminality, ranging from serious public order offences to large-scale shoplifting expeditions around the country.

In my role I was thus tasked with coming up with a plan to tackle the 'Zulu Warriors', and the seeds of what was to become 'Operation Red Card' were sown.

In the initial stages I approached the Metropolitan Police, who were already conducting several undercover operations at clubs in London, and learnt in some detail how they approached evidence-gathering. With a small observations team, I also started monitoring some of the 'home' and 'away' Birmingham City FC games, and started to identify potential targets.

On the 28th February 1987, we had some luck when efforts to draw police officers into an ambush on the terraces at St Andrews was witnessed and captured on CCTV.

In due course a full-scale operation was sanctioned at the highest levels of the Force and I recruited six officers, who would work undercover, as well as two uniform spotters and an evidence-gathering team. Now the real work was to start.

Much of our focus was also on 'The Crown' Licensed House in Hill Street, in Birmingham City Centre, which was the unofficial headquarters of the 'Zulu Warriors'.

***

On the 20th February 1987, Clinton McCurbin died in Wolverhampton during a struggle with police officers, while being arrested for alleged shoplifting and use of a stolen credit card,

His death subsequently led to incidents of public order and social unrest resulting in confrontations with the police in Wolverhampton Town Centre.

Figure 105 Police cordon in Wolverhampton Town Centre, courtesy of the Express & Star

***

Michael Layton continues outlining events relating to 'Operation Red Card'.

'On Saturday 11th April 1987, Tottenham Hotspur were due to play Watford at Aston Villa's ground in one of the football season's two FA Cup semi-finals. Before the match supporters from both teams were drinking in Birmingham City Centre, as were the 'Zulu Warriors', who were out in force and gathered at 'The 'Crown'.

I had placed undercover officers inside the pub and from a vantage point nearby we were able to covertly film the comings and goings of people. What followed was a pre-planned fight involving 'Zulu Warriors', who at about 1.20pm, poured out of 'The Crown' to confront a large number of Tottenham supporters who had previously been drinking at the nearby 'Craven Arms' pub. The chants of 'Zulu' reminiscent from scenes in the film of the same name could clearly be heard below us.

In the violence that followed, one person was stabbed and nearly died, as the two sides used various weapons against each other. The actual fight involving scores of people lasted just a couple of minutes and most had dispersed prior to the arrival of police. We had however captured scenes of pandemonium on video during the fighting and in due course were able to identify 27 suspects for violent disorder.

As months of evidence-gathering continued, the undercover officers continued to put themselves in harm's way. Indeed, at the end of May 1987, four of them were subjected to a 'kangaroo' court inside 'The Crown' licensed house when the doors were barred preventing them from leaving. As they were questioned closely by men armed with snooker-cues they were undoubtedly saved by their resolute and brave conduct in facing them down, but also because their accusers made the mistake of accusing a fifth man of being a police officer who took great exception to the accusation and responded vociferously!'

***

Retired officer Bob Moon recalls a particular *'death message'* that he had to deliver in Knowle, in Solihull in the Spring of 1987– a duty which most police officers must cope with during their service, and which brings home the human tragedy behind road traffic accident statistics:

'I was alone and on patrol one Sunday. Normally these days were okay, and we could look forward to getting all the paperwork sorted from the week's work. So I had spent a few hours doing that and then went out.

It was at about nine o'clock that I got a message that there had been a smash on the M5. At that point it was purely for information purposes because my patch was on the border and the adjoining Force was dealing with it.

About an hour later I was asked to visit a house to enquire about the occupants. Had they travelled down the M5?

The local police had found four dead folks, and a parrot! There was a car with registration plates and dead people. Needless to say the Police National Computer provided the name and address of the registered keeper.

When I pulled up at the house, a young girl was playing a piano in the main hall; a small girl was playing a viola. This was a picture of peace.

I was so scared. I knew that their life would end with my words. I had to ask some questions that then confirmed that their family were in that car. I knew they were dead. Then I had to tell the two girls that every single member of their family was gone.

How can you do that? It does not matter how hard you are, how much you have fought, how tough you are, nothing can prepare you for that. It broke my heart, and I broke theirs. I felt like the 'harbinger of doom'. Those two young girls hated me as I said those fateful words, but I had to be honest.

I had to find a family friend to help out, and I did, but that was hard because I had to explain to him that his best mate was dead. It was a nightmare.

To tell so many people that so many people were dead is not easy. One has to be professional and deal with the implications of what one is saying. But it breaks your heart. I cried, and cried, cried! Not in front of that family, but back at the station, in the locker room and sometimes after when I've thought of it.'

***

On the 11th August 1987, PC Martin Andrew Laucht, aged twenty-eight years, died in a motorcycle accident, riding pillion, whilst on his way to carry out surveillance duties.

Retired officer Andy Belcher recalls:

'Martin and I were great friends in the late 70's, early 80's. We shared the same birth date and were both Police Cadets although I am pretty sure that Martin joined the year before me. We didn't know each other before, but we both became Police Constables on the 26th May 1977, and went off to Eynsham Hall District Police Training Centre in Oxfordshire for our initial training. We went on holidays together with my family, had many adventures, and generally became good 'buddies'.

Martin loved cars and later motorbikes. He had a nickname 'Vitus' because you could never get him to sit still for a minute. He later went onto traffic and subsequently started to do surveillance work.

He was just a really nice kind guy – always fun to be around and a ray of sunshine who lit up the room when he entered.'

Retired officer Carol Joy also remembers Martin, having been a Police Cadet at the same time, and recalls him being a *'lovely man'*.

Figure 106 PC Martin Laucht & PC Paul Lewin, courtesy of P Lewin

***

Michael Layton continues events relating to Operation *'Red Card'*.

'On the 7th October 1987, nearly 200 police officers executed search warrants at nearly 40 addresses in a targeted arrest phase for Operation 'Red Card', looking for 40 specific individuals.

I was sat in 'Alpha Control' at Force Headquarters after the briefing, as all of the names of the targets were put up on dry-wipe boards. We had an officer whose sole job was to act as a 'plotter' updating the boards as the day progressed and news came in. I imagined it feeling a bit like Bomber Command in World War II as the sense of anticipation rose.

After two years in the planning stage, the new 'Alpha Control' centre had opened. Its primary function was to provide a purpose-made centre for the management of major incidents or large-scale operations in the Force.

By the end of the day 39 of our 40 targets had been arrested and were in custody at various police stations throughout the West Midlands.

A second wave of arrests was conducted on the 14th October 1987, when 10 more targets were arrested.

In all, throughout the course of the operation 67 persons were arrested, the vast majority of whom were charged with various offences and had their day in court. The majority of the defendants charged with public order offences pleaded guilty, and the undercover officers were never required to give evidence, or disclose their identities, which remain unknown to the public to this day.

I wasn't naïve enough to think that we had dealt a mortal blow to the 'Zulu Warriors'. We had won a battle but not necessarily the war. This was however the first operation of its type in the West Midlands area and sent a clear message to those involved in organised football violence that they needed to start looking over their shoulders.'

'ZULU' GANG SMASHED IN POLICE RAID

By STEVE WARREN

A man covered by a blanket is taken into Digbeth police station, Birmingham, after being arrested at his Oldbury home

A **NOTORIOUS** gang of West Midland football thugs known as The Zulu Warriors was smashed by police today.

Delighted police chiefs hailed the crackdown — Operation Red Card — as a huge success after a series of dawn raids by nearly 200 officers.

They netted a total of 37 men, both black and white, alleged to have been involved in a three-year reign of terror in Birmingham city centre and at football grounds around England.

The gang purport to be supporters of Birmingham City but police say they are more interested in violence and mayhem than sport.

Police recovered a large quantity of weapons believed to have been used by the thugs. They included an umbrella with a sharpened steel tip, machetes, a meat cleaver, a large number of knives, and home-made clubs and coshes.

Operation Red Card marked the culmination of eight months work by a team of undercover detectives who managed to infiltrate the gang and identify the leaders.

Police said those arrested would be charged with a variety of offences arising from incidents of public disorder, violent assault — including one case in which a stabbing victim nearly died — muggings and organised shoplifting.

'BROKEN THE BACK'

Those arrested were taken to six police stations in Birmingham, and they are expected to appear before the city's magistrates tomorrow. One hundred and eighty officers armed with search warrants were involved in the raids, which included homes in Birmingham, Oldbury, Streetly, Great Barr, Cannock, Lichfield and Redditch.

Teams of plain-clothed and uniformed men, joined by officers of the British Transport Police, were given a 5am briefing at the West Midlands Force training centre in Edgbaston before the operation got under way.

Chief Superintendent Clive Roche, who is leading Operation Red Card, said the suspects were all aged over 18, with some hard-core members of the gang up to 40.

He was confident today's operation would have "broken the back" of the Zulu Warriors, who take their name from a bawdy rugby song. But he added: "We shall be making follow up inquiries and there could be more arrests."

Police also recovered 'scrap books' from two addresses containing both press clippings and original photographs of violent incidents in which those arrested had allegedly been involved.

Operation Red Card was co-ordinated from Alpha Control, the West Midlands Force's new high-tech nerve centre at its Lloyd House HQ in Birmingham.

Figure 107 Courtesy of the Express & Star

Slumbering suspects are seized

By Paul Fulford

Early morning briefing for police officers before today's operation

They arrived before the milk, quietly, swiftly and without drama. A soft knock on the front door got no response, so the bearded man rapped it a little harder. A light came on in the next semi-detached house in a side street off the main Birmingham to Wolverhampton road in Oldbury.

Assistant Chief Constable Paul Leopold holds one of the knives confiscated during operation Zulu.

The door opened slightly and a young man, still bleary with sleep, peered through the darkness at the three figures standing there.

"West Midlands police," said the casually-dressed bearded man flanked by two uniformed colleagues.

Another uniformed officer stood in the front garden, in case the suspect tried to escape.

But he was not needed as his colleagues merely had to show the warrant they were carrying to be allowed inside without any problems.

Within minutes, they had arrested the 19-year-old suspect and, in front of his stunned parents, began to search the house.

The scoop carried out just after 6am, when even Wolverhampton Road was free of traffic, was part of a co-ordinated series of raids carried out by West Midlands police to net more than 30 young men suspected of football hooliganism.

At 4.45am, 180 officers gathered at the Tally Ho! Police Training Centre, Edgbaston, Birmingham, to be briefed about the operation, the culmination of eight months of planning.

Fifteen minutes later, a fleet of vans was trundling along roads that were nearly deserted.

Stooping

Surprise was the key to success. Senior officers did not want suspects to five or to dispose of any item, such as a weapon, that could be used as evidence in a court case.

Woken from their slumbers, the Oldbury "target" was certainly surprised.

As police searched the house, his father appeared at the door and called over to an officer standing unsteadily.

He was angry that the Press had been tipped off and threatened to throw a blanket over the waiting photographer.

He need not have worried. The teenager who emerged had his head hidden by a blanket.

Officers flanked the tall, stooping lad, who was wearing jeans.

He was ushered into the van, which reversed and sped to Digbeth police station in the city centre.

Other vans, too, were bringing in their cargoes and the scene outside the police station was one of bustle and hustle as uniformed and plain clothed officers arrived and left.

A mile away, at Steelhouse Lane, the scene was the same.

"We've got them all except for a couple," said a senior detective as he got out of his car.

"They went out on the drink last night and weren't at home. But we're looking for them."

'Zulus' smashed

As it drew to a close, with just the suspects still to be heard, Mr Beake said: "It's gone very well, we're extremely pleased."

Operation Red Card was made possible by the courage and dedication of a 14-strong team of officers who have worked full-time on the case since the beginning of the year.

Their top-secret investigations are mounted from an outpost room at West Midlands police headquarters, and co-ordinated close liaison with British Transport Police.

West Midlands Police chiefs will not reveal just how many of the officers actually went undercover.

"It is extremely difficult to carry out one of these operations," said Assistant Chief Constable Paul Leopold.

The officers are in constant physical danger and to talk about how they did it would be liable to jeopardise their safety and any future operations."

But Mr Leopold said his men had to match the language of the football hooligans and wear the expensive designer label clothes so popular on the terraces, in order to win the thugs' confidence.

The covert operation took the undercover officers on rail specials to away matches as far afield as Leeds in the north, and Torquay in the south.

All the while these officers were compiling the dossiers of incriminating evidence which led to today's action.

Clashes

Operation Red Card is the biggest blitz on football hooligans yet seen in Britain, and one of the biggest operations of any kind ever mounted by the West Midlands Force.

The Zulu Warriors were at the forefront of one of Britain's worst-ever football riots, at Birmingham City's St Andrew's ground in May, 1985.

A 15-year-old Northampton boy died when a wall fell on top of him during ugly clashes between Blues and Leeds United fans.

Unlike other gangs of football hooligans around the country, and particularly in London, police do not believe there is any right-wing political infiltration of the Zulu Warriors.

An arrested man, his head covered, is taken into Steelhouse Lane police station

Figure 108 Courtesy of the Express & Star

***

On the 25th November 1987, PC Geoffrey Ernest Collins, aged thirty-eight years, was fatally injured in a collision with a lorry, in the Cannock Chase area, while on a motorcycle course.

Retired officer Stuart Griffiths recalls Geoff:

'I first met Geoff when I joined 'C' Unit at the old Bloxwich Police Station in early 1976. It could be intimidating joining a new shift, but Geoff made me feel at ease. He helped me out with paperwork and always had time for you. He was very easy-going and always had a smile on his face. My wife worked at 'Pelsall Social Club', commonly known as 'The Scatter', as a barmaid. Geoff's dad was a member and Geoff used to have a drink in there with him. Geoff was an only child and his death devastated his parents. Roy Marrat was our Sergeant on the shift at the time.

To illustrate the kind of person he was I remember that he befriended a couple called 'Mr and Mrs G' who lived in Church Street, Bloxwich and were well-known in the local community. They were both in their mid-seventies and Geoff used to help them as much as possible, even taking them to places if they needed to get somewhere and ultimately attended their funerals. He was just a really kind person who would do anything for you.'

*** *

On the 29th November 1987, PC Colin John Hall, aged forty years, a dog handler, collapsed and died after helping to quell a disturbance.

Retired officer Ken Rowley recalls:

'I was the Duty Inspector at Willenhall on the night of Colin's death. We got a report of a 'noisy party' in a block of flats near Bloxwich and I attended with four or five officers, including Colin. I remember that for some reason we used the stairs, rather than the lift, to get up several flights to the flat in question.

I knew the occupier and we managed to sort things out and eventually left with no offences being disclosed. Colin and I walked back down the stairs together and as we were walking across a patch of ground to get back to our vehicles, I was suddenly conscious of Colin collapsing to the ground behind me. We called for an ambulance immediately and Colin was taken to the Manor Hospital but sadly he died. It came as a great shock to us all. As a dog-handler Colin was always ready to back us up when help was needed.'

Retired officer Norman Langford recalls:

'I was the Sub Divisional Commander at Walsall when Colin died. I was called out at around 3.00am when he had collapsed and died whilst on duty. There had been a riotous party taking place that Colin, along with other officers had attended. Colin was a dog handler but did not deploy his dog at the incident. When it was all over, he was outside the premises when he collapsed and died. When I arrived, I ascertained that Colin had gone into one of the rooms at the premises alone to assist in dealing with the incident. I was very concerned that something may have happened in that room that had contributed to his death and therefore told the Control Room at Bournville I needed an immediate post-mortem. A pathologist arrived within the hour and I was present at the post-mortem at Walsall Hospital where it was quickly ascertained that Colin had died from a heart attack and there were no signs to indicate he had been attacked by violent behaviour from anyone at the incident. His death therefore was from natural causes. This brought my concerns that he may have been attacked to an end. I then had the sad task of informing his wife, Kate, of Colin's death.'

*** *

Hard on the heels of Operation *'Red Card',* a second covert operation commenced on the 30th November 1987, under the operational name *'Growth'* which stood for *'Get Rid Of Wolverhampton Troublesome Hooligans'.*

One of its catalysts was the serious disorder when 4,000 Wolverhampton Wanderers supporters had attended an 'away' game at Scarborough that August. This was coincidentally the same day on which *'Zulu Warriors'* were fighting with Stoke fans in Birmingham. The Wolverhampton hooligan elements were known as the *'Subway Army',* and the *'Bridge Boys',* named after a bridge opposite Wolverhampton Railway Station which was a favourite ambush spot, and they had a sizeable following.

Using the same tactics successfully adopted on *'Red Card',* officers were able to identify some 300 potential suspects in its early stages, and resulted in a series of dawn raids in March 1988 when 250 officers raided 68 homes.

Figure 109 Courtesy of the Express & Star

Figure 110 Courtesy of the Express & Star

More than 30 additional targets were dealt with in follow-up raids.

The attitude and courage of the undercover officers to the dangers they faced during both of these ground-breaking operations was summed up in the book *'Hunting The Hooligans'*, co-written by Michael Layton, by one of those officers using the name *'Steve'*:

'I felt physically drained at the end of the operation. I used to go home in the dark to avoid the neighbours seeing what I looked like……I found it really hard to fit back into normal policing. That said, I would have done it again.'

***

On the 23rd December 1987, sisters Alice Rowley, aged 87 years, and Edna Rowley, aged 77 years, were found brutally murdered at their corner shop flat in Greswolde Road, Sparkhill, Birmingham. The spinsters were well-known and much-respected within the local community.

Police officers forced entry into the premises after a concerned neighbour made contact to say that they hadn't seen them all day. Alice was discovered in the living room of the flat which adjoined the shop, and had been strangled, whilst Edna was found suffocated in an upstairs bedroom.

The murders were the subject of a huge police enquiry during which they took the unprecedented step of offering a reward of £10,000.

Detective Superintendent Mick Foster led the enquiry at the time and commented, *"This was a heinous and cowardly crime. Alice and Edna were kindly old ladies who were loved in the community."*

During a 5 month period, 6,000 names were entered onto police computer systems, plus 3,000 addresses, and some 5,000 actions completed as more than 1,600 witness statements were taken.

Despite these efforts this brutal crime remains unsolved to this day.

***

At the end of 1987 the West Midlands Police reported an increase of just 1.5% in reported crime overall, which was a significant decrease on the previous year. At the same time the detection rate rose to 36.1% and more than 6,000 fewer burglary dwelling house burglaries were recorded.

***

In the financial year 1987/88, the West Midlands Police Authority manpower budget had provided for an extra 100 police officers, 125 civilians and 49 Traffic Wardens to be recruited, however the Home Office approved no additional officers and instead agreed to an additional 328 extra civilians being recruited.

1988

The Murder of PC Gavin Carlton

As of the 31st March 1988, there were 6,639 police officers in post in the Force with 2,213 civilian staff, and 39 Police Cadets. The Home Office approved the recruitment of an additional 70 police officers, and 50 civilians for the financial year.

***

In 1988, the Force pioneered the use of 'video cars' to deal with bad drivers.

In another traffic innovation, the Head of Traffic, Chief Superintendent Bob Smalley, discovered in a research document from America, that blue and yellow liveried police cars stood out better in the dark than those using the colour orange, which tended to fade. In due course arrangements were made for this to be piloted on vehicles in the Force, and eventually other Forces in the UK followed suit.

Figure 111 Chief Superintendent Bob Smalley & ACC Paul Leopold with new liveried police vehicle, circa 1988, courtesy of B Smalley

In August 1988, crime figures released showed that whilst overall crime was down by 10% and the detection rate had increased to 42.4%, violent crime had in fact increased by a fifth. Only 3 months earlier the Force had concluded a month-long weapons amnesty which led to the recovery of 319 knives, 43 Rambo knives, 156 flick-knives, 17 swords, 29 bayonets, 42 machetes, 13 flails, 8 catapults, and 42 home-made weapons, in an effort to stem the flow of weapons being used in violent attacks on the streets. In addition 112 firearms and 6,000 rounds of ammunition were also handed in.

***

During the year the Force announced that it was recruiting *'brighter bobbies'* revealing that 8% of recruits to the Force had University degrees, with 10% having two or more GCE 'A' Levels and a further 30% possessing 5 or more GCE 'O' Levels.

***

On Wednesday 10th August 1988 at 9.45am, a security guard was stabbed to death in Birmingham City Centre as he fought off robbers who attacked him as he was delivering cash to a bank. A 26 year-old window cleaner who went to his aid was stabbed in the stomach and spleen, and suffered serious injuries. More shocking was the fact that the murder took place outside Barclays Bank in the High Street, which was packed with shoppers at the time.

The security guard, 44 year-old John Worwood, bravely hung on to his steel briefcase containing cash as he was attacked and stabbed fatally in the chest, severing a major artery, and in the arm. Despite being rushed to hospital in a police vehicle, doctors were unable to save him.

More than 160 officers were deployed to the investigation, and on the 2nd September 1988, two men were arrested.

The murder ignited the debate on capital punishment, with local MP Anthony Beaumont-Dark calling for a return of the death penalty, but history confirms that the Government and society as a whole were not for turning.

***

At 10am on the 19th December 1988, , two men burst into the Midland Bank in Tile Hill, Coventry, and stole £600 during the course of a robbery. The bank clerk managed to press a 'panic button' to alert the police.

As they were making off from the scene, a garage cashier tried to block their getaway vehicle but they managed to escape.

PC Gavin Carlton, aged 29 years, was one of a number of officers who responded to the call. He was the first on the scene and was following the two men when a shot was fired at his car.

He swerved to avoid it, hitting a bollard in the road as he did so. As he tried to reverse, the gunman got out of his Cortina car and shot him at point-blank range with a sawn-off shotgun, killing the officer.

Minutes later DC Len Jakeman and DC Trevor Ginn responded to the call in a CID Metro car, having heard it on their police radio, whilst on the way to court.

They sighted the robber's vehicle, caught up with it and followed them until they saw it get stuck behind a skip-lorry. The Cortina car was then rammed by the Metro in traffic on the A45 and the two officers left their vehicle in an effort to arrest the suspects.

The robbers abandoned their vehicle before running to some nearby flats where a second getaway car was parked, chased by the officers.

During a confrontation which ensued DC Jakeman, was shot in the stomach but was rushed to hospital and survived, after surgery which left him off work for 20 months.

DC Ginn and other officers continued the chase, which eventually led them across a golf course, and a police helicopter tracked the suspects to a house in Stoneleigh Avenue, where they smashed their way into the unoccupied home.

Neighbours were evacuated, as well as residents in nearby Warwick Avenue, and after reports of shots being fired at the helicopter it pulled back from the scene.

20 armed officers, supported by 30 unarmed officers, then sealed off the area as negotiators moved into a house opposite the one occupied by the two men, in an effort to engage with them.

At about 11.30am, one of the robbers left the house unarmed and gave himself up.

Shortly afterwards a shot was heard from inside.

Officers waited until they were able to get safely closer to the house where at some point officers could see, through partly-drawn curtains, a figure slumped in a chair.

At 2.40pm the house was stormed and the gunman, David Fisher, aged 22 years, was found dead with a shot to the head, having turned the gun on himself.

His accomplice, Nicholas Hill, later received a fourteen year prison sentence for armed robbery.

PC Carlton joined the police service in 1981 at the age of 21 years and was based at Fletchamstead Police Station in Coventry.

In 1990, a memorial was unveiled in Torrington Avenue at a ceremony organised by the Police Memorial Trust, and attended by dignitaries including Chief Constable Ronald Hadfield. The Home Secretary, Mr David Waddington, unveiled a marble commemorative stone on the spot where Gavin Carlton was murdered.

Figure 112 Gavin Carlton Memorial Stone, courtesy of K Blakeman

Figure 113 Gavin Carlton memorial ceremony, courtesy of K Blakeman

Retired officer Kerry Blakeman reflects:

'At the time of Gavin's death I was based at Chelmsley Wood Police Station, but living in Coventry. I had only been on patrol for six weeks having left Ryton Police Training School after my initial course. I was on a 2pm -10pm shift that day and his loss had a profound impact on the Force. After finishing my shift I drove to the scene of the shooting.

The police cordon had been lifted but the signs of the impact were evident on the road and the bollard where his vehicle had got stuck. I stood in quiet contemplation thinking about Gavin, his family and his shift.

The death of Gavin prompted speeches in the House of Commons by the then Prime Minister Margaret Thatcher, and in June 1990 Gavin was posthumously awarded the Queen's Commendation for Brave Conduct.

In September 1990, a memorial was unveiled in Torrington Avenue where Gavin was shot. Each year on the anniversary of his death, friends and former colleagues gather at the memorial to remember the sacrifice he paid in service.

In 2002 I transferred to Coventry, at which time Gavin's picture and award were situated at Fletchamstead Police Station. At that time the main parade station was Chace Avenue and there was nothing to remember Gavin at this location. As a result I approached Superintendent Clive Burgess and he gave his approval for the parade room to be named in his memory. In 2004 Gavin's family were invited to the formal opening.

With the passage of time, as a result of various restructures in the Force, the area of Coventry became one Operational Command Unit. In 2010 as the new Chief Inspector responsible for 'Local Policing' in the City I arranged for the naming of a dedicated conference room in memory of Gavin at Little Park Street Police Station.

A plaque inside the room named in his honour reads: 'A modest, decent, honourable man who will forever live in our hearts because of the gallantry shown at the time of his death. By that he became wholly outstanding. He was an exemplary example, a shining inspiration to us all'…….'

Figure 114 Kerry Blakeman in the 'Gavin Carlton Room', courtesy of K Blakeman

Dc Jakeman subsequently received the George Medal in recognition of his bravery, whilst DC Ginn received the Queen's Gallantry Medal.

Sergeant Leonard Yeomans, PC Robert Kiedron, and PC Greg Oly received the Queen's Commendation for Brave Conduct, as did PC Gavin Carlton, whose commendation was awarded posthumously.

Figure 115 PC Gavin Carlton, circa 1981, courtesy of D Menzel

***

At the end of 1988, the West Midlands Police recorded an 11% reduction in overall recorded crime which equated to 28,000 fewer offences, and an overall detection rate of 42.4%.

All 41 cases of murder were detected, but violent crimes against the person, predominantly involving male victims and offenders aged between 16 and 23 years, increased.

Following the death of PC Carlton, retired officer Roy Shotton recalls:

'Following the officer's murder I was asked to become part of a two-man 'Armed Response Vehicle' (ARV) for the Force on a full-time basis, so I left Traffic and in fact never returned. It was a forerunner for a new full-time Firearms Unit, and I was a firearms officer for many years, during which time I completed a Firearms Instructors Course, and was trained as a sniper and in hostage rescue. The teams used to deploy to all aspects of firearms work including ARVs, surveillance, and pre-planned operations.'

Figure 116 Roy Shotton with sniper rifle, courtesy of R Shotton

Figure 117 Hostage rescue training, courtesy of R Shotton

Figure 118 Roy Shotton with firearm, courtesy of R Shotton

At the end of the reporting period 1988/89 Chief Constable Geoffrey Dear said, *'Assaults on police give considerable cause for worry. There are indications that some small sections of society continue to offend disproportionately more than most and I have called for a special study of this problem.....It is a wholly unacceptable fact that police officers face, on a daily basis, a level of danger and violence in their work which was not present only a few years ago, and it is to their credit that they continue to work with such dedication, notwithstanding the risks they run. The year under review closed with the tragic death of Police Constable Gavin Carlton in Coventry in circumstances of great savagery, and great bravery both on his part and on the part of others. It was a salutary and grim reminder of the risks accepted by officers at the leading edge of policing.'*

1989

The War on Drugs

On the 16th April 1989, PC Anthony John Salt, aged thirty years, and a father of three, was fatally injured while on surveillance duty.

During the evening of Saturday 16th April, PC Salt and another colleague, were on duty in plain clothes, assigned to maintaining observations on a suspected illegal nightclub in the Small Heath area of Birmingham. They kept watch from a flat in Whitehall Road but at some stage both of them left the observations point and ultimately became separated. PC Salt was subsequently found with a serious head injury, which proved to be fatal.

Figure 119 PC Salt's plaque at the National Memorial Arboretum, courtesy of M Layton

Figure 120 PC Salt's plaque in 'The Beat', courtesy of M Layton

More than 350 officers from the West Midlands Police took part in an investigation unprecedented in British police history – to piece together what happened in the football disaster at Hillsborough Football Ground on the 15th April 1989. The investigation was headed by the Chief Constable Geoffrey Dear.

***

In April 1989, brothers Chris and Steve Rowe found themselves featured in a local newspaper article alongside their dogs, having become the first brothers on record to become members of the Police Dog Section at the same time. They both went on to become police dog trainers at the Unit's base in Balsall Heath, from where they eventually retired.

Figure 121 Chris Rowe (L), with PD 'Zimba', & Steve Rowe (R), with PD 'Jamie', courtesy of C Rowe

***

The Force took delivery of a brand new *'Squirrel'* twin-engine helicopter, forming the new Air Operations Unit.

***

In May 1989, a riot occurred in the Heath Town area of Wolverhampton following a drugs raid on the *'Travellers Rest'* pub. 5 people subsequently appeared in court specifically in relation to the raid whilst a further 13 people were arrested in relation to the subsequent disturbances.

Figure 122 Courtesy of the Express & Star

On the 23rd May 1989, the police raid on a suspected drugs dealing operation at the Public House in the Heath Town district of Wolverhampton, led to a riot in which up to 500 people threw missiles and petrol bombs at police officers.

120 police officers mounted the drugs raid on the *'Travellers' Rest'* pub in the Heath Town district of Wolverhampton. Fifteen minutes later, youths converged on the building and more than two hours of street violence followed with youths pitted against 250 police in riot-gear.

Figure 123 Courtesy of the Express & Star

Figure 124 Courtesy of the Express & Star

Figure 125 Courtesy of the Express & Star

Figure 126 Courtesy of the Express & Star

Local anger and liberal misgivings over the raid were overshadowed by reaction to the 'ominous' discovery of 14 wraps of 'crack cocaine' reportedly worth £140 – 'this truly diabolical substance', as *'The Times'* newspaper put it at the time. Invited to congratulate the police on their actions, Margaret Thatcher said they were 'entirely right', as 'crack peddlers must know they have no haven' *(Hansard, 25 May 1989)*.

West Midlands police at first suggested that the Heath Town 'riot' was organised by drug dealers, and for Home Secretary Hurd it was confirmation that "drug trafficking leads to violence" *(Daily Mail, 2 June 1989)*.

For other observers it was confirmation that years of 'poor policing' and deteriorating relations between police and local black youths in a socially deprived area had borne fruit. 'Crack', it is suggested, both here and in America, was used as an alternative to less comfortable explanations of social disorder. *(Searchlight, 1989, issue 169)*.

***

In August 1989, Chief Constable Geoffrey Dear disbanded the Serious Crime Squad with immediate effect, and the officers who had served on it since 1986 were posted to non-operational duties. A major inquiry led by West Yorkshire Police was then mounted into all cases dealt with by the Squad from that date.

Ultimately a number of court cases were appealed and convictions quashed.

(Postscript: On the 19th May 1992, the Director of Public Prosecutions, Barbara Mills QC, announced that there was insufficient evidence to prosecute any officer in respect of any of the cases referred to them by the Enquiry Team.)

***

Peter Walsh is an author and publisher specializing in organised crime. In 2018 he concluded a project lasting 6 years and published '*Drug War: The Secret History*' – the first modern history of the UK's fight against illegal drugs. It chronicles the activities of high-level traffickers who drugged Britain, and the work of Her Majesties Customs and Excise who, together with other agencies, engaged in a 50 year battle to stem the tide of cannabis, cocaine and heroin. The details below are drawn from extracts in his book and provide a mere 'snapshot' of how the West Midlands and Birmingham featured in the illicit trade.

What became known as '*Indo-Pak*' cannabis importations were operating in the late 1960's. One company based in London ostensibly imported food, spices and Indian medicines, allegedly for growing Asian communities in London, Birmingham, Manchester and Bradford, but hidden inside the consignments were blocks of cannabis.

The man behind the operations was importing what were said to be the largest amounts of cannabis into the UK at the time. Often loads were consigned to accommodation addresses or fictitious firms among growing Pakistani and Indian communities in Bradford, Birmingham, and Southall where friends and relatives from the same villages tended to congregate. They were difficult to penetrate.

In January 1968, a famous 'film mogul' was arrested in Birmingham for a minor offence but intelligence subsequently led customs investigators to a plot to import drugs inside pickles.

In Birmingham, immigrants from the sub-continent were also being advanced the travel fare to the UK, to be repaid at inflated rates of interest after their arrival, as an incentive to bring in drugs to pay off the debt.

In the mid-1970's the Chinese heroin trade took off. One group was linked to the '*14K Triad*' with connections to Birmingham, whilst a second group based in Manchester's Chinatown were said to use a barber shop in Birmingham as a depot, with heroin hidden inside food cargoes.

In the mid-1980's a man described as 'Birmingham's biggest cannabis supplier' was alleged to be importing multiple tonnes from Holland. At one stage he turned up in Spain among other British criminal elements that went to the '*Costa del Crime*' to escape from the prying eyes of British police and to establish new networks. He was very good at organising transports and remained active into the early 90s.

His gang was said to have gained corrupt access to the computer system at Felixstowe Terminal. He was wanted in connection with a number of large importations – literally tonnes of cannabis from Holland inside container lorries carrying consignments of wax, which were unloaded in a warehouse in Birmingham. Most of the drugs went to London and in one 6 month period alone £4,000,000 was laundered back to Holland.

In the mid-1990's came the identification of a London money-mover and transport organiser, who turned out to be the connection between several of the most powerful groups in the country, a hub at the centre of a wheel. This included men who were high-up in the Aston Villa 'football hooligan' fraternity.

Birmingham did not feature as much as some other UK cities because it was not an entry port for importation, unlike the major ports, but more for subsequent distribution.

In one case in the mid-1990's, a feature of HMCE tactics of the period resulted in a 'controlled delivery' of heroin from Pakistan ending up in Birmingham.

A young man called Jameel Akhtar was arrested apparently receiving 20 kilos of heroin in the car park of Birmingham New Street Station, which was said to have been sourced in Pakistan through a powerful 'khan', or boss. Akhtar was jailed for 13 years in January 1997. The circumstances of his arrest were controversial, however. He initially appealed, without success, but in 2005 his conviction was quashed after a review ordered by the Criminal Cases Review Commission.

This was the backcloth to some of the 'battlegrounds' the West Midlands Police Drug Squad found themselves operating in as they also attempted to stem the tide of drugs dealing at a local and Force level.

Retired officer Dave Faulkner recalls:

'I was fortunate to work on many departments during my thirty-two years with the West Midlands Police. The most exciting and rewarding though was the West Midlands Police Force Drug Squad between 1989 and 1996.

We enforced the law relating to illegal drug-misuse and more importantly illegal supply. The people we investigated were, by and large, engaged in an activity that was extremely financially lucrative and consequently they were determined. Violence was the backdrop to their activities.

We had three offices at Coventry, Birmingham, and Darlaston in the Black Country. At the height of recruitment, we were able to mobilise more than sixty officers. We were recognised as the leading drugs investigative body outside of the Metropolitan Police Area and, with some justification, considered ourselves to be the national number one drugs investigative body.

Most police officers are familiar with the term 'Nigel'. This is the name given to modern-day door-forcing rams. It originated in our office, we developed a Ram and it was painted in black enamel paint. At the time Nigel Benn, a force within world middleweight boxing, was challenging for the world title, he was known as the 'Dark Destroyer' and so our Ram became 'Nigel'.

During my years on the Drugs Squad, at different times, we were responsible for the largest mainland seizure of Ecstasy, Cocaine and Heroin. To give you a flavour of the type of targets we had, the Ecstasy seizure was directly connected to a Northern Irish Terrorist organisation. At times we worked closely with officers from Her Majesties Customs and Excise and generally got on well with them at an operational level, indeed I played sport with some of them.

We were an unarmed unit but often recovered firearms owned by our targets. The presence of firearms, if known, could be addressed by the Firearms Tactical Unit, but often we had no knowledge that firearms would be present.

This led us to become extremely proficient at fast-entry into premises and 'hard- stopping' of moving vehicles. From these experiences and following the 'time honoured' use of police humour, one of our number was known as 'Triplex' - look at your vehicle windscreen and the chances are the manufacturing company is Triplex.

Our 'Triplex' made sure that any car we were 'hard-stopping' would be a new customer for a windscreen. An outsider may think that smashing a windscreen with a target inside was unwarranted, but it was designed to disorientate the persons inside in order to give us time to open the doors and secure the occupants. We often recovered firearms from vehicles.

Such was our reputation that the Home office on occasions sent to us interested parties to witness our working methods, such as academics, the Military, and overseas Police Officers who were often posted to the department.

The picture below shows a group of us after the stopping and searching of the lorry in the background. The man wearing the red tie was Lieutenant Jack Killachy of the Chicago Narcotics Squad, who visited us as part of an exchange. Jack was and I hope still is, a fantastic, humorous, individual; it's hard to believe that picture was taken twenty-six years ago.

Another party sent to us was a Major, I will not name him, but he was being posted as a Military Attaché to a distant part of the world to help assist and coordinate British military assistance to foreign governments. He wanted to understand the effect that drugs, particularly Class A Drugs, had on the streets of his country. He spent a week with us and on leaving gave us a little speech over a small dry sherry. It filled me with pride to hear him recount his small but eventful experiences with us, stating that he would not have sent his men into similar situations, without being armed, yet we did it week on week.

It saddened me when the West Midlands Police re-structured, and deployed officers from the Force Drug Squad to Divisions and thus ended on a daily basis, the investigation into Level 1 criminality with a dedicated resource.'

Figure 127 Dave Faulkner, colleagues, and Lt Jack Killachy from the USA, courtesy of D Faulkner

1990

One Out & One In

During the first 3 months of the year, traffic officers throughout the Force were heavily engaged as a result of the Ambulance dispute and the escorting of military ambulances.

Retired officer Paul Rainey was a police motorcyclist during the dispute and spent much of his time escorting military ambulances responding to emergency calls.

Figure 128 Ambulance dispute 1990, courtesy of P Rainey

Figure 129 Ambulance dispute 1990, courtesy of P Rainey

***

In March 1990, Sir Geoffrey Dear left the Force to join Her Majesty's Inspectorate. He was replaced as Chief Constable on the 1st June by Ronald Hadfield, who was to serve for 6 years.

Ronald Hadfield joined the Oldham Borough Police in 1958, a factor which was to feature in a quite well-known nick-name which some members of the Force later adopted. After serving in several Forces, he became the Chief Constable of Nottinghamshire Constabulary in 1987 before moving to the West Midlands.

***

The strength of the Force in 1990 stood at nearly 7,000 officers and 3,000 police staff, serving a population of 2.7 million people with a budget of £238,000,000.

By the end of the year just 165 of those officers were from a visible ethnic minority background.

***

In March, the Central Motorway Police Group was formed with the agreement of West Midlands Police and West Mercia Police. Headed by a West Mercia Superintendent, it became responsible for policing 73.2 miles of the M5, M6, and M42 motorways, controlled from the restructured Motorway Control Room at Perry Barr.

The critical work undertaken by motorway policing officers was highlighted during 1990 when in a single accident on the M42 motorway, an articulated lorry carrying steel rods collided with a queue of vehicles waiting to exit Junction 6, killing 6 people.

***

On the 10th March 1990, PC Colin Graham Pursall, aged twenty-seven years, died in a road traffic accident while travelling to report for duty.

He worked at Belgrave Road Police Station in Birmingham, and retired officer Tony Everett recalls:

'Colin was a panda driver on 'C' Unit with me at Belgrave Road 'B1' at the same time as myself. He was a really nice guy – a true gent. The driver of the other vehicle involved in the accident made off afterwards but was later traced. It was a really difficult time for members of Colin's shift who were shocked at his death, and I remember that colleagues from Bournville and Kings Heath covered our area in the first few hours afterwards to help out. Colin was a sad loss to his family, friends and colleagues.'

***

189

On the 28th March 1990, PC 9650 Mark Anthony Gumbley, aged twenty-seven years, died after being in a collision with a lorry while on a police motorcycle course, in Worcestershire.

Mark was based at Digbeth Police Station, but at the time of his death was on a traffic attachment. He was a married man and had been with the Force for about 9 years, achieving several commendations for good police work.

He was travelling towards Kidderminster in convoy with a group of officers when the accident happened at about 3.35pm.

One media report detailed the fact that *'the officer died instantly when his 600 cc Norton motorcycle collided head-on at Honeybrook on the A442 Bridgnorth to Kidderminster Road. He was going around a left-hand bend when he appeared to lose control of the powerful machine which crossed over to the other side of the road and slid under the wheels of the oncoming lorry'.*

He was described by colleagues at Digbeth in the article as being a, *'dedicated, highly-motivated, and enthusiastic officer'.*

Figure 130 Mark Gumbley, courtesy of D Menzel

***

At 11am on Wednesday 25th July 1990, a fire occurred at Birmingham Powder Coatings Limited, Clonmel Road, Stirchley. At an early stage the police were alerted by the Fire Service, to the effect that life-threatening gases were being given off. The Force helicopter was used to direct residents to a nearby school, and others to stay inside, no doubt contributing to the preservation of life, with the fire then subsequently being successfully brought under control.

***

On the 30th October 1990, Special Constable 244 Neil Coleman, aged twenty-seven years, was killed when hit by a bus while on traffic duty after a football match at Villa Park football ground.

Figure 131 SC Coleman, courtesy of D Menzel

***

The 50th anniversary of the *'Coventry Blitz'* was marked by a visit of HM The Queen Mother, which necessitated a policing operation involving over 450 officers. Dignitaries from across the world participated in a wreath-laying ceremony at a communal grave, for those who died as a result of the air raid. In the evening, up to 150,000 people flocked to the city to witness Dame Vera Lynn switch on the Christmas lights.

***

In November 1990, as civilianisation continued within the Force, one particular success was recalled by co-author Michael Layton:

'One of our successes in the Force Intelligence Bureau, where I was a Detective Inspector, was the appointment of nineteen-year-old Darren Ratcliffe, who was profoundly deaf, had no speech, and also suffered from Ushers Syndrome which affected his vision.

He was employed under a Supernumerary scheme. He loved computers and fitted in quickly with staff, some of whom started to learn sign-language to communicate.

Darren always found a way, with a bit of a 'cheeky grin', to get his message across. He subsequently received a regional West Midlands Young Deaf Achiever Award and went to London as part of the Force's bid to win an award in relation to disabilities, which was duly awarded a third place.'

Figure 132 Force Intelligence Bureau staff, Darren Ratcliffe on far right, courtesy of M Layton

***

At the end of 1990, every Division in the Force found themselves recording an increase in recorded crime. For the first time in 3 years, overall crime was up in the Force, with a total of 258,179 crimes being reported, an increase of 15.9% compared to 1989. The total value of property recorded as stolen was just over £178,000,000.

37 homicides were committed during the course of the year, 3 of which remained undetected. Of these 36 were recorded as murder, and one of manslaughter.

In terms of robberies, the phrase *'muggings'* emerged in the press to describe 'street robberies' that appeared to be on the rise.

One particular operation in relation to burglaries which achieved notable success in 1990 was aimed at focusing on so-called *'bogus official'* offences, which often involved elderly and vulnerable victims. 32 offenders were arrested, leading to the detection of over 600 offences.

During the year, proceedings were initiated against 121,732 persons in respect of offences of all types, an increase of 6.5% on the previous year.

A staggering total of 1,781 members of the Force were assaulted whilst on duty, which included 103 female officers, an increase of 26% on the previous year. Of these assaults, 845 were of a serious nature.

1991

It's A Dog's Life

In January, the West Midlands Police Dog Branch was represented at *'Crufts Dog Show'* for the first time, giving daily demonstrations of their skills in the show ring, following the event's move from London to the National Exhibition Centre.

One of the officers working on the Dog Section during this period was PC Paul Richards who handled a number of dogs. Based in the Borough of Walsall much of his local training took place at the Old Walsall Airfield in Aldridge. He was one of 8 other dog-handlers working in the Borough, with their supervisor at the time being Sergeant Graham Burton.

Figure 133 PC Richards with PD 'Max', courtesy of P Richards

Figure 134 PC Richards with PD 'Jake', courtesy of P Richards

***

In March, the Force Drug Squad arrested 4 people near Birmingham Airport in possession of 2 kilograms of heroin. The *'street value'* of the drugs was £500,000, the largest seizure by the Drug Squad in recent years.

On the 11th March, 3 officers from the Firearms Operations Unit were on duty in Birmingham City Centre, when a vehicle was pointed out to them as having been involved in an armed robbery. The officers pursued the vehicle for some distance during which it crashed and the occupants commandeered another vehicle at gunpoint. The chase continued until that vehicle also crashed and 2 men were arrested. A sawn-off shotgun and a loaded pistol were recovered.

***

In April 1991, Plain Clothes Unit officers conducted the biggest raid of its kind in the Midlands against a major distribution network for pornographic materials. Thousands of videos and magazines with a value of £250,000 were seized during raids on 29 premises.

***

Birmingham University produced a report at the request of the Police Authority, which revealed that 5 police officers on average were assaulted every day in the Force area. It was predicted that a quarter of all serving officers were likely to be assaulted during the year.

Analysis of 200 cases revealed that 75% of the samples were assaults where officers encountered an incident whilst on routine patrol. Two thirds of offenders had a history of using violence, and it was officers in the early stages of their careers that were most at risk.

In fact, a total of 1,560 assaults on West Midlands Police officers took place in 1991 which, although a reduction on the previous year, was still remarkably high and remained an upward trend. 70 female officers were among those attacked.

The Force faced a recruitment freeze following a £14,000,000 budget shortfall and plans to recruit an additional 200 officers had to be scrapped.

***

During the course of the year, the Force policed 28 Royal Visits including on the 12th June, the opening of the Birmingham International Convention Centre by Her Majesty the Queen, accompanied by the Duke of Edinburgh.

***

During the evening of the 2nd September, a large fire which started in premises in Piers Road Handsworth, caused an electrical sub-station to fail. During a total black-out in the Handsworth and Lozells areas, looters took the opportunity to break into 56 premises and steal property valued at £200,000 with significant damage being caused.

Following the swift deployment of officers from several Divisions, 29 people were charged with a variety of offences.

Co-Author Stephen Burrows recalls:

'The third Handsworth 'riot' occurred on the 2nd September, when a power-cut plunged the area into darkness and sparked a looting spree in local shops. Two hundred police officers in riot-gear were called in to bring the unrest under control. Shops and houses were looted, and cars were stolen.

I was a Sergeant at Steelhouse Lane, public-order trained, and on duty. I was 'scrambled' to attend Handsworth, in charge of a van containing ten Constables, including a driver. This was known as a 'one-ten', and three of these van-loads comprised a Police Support Unit (PSU), with an Inspector in charge. I had been in the previous riots in 1985, but we were much better trained and equipped by 1991, with knee, shin and elbow armour, better shields, boots, radio communications and batons.

We knew what we were doing, and I think everybody was determined that we weren't going to have a repeat of the carnage of 1985.

Upon arrival, we were initially deployed to Soho Road. The situation was chaotic. All the lights were out, lots of people running around, clearly intent on looting, and there were groups of Asian shopkeepers guarding their premises, some armed with hockey sticks and the like. I saw people carrying off televisions and other electrical items, no doubt looted from local shops.

This had no 'feel' of disorder borne of social unrest, it was criminal opportunism. The lights had gone out, and the vultures'' had descended upon Handsworth, determined to steal as much as they could. There was a Chief Inspector in charge on the ground. He said that the rioters had built a barricade across Soho Road and that it needed clearing before order could be restored. There were reports of petrol bombs being stockpiled too. It was decided that this time there would be no 'stand-offs', the rioters would be cleared from the streets with whatever degree of force was required.

Happily, there were no tactical masterminds amongst the rioters, and they did not know that their barricade was easily outflanked. We were sent with other vans via side-streets to the rear of the barricade, whilst other PSU's were drawn up ahead of the barricade, the focus of the rioter's attention. In a coordinated action, we hit the barricade from front and rear, disgorging from the vans in full riot gear and brooking no resistance. It was all over in minutes and the crowd fled. The disorder pretty much ended then. The rest of the night we prowled the streets mopping up any stragglers.'

Just 5 days later, 500,000 visitors went to Handsworth to enjoy the carnival.

***

During the year, overflow and remand prisoners from HM Prisons were held in approved cells in the Force area. The maximum number detained reached a peak on the 21st/22nd September, when 115 prisoners were in custody in police cells.

Co-author Stephen Burrows recollects:

'At the time, I was a Sergeant at Steelhouse Lane Police Station, which adjoined Central Lock Up. I was custody trained and there were remand prisoners from prisons held there. Four hours overtime was on offer at the end of 2 x 10 shift to 'put the prisoners to bed' and I regularly performed that role. It was quite a surreal experience. Because they were on remand, they were not subject to the strict prison discipline. We used to sit and watch television with them until their 'lights out' time, when the round of dispensing their prescribed drugs would commence. From memory, every single one was on Temazepam or similar, doled out through the cell hatch with a plastic cup of water to take them with. There was never any bother with them and I felt safe even when sat amongst them, in fact there was plenty of chat and banter between us. All of us in prison, but for different reasons...'

***

In 1991, crime increased by 14.3% on the previous year and demands from the public increased by 8.5%.

A total of 38 homicides were recorded as murder, all of which were detected. In addition 46 cases of manslaughter/infanticide were recorded with all bar one shown as detected.

***

The 1991 census figures indicated that 51.3% of the population were female and 14.6% of the population indicated that their ethnic group was other than white. Based on this figure it was estimated that a total of 365,000 residents of the West Midlands were from ethnic minority groups, mainly from Commonwealth countries.

1992

The Stephanie Slater Kidnapping

One of the largest manhunts ever undertaken in the West Midlands took place following the kidnapping of Estate Agent Stephanie Slater. Operation *'Kaftan'* involved hundreds of officers. Stephanie was released by her kidnapper after 5 days. He was eventually arrested.

Co-Author Michael Layton, who at the time was a Detective Inspector in the Force Intelligence Bureau, recalls:

'On the morning of Wednesday 22nd January 1992, Stephanie Slater, aged twenty-five-years, was kidnapped by Michael Sams, a toolmaker with one leg. Not known to her at the time, he had already murdered eighteen year-old Julie Dart, after abducting her in July 1991 from a street in Leeds.

Using a false name, and after some meticulous pre-planning, he arranged to meet Stephanie Slater, a sales negotiator with Shipways Estate Agents, ostensibly to view an empty semi-detached property at 153 Turnberry Road, in the Great Barr area of Birmingham.

At the property, the viewing of the house started as normal until they entered the upstairs bathroom, whereupon he attacked her, and tied her up, before removing her from the house and taking her away in a vehicle. She was then kept prisoner in a workshop by the River Trent in Newark in Nottinghamshire. For eight days she was blindfolded, bound and gagged, whilst being kept in a home-made 'coffin' inside a wheelie bin, which had been laid horizontal, in conditions which were clearly meant to terrify her into submission.

Within hours Sams made a ransom demand and during one of the calls which were made he was described as having a Nottinghamshire accent. One call was subsequently traced to a public call box at a service station in Nottinghamshire.

The Force Intelligence Bureau was tasked with setting up a dedicated Intelligence Cell as part of the Major Incident Room at Nechells Police Station under the operational name 'Kaftan'. It very quickly became a linked enquiry with West Yorkshire Police, and other national law enforcement agencies, and the gathering of intelligence was put at the very heart of the investigation. Suddenly we were put under a very large 'spotlight'.

The new head of FIB was part of the senior management team, as well as acting as the Intelligence Coordinator, and Regional Crime Squad liaison officer, whilst I was the Intelligence Cell Manager and ran the team from two portacabins in the back yard of the Police Station.

Two of the staff worked full time conducting intelligence analysis, and the whole of one wall of one of the portacabins was covered in a continuous 'sequence of events' chart which was constantly pored over for clues. You could not afford to be distracted with this type of work and it was sometimes difficult for the two of them to get the 'peace and quiet' they needed to get on with their job, due to problems with space.

Other members of the Intelligence Cell, included Detective Sergeant Eric Hughes, who was a meticulously hard worker, a gentleman, and extremely loyal to me personally.

We were tasked with various intelligence functions and Eric's job was to maintain a complex file, with DC Kelly, which contained comprehensive details in relation to profiles of the 'Victim' and 'Kidnapper(s)'. It was a hugely important job and senior investigators relied on the information to assist in some of their decision-making. There were lots of senior officers on the investigation, all occupying different roles, which made it difficult at times for us to deal with competing demands.

In the early days of the investigation, some senior CID officers in the Force were openly sceptical about what the Intelligence Cell could produce, and West Yorkshire Police did not put a similar structure in place for their enquiry.

One officer was imbedded within the Regional Crime Squad, whilst two others, including Richard Shakespeare, were responsible for Prison Intelligence. Another officer was employed full-time on researching financial lines of enquiry, and leads from recovered exhibits, which provided valuable information to police search teams at a later stage of the enquiry. All of them were initially posted to ten hour shifts but they soon became the very minimum hours of working.

A further five officers worked directly to the head of FIB, doing twelve-hour shifts around the clock to give us a 24/7 intelligence and communications capability with which to provide support to some of the staff deployed covertly.

Whilst there might be long periods waiting for the phone to ring, or a radio to transmit, they would have to act swiftly and in accordance with some very complex procedures if certain things started to happen on the ground. It was the biggest deployment of FIB staff in the new structure that we had ever undertaken, and a big challenge to our reputation as an effective department.

As part of the contingency plan for Operation 'Kaftan' we attended all of the daily briefings for the operational teams, and provided an intelligence update, as well as conducting specific intelligence briefings. We always encouraged staff to be open in these sessions.

Other members of the police staff in FIB assisted within an Incident Information Centre set up by the Force Operations Department, at Force Headquarters, which took calls from members of the public in response to press appeals.

We left a 'skeleton staff' at Headquarters to try to keep the day job going. At one point this team was near to breaking point, and I had to fend off requests to take even more staff away. This was a 'highly charged' enquiry where staff routinely worked at least twelve hours a day, day-in-day-out, and stress levels were high. These were the jobs that made careers, or broke them, and all the time there was a victim out there who needed help.

On the 29th January 1992, the manager of Shipways followed some complex instructions from Sams as to how to deliver a cash ransom, which was ultimately left on the bridge parapet over a disused railway line in the Pennines near Barnsley.

Despite a huge effort involving covert policing techniques Sams managed to take the money and escape from the scene, using a moped to avoid being tracked by police.

Throughout these events I was in the office, with members of my team watching events unfold. I had already been on duty for nearly twelve hours, but I had to be there, it would have been unthinkable not to be.

It was an extremely tense time and I felt for the senior officers who were tasked with making massive split-second decisions in such a charged environment. The moment when the cash disappeared along with the attacker was a 'black moment' which was felt personally by everyone, whatever role they were performing. The next move would be in the hands of the kidnapper, and now that he had the money people feared the worst, and yet within hours he was to surprise many of us with a move that had not been predicted.

In the early hours of Thursday 30th January 1992, Stephanie was dumped by Sams at the end of the road where she lived with her adoptive parents, and he drove away undetected into the darkness.

Figure 135 Police officers outside the home of Stephanie Slater, courtesy of the Express & Star

Whilst this was a huge relief for the enquiry team it was clearly far from over, and if anything, people became even more determined to find the kidnapper. Thus far he had been playing a very successful game of 'cat and mouse' with organisations which had vast resources at their disposal, as well as numerous experts. It was simply unthinkable that he would be allowed to win.

This was proving to be a massive investigation with many lines of enquiry all over the country. The HOLMES, (Home Office Large Major Enquiry System), staff were working flat-out maintaining the computer inputting, indexing, statement reading, and allocating 'Actions' to the outside enquiry teams, who knew that any one of those 'Actions' might hold the key to the enquiry.

From a regional perspective, West Midlands Police, as the second biggest force in the country, saw themselves as 'key players' whilst West Yorkshire Police, as the biggest force in the North East, regarded themselves as equals.

During the month of January 1992, I worked fifty-eight hours overtime, which increased to ninety-seven hours overtime in February 1992, the equivalent of working six weeks in a normal four week period. Even in March 1992, until I left the investigation, I worked another thirty five hours overtime and the reality was that home life in that three months consisted of sleeping, one hot meal a day, and possibly one day off a week, if we were lucky.

Everyone was in the same boat – it was unrelenting as people pored over every minute detail of the case, even down to the type of food the victim and offender had consumed.

Criminal intelligence analysis was still a relatively new concept in policing and we had to manage the expectations of the uninitiated, who often thought that the process could produce some sort of magical answer. Following Stephanie's release we also started looking more at identifying radius areas based on predictions of the minimum, and maximum, times she might have travelled from the place of kidnap to her home following her release.

Another member of FIB, DC Joe McCallion, was responsible for traffic intelligence, and he was supported by PC Bob Nockalls, who focused on mapping and routing issues. We used traffic officers, mainly officers on motorbikes, to physically drive all of the possible routes, within speed limits, and came up with options for other officers to explore, given that by now we were looking for other 'landmarks.'

One of those radius lines was in fact very close to the area in which Sam's had his workshop in Newark, but at that point it was just one possibility in a 'haystack' of others, as the walls in our porta cabins filled with yet more charts and maps. As enquiries continued however we became more and more convinced that the place in which Stephanie Slater was detained was in an area to the east of Nottingham which became colloquially known as the 'Golden Triangle'.

Ultimately Sams was a man who transcended a number of force borders during the course of his criminal activities which made the task of apprehending him even more difficult. Parts of the investigation related to the rail network and once more I found myself liaising with old colleagues from the British Transport Police, and an officer was seconded to us for a time.

At the same time, Helen Skelton, the Senior Analyst who I had recruited into FIB, spent valuable time doing a detailed comparison of the Stephanie Slater and Julie Dart incidents to identify common features, of which there were many. This work provided a valuable insight into the skillset of the suspect – all we needed was a name.

In early February 1992, an artist's impression, in colour, of Stephanie's attacker, wearing glasses, was released to the media, and although not known at the time it proved to be a remarkable likeness. Ultimately it was the power of the media that would be a 'tipping point' in the enquiry and Sams' undoing. The Force Intelligence Bureau also circulated a Special Police Bulletin, to all Forces in the UK, which included a description of the suspect that now described him as having a soft Yorkshire accent.

A 'voice analyst' who had listened to tape recordings of his voice had confirmed it as being from a specific area in the north of the UK. Later that month a second bulletin was circulated with a description of an Austin Metro which was believed to have been used by Sams, as yet another piece of the jigsaw puzzle was put in place.

On Thursday 20th February 1992, the TV show, 'Crimewatch UK', featured details of the case, and the police made public a tape recording of the kidnapper's voice which was recognised by Sams' first wife.

On Friday 21st February 1992, Michael Sams, who had an address in Nottinghamshire, was arrested, and his workshop was located at Newark on Trent. He was initially taken to a police station in Birmingham for questioning and on Sunday 23rd February 1992, was charged with the abduction of Stephanie Slater, as well as blackmail and unlawful imprisonment.

Following court appearances in Birmingham he was then taken to West Yorkshire where he was interviewed about the murder of Julie Dart and subsequently charged.

Figure 136 Scenes outside Central Lock Up, Steelhouse Lane during Sams' court appearances, courtesy of the Express & Star

The evil trail of Michael Sams

July 9 1991: Teenage prostitute Julie Dart snatched from near her home

February 22 1992: Sams arrested at his tool repair shop at Newark

January 29 1992: Kevin Watts delivers £175,000 ransom to be collected from disused railway bridge. Sams slips the police cordon and escapes with the cash.

July 3 1991: Attempted capture of Crewe estate agent Carol Jones

January 22 1992: Shipways estate agent Stephanie Slater kidnapped at Great Barr while showing man around house. Ransom demanded

GRANTHAM: July 19 1991 body of Julie Dart found in field

COVENTRY: Blanket found with Julie Dart's body linked to city laundry

LEEDS • BARNSLEY • OXSPRING SUTTON-ON-TRENT SOUTHWELL NEWARK CREWE GRANTHAM NOTTINGHAM BIRMINGHAM COVENTRY

Figure 137 Courtesy of the Express & Star

Sams gave detailed accounts of his involvement in the kidnapping of Stephanie Slater, and the work of the Intelligence Cell continued unabated for a while, to support the enquiry team, which was now focused on preparing a detailed prosecution file.

Michael Sams was eventually sentenced to life imprisonment for the kidnap and murder of Julie Dart and the kidnap of Stephanie Slater. At his trial he admitted the kidnap of Stephanie Slater, but denied the murder of Julie Dart, however three days after being convicted he confessed.

(Postscript: At the beginning of October 1993, the media announced that Stephanie Slater had been awarded the sum of just £5,000 in compensation from the Criminal Injuries Compensation Board for 'suffering and distress.' At the time she was quoted as saying "Some people have said that I should have got more but I am quite happy. No amount could compensate for what Sams did to me."

Taking all the circumstances into account this case could only be described as a truly remarkable story of 'survival against all the odds' and a unique enquiry which I have never forgotten.

In February 1995, Stephanie Slater released a book titled, 'Beyond Fear', about her ordeal, in which she disclosed that within hours of being kidnapped she was raped by Sams, in his workshop, whilst handcuffed, naked, and blindfolded. She said that she had kept her secret for two years because she did not want to upset her family or want people to know that she had had sexual contact with her kidnapper.

She was quoted in the press as saying, "I went through hell at that man's hands, but I didn't want people to know he had touched me because I felt dirty enough. I became obsessive about cleanliness. I used to have a bath twice a day, shower three times a day, scrub myself until I bled."

Sadly, Stephanie Slater died, aged just fifty-years, after losing a battle with cancer on the 31st August 2017.')

***

On the 26th January 1992, PC Mark John Woodhead, aged thirty-two years, collapsed and died while on duty at Fletchamstead Police Station.

Figure 138 PC Woodhead, courtesy of D Menzel

***

In February, Operation *'Marigold'* was successfully concluded by Drug Squad officers in Birmingham, when 3 men were arrested in possession of 3.5 kilos of heroin with a street value of over £1,000,000– the biggest seizure ever in the West Midlands.

On the 24th February 1992, a fourteen year-old girl sustained multiple fatal stab wounds to her back and legs during an argument with a group of girls and the parent of one of them. The incident took place in Hungerford Road, Castle Bromwich following previous disputes. Two sisters aged15 and 14 years, and their father, were later charged with murder.

On the 29th February 1992, Birmingham City FC played Stoke City in a league match at St. Andrews ground. A serious disturbance took place involving a pitch invasion towards the end of the game. A post-incident Operation, *'Mission'* ,was set up to compile evidence and to retrospectively arrest offenders. This resulted in 66 persons being arrested and charged.

Former officer Mark Wardle recalls events leading up to this match:

'This was probably the first football match I was involved in policing. I'd tried to get on the Divisional Police Support Unit on other occasions but hadn't been successful as I was still a probationer, and more senior colleagues usually got posted to it for events. So, being a football fan, albeit Villa, and despite the match being Birmingham City v Stoke, I was pleased to have got a place. It felt as though I was making some progress on the Division and was, slowly but surely, being accepted as part of the team as my probation came close to finishing.

We were, as I recall, to be a serial made up of a Sergeant plus seven Constables, a one and seven as they were referred to. I can't recall any of the other officers or the name of the Sergeant, but I do recall the Sergeant was from 'L1', Solihull, and we set off from there to collect the others from 'L2', Chelmsley Wood.

We stopped at 'L2' for refreshments, a huge cooked breakfast I think, where there was some confusion over meal tickets! The Sergeant briefed us all at the table, and off we went.

I vaguely recall a pre-match briefing held somewhere in the bowels of St. Andrews Stadium. I'm not sure why I was there, but I seem to recall that, for the most part it was senior ranks, PSU Sergeants and Football Intelligence officers from West Midlands Police and Staffordshire Police. Perhaps the Sergeant took me along as it was my first match.

I can remember feeling a little concerned at the end of the briefing, although I am not sure why exactly. It may have been because our posting for the match became clear – we were to be positioned behind one of the goals, and were to form part of the 'thin blue' if not 'fluorescent line', in our jackets, between the opposing supporters.

It promised to be a 'baptism of fire' for my very first match and I was full of nerves, but looking forward to getting involved. As an ex-serviceman who enjoyed the game, I didn't have time for the hooligan element who thought they were as 'hard as nails' and were intent on ruining the game. I'd served in Northern Ireland and the Falklands War alongside some fellas who were really tough and I thought that this lot would not compare!

I was to come to realise quite quickly however, that the 'L' Division PSU probably wasn't going to be much of a match for the hooligans of both Stoke and Birmingham City. Stuck between the two I was left feeling quite vulnerable. As much as they hated each other, neither of them liked me or my fluorescent-clad colleagues either.

We took up our position alongside some sort of fencing I think, that was about six feet high. Whilst intimidating, pre-match, it wasn't too bad on the whole – there was plenty of banter, a lot of bad language, I recall thinking that I'd easily get a 'Section 5 Public Order' arrest when the time was right.

Things changed around kick-off time, when I recall a hard-core of, I think, Stoke fans, pitching up dressed in sunglasses and 'Blues Brothers' hats. It was difficult to estimate numbers, but there was an amount significant enough to be noticeable and they took the hooligan lead.

Verbal exchanges started, these became increasingly hostile, the language was foul and abusive, and the situation started to go downhill from there. Their approach, of course, riled up the opposition supporters and we entered a downward spiral rapidly heading towards serious public disorder – a loud, threatening and intimidating situation already, when missiles were added to the mix.

I recall the Sergeant looking up and down our line anxiously, trying to encourage us to hold the position. The truth of the matter was, we were a mixed bunch of probationer and more seasoned officers, we hardly knew each other, never mind our strengths and weaknesses, plus our public order training had been minimal if my own experience was anything to go by. We were far from a coherent team.

As the situation became more heated between the rival fans, the Sergeant in charge of our serial gave the order to withdraw from our position and to head for the pitch. I recall thinking this wasn't the 'military' way of dealing with things, however as I reflected upon the situation afterwards, quickly came to realise that it was, without doubt, the right decision. Had we stayed, as the violence escalated, there is little doubt that both sets of supporters would have put aside their rivalries and united against us.

We ended up on the pitch, just outside the goal area where we were quickly formed up into a cordon with other officers who were either already there, or quickly making their way there. I recall that there were several dog handlers on the pitch too, and we were all employed separating those on the terrace from being joined by more supporters keen to give the Stoke fans a bit of a kicking.

I think the cordon worked, and, thanks to the pragmatic decision-making of our Sergeant, the 'L1' serial was intact and we left the scene unscathed - but only just.

This incident was probably my first experience of mass-violence. It spurred me on to join the 'OSU', where I served for three years on 'B' serial and became a regular at all the football stadia across the West Midlands.

I loved my time on 'The Group' and took a great deal of pride with the manner in which we policed football matches as part of a dedicated, well-trained team.'

Rival supporters fighting on the edge of the pitch   Fans invade the pitch at St Andrews bringing the match to a halt

Club faces closure as crowd riots

Birmingham City faces wrath of the Football Association after hundreds hooligans went on the rampage at the St Andrew's ground.

Fans invaded the pitch set upon rival Stoke City supporters, bringing Saturday's Third Division clash to a

Blues' League match with

Swansea City tomorrow evening has been given the go-ahead by police, who said the club could not be licensed for Saturday's disturbance.

The club would, however, be forced to play future matches behind closed doors, have a hefty fine imposed, or have points docked when an FA inquiry is held into the incidents.

Trouble flared on Saturday after referee Roger Wiseman allowed a controversial Stoke equalising goal with just two minutes of play left.

The crowd's anger turned to fury when an appeal by Blues players for a goal was turned down less than a minute later.

Hundreds charged on to the pitch, tore down advertising hoardings and hurled missiles.

They then attacked Stoke fans in the Tilton Road end and a pitched battle broke out. The fighting continued outside as the Stoke fans tried to leave.

Express & Star journalist Mr Dave Knight, who had gone to the match as a spectator, said: "It was 15 minutes of anarchy."

"The men took over. There were not enough police to do anything, they just made a few token arrests."

There were 200 police on duty at the match and 150 club stewards.

Figure 139 Courtesy of the Express & Star

***

In April the Force launched a month-long force-wide weapons amnesty when people were invited to *'Bin Their Blades'* with no questions asked, in secure containers at more than 50 police stations. By the end of the amnesty, 480 weapons had been handed over, including 360 knives, as well as 630 rounds of ammunition.

***

On the 15th May 1992, a 14 year-old girl and her mother were shot dead at their home in Ludlow Road, Alum Rock, Birmingham. The offender, a 41 year-old man, and the husband and father of the victims, then shot himself dead.

A second daughter, aged 17 years, also received serious gunshot wounds and died from her injuries two weeks later.

On the 24th May, a 3 year old Coventry boy, Carl Kennedy, was found battered to death in undergrowth near to his home. The murder attracted enormous media attention. Two weeks later a local youth, aged 15 years, was arrested and charged with his murder.

**

On the 31st July, HRH Princess of Wales opened the new Wolverhampton Police Station in Bilston Street. Specially invited guests included 500 schoolchildren. During the course of the year the Force was engaged with 25 Royal Visits in total.

**

In the summer of 1992, Bob Moon recalls a rather unusual robbery arrest in Highgate, Birmingham:

'Early evening, one week-day, myself and another Sergeant known as 'Judge' were on patrol when we heard a shout come up to a pub-fight in a run-down and dangerous part of the city. We were not far away and so decided to go. Having informed our Controller, we went to the pub.

The licensee met us at the door and tried to reassure us that all was fine. We ignored him and had a stroll around the place. Typical of the area, no-one wanted to speak to us. We saw a few broken glasses and blood on the floor, but the boss 'blagged his way' through our questions – a bar worker had cut her hand on a glass, and gone home to sort it out. Complete rubbish but we couldn't prove otherwise.

In any event there was no disorder taking place, no injured people – nothing. We knew what had happened but without witnesses we were stuffed. There had been a fight, probably between rival drug dealers, but with no information forthcoming we left. The licensee shook our hands smiling, knowing that his license was okay.

When we walked out of the pub towards our car, I noticed that the door of the post-office opposite was ajar. It was gone seven o'clock in the evening and the post office should have been shut and shuttered. I mentioned this to 'Judge', and we decided to take a look.

Having radioed our intentions, we went across the road to the post office. I gently opened the door and stepped inside. For a moment everything seemed quiet, empty, almost like someone had forgotten to lock the door. Then in a reflection on the armour glass I saw a woman on the floor with tape over her mouth.

I didn't panic. I nudged 'Judge' and whispered to him what I had seen. He went back outside to radio for help. I walked towards the counters and as I did so a man appeared with a large knife but he was behind the counter and the armoured glass.

There then followed an almost comical run-around. I could not get to him and he could not get out. I began trying to smash the glass but it lived up to its name. I shouted to the Sergeant and he came running back in to tell me that a Unit of OSU were almost here. I told him to get them to the back of the building to stop the bloke from escaping. All the time he was trying to get through the glass at me, and I was trying to get at him.

I could, at the same time see the safe open, a man was on his knees tied up, there were three women in the same position, all tied and taped. The fear in their eyes was palpable. All the time I was smashing at the glass and the doors but to no avail.

Within a few minutes a bunch of OSU burst through the back of the post-office and beat the man to the ground. At the same time I had managed to smash a door down and dived into the fray. His knife nicked my arm.

He was taken away, and we then set about releasing the staff and preserving the crime scene.

This man had held three women and the postmaster hostage for over three hours, forcing them to open the safe. The prisoner spent a few days in hospital because of his injuries and then came to my Police Station to be charged.'

***

In August the body of 55 year-old Spyros Georghiades was found at Moseley Snooker Club. He was the night-manager and suffered fatal head injuries and stab wounds to his back after a violent attack.

***

On the 16th October, the International Convention Centre, in Birmingham, played host to the Special European Council. This involved over 100 Traffic Division officers escorting 14 cavalcades from Birmingham International Airport to the City Centre. The conference was also attended by the Heads of all 12 Member States, and attracted 2,000 media representatives.

***

On the 2nd December 1992, officers were called to an address in Northfield where they found the bodies of a 71 year-old man, his wife aged 72 years, and their 47 year-old disabled son. All 3 had suffered head injuries and multiple stab wounds.

***

During the course of the year a total of 1,645 officers were assaulted, of which 790 related to serious injuries. These attacks resulted in 1,979 days being lost due to sickness.

Some examples of these attacks included an officer from Coventry who needed 15 stitches to severe ear injuries, an officer from Walsall who suffered a fractured cheekbone and severe eye injuries, one from the 'C' Division who suffered a broken arm, and a female officer from the 'F' Division who sustained broken ribs.

110 of the serious assaults were on female officers, and included 3 indecent assaults.

***

Members of the Force responded to 308,041 '999' emergency calls during the year, and the Command and Control system recorded details of 873,263 incidents.

The Force recorded 321,814 crimes during the year, which was an increase of 26,782 on the 1991 figures.

During 1992 there were 56 cases of homicide, of which 53 were recorded as murder and 3 as manslaughter. Of these 48 cases of murder were detected, which included one murder recorded in the previous year.

On the roads, officers dealt with 6,462 people for drink/driving offences, and nearly 1000 for drunken behaviour on the streets.

During 1992 a total of 1,889 persons were arrested for drugs-related offences, of which 272 were arrested by members of the Force Drugs Squad. The Force conducted 19 joint operations with the Regional Crime Squad and 10 with HM Customs.

***

In December 1992, the resident population of the West Midlands was estimated at 2,619,000, resulting in a police to population ratio of one officer to every 375 persons. This was substantially better than the national average at the time, which was one to 446 persons, but was similar in number to other 'metropolitan' style Forces outside London.

1993

The Birth Of DCU's

On the 6th January 1993, a public outcry attracted media attention following the death of a 13 year-old schoolgirl who was knocked down and killed by the driver of a stolen car who failed to stop at the scene in Walsall.

***

On the 18th March 1993, PC Philip Joseph Kurlinkus, aged thirty-nine years, died in a motorcycle accident responding to an emergency call.

Retired officer Stuart Knight recalls:

'I commenced my initial training course at Ryton On Dunsmore on the 2nd July 1972, on 'A' Syndicate of Course 484.

Philip was on the same course but in another of the syndicates, but I remember him as a fellow 'Brummie' who like me had joined Birmingham City Police.

Philip became known as 'Klink' to his friends and after serving on the 'E' Division he went onto Eastern Traffic as a motorcyclist. Police bikers are affectionately referred to as 'scruffies' due the 'all-weather' leathers they wear.

It was a great shock when I learnt about his death.'

Retired officer Paul Rainey recalls;

'Phil (Klink) and I joined Birmingham City Cadets in 1969 with many others. He was a great guy who will always be sadly missed.'

***

In April, Divisional Crime Support Units were established Force-wide after 3 pilot schemes, during which 1,400 arrests were made and 3,600 crimes were detected, were evaluated. The new teams achieved some notable successes in combating crime during the course of the year.

The disbandment of the Serious Crime Squad had left the Force without a unit dedicated to the co-ordination and investigation of serious crime Force-wide, and these Units were formed to fill that gap. Each was headed by a Detective Chief Inspector, with a Detective Inspector having operational responsibility for a mixture of CID and uniform officers, plus an input from the Force Drugs Squad. During this period the term 'intelligence led' was born, as senior officers sought to maximise 'value for money' by deploying resources to 'hot spots' and persistent offenders, using criminal intelligence, which included crime pattern analysis.

***

In May, a 43 year-old garage attendant, Mohammed Hanif, failed to return to his Edgbaston home after work. It was later discovered that the garage had been robbed and the burnt-out wreckage of his car was found 3 miles away. After an intensive search over several days, the man's body was eventually found in a field in Earlswood, Warwickshire. He had died of asphyxia following a violent assault. A 26 year-old man from Balsall Heath and an 18 year-old man from Druids Heath were later charged with his murder.

***

In May 1993, unemployment rates in the West Midlands averaged 13.1%, with a high of 18.9% in Birmingham and a low of 10.3% in Solihull. These represented averages for other Metropolitan Boroughs, but in specific areas unemployment rates reached a high of 33%.

***

On the 8th June 1993, PC David Brennan, aged thirty-seven years, was fatally injured in a road traffic accident on his way to report for duty.

Retired officer Julie Maley, nee Whild, recalls David:

'I worked with Dave Brennan on the Special Plain Clothes Unit in the early 80's.

He was a really nice man and had an Austin Princess when I worked with him, which was an automatic. My Dad at the time was buying an automatic car, so Dave gave me some tuition in driving his, to get used to the differences. He was a laid-back and calm man.

We had some fun on the team, with Chris James and Bob Vercesi. On one occasion, Dave and I were in the back of a transit van watching a suspected brothel, using a long-lens camera up against the blacked out rear windows. There were small spy holes in the side of the van too. Suddenly a large man came out with a hammer and machete in his hand and approached the van.

We were parked in a small yard. Dave held onto the camera which was a few inches from the man looking through the windows. I had my fingers in each spy hole as the man started shaking the van. We both held our breath fearing the worst, especially as the only way out for us, was through those doors. Surprisingly the van stayed put and so did the camera.

After about ten minutes the man left a child sitting in the yard to watch the van and see who came back to it. He was told to go and tell the man when the driver returned. We had no mobile phones in those days, so it was scary.

A while later the young child wandered into the building and Dave quickly got out of the back of the van and into the front. I stood in the back holding the camera, while Dave did a very quick reverse, turn and escaped. I think we both lost one life that day.

We got some excellent photos though!'

Figure 140 David Brennan, courtesy of D Menzel

***

Also, in June the body of Miss Betty Barrett, aged 67 years, was found hidden in a linen-basket at her home in Cawdor Crescent, Ladywood. The house had been ransacked and she had suffered head injuries. A man from Newtown and a youth from Belfast were later charged with her murder.

***

On Monday 25th October 1993, the Force announced the results of Operation *'Plato'*, a week-long operation which resulted in the recovery of stolen property valued at nearly £60,000, the recovery of several thousand pounds worth of heroin, and 128 arrests.

***

On the 2nd November, Operation *'Tom'* took place as part of a force-wide initiative to tackle MOT fraud, involving forged documents and excise licences. 500 officers made 110 arrests on the day, with the potential for the same number to be arrested in follow-up operations.

***

In December, a murder enquiry was launched after a man from Moorcroft Place in Nechells was beaten about the head with a pick-axe handle by his neighbour. Mr Thomas Spence aged 47 years had just returned from collecting his dead father's ashes and was sprinkling them in the front garden when he was attacked.

***

In 1993, a total of 965,377 incidents were recorded and 333,550, *'999'* emergency calls handled by the Force.

A total of 323,587 crimes were recorded, of which 86,809 crimes were detected.

Crime as a whole in the UK was big business, with property valued at £10,000,000 being stolen each day. In the West Midlands alone there had been more than a 100% increase in the value of property stolen, from £117,000,000 in 1988, to £237,000,000 in 1993.

A total of 1,676 assaults on police officers took place with an average of 4 assaults a day. In one instance in April, Drug Squad officers executing a warrant were attacked by a man with a machete. One officer had some of his toes partially severed, which required micro-surgery. In May, 6 officers from Erdington received eye injuries after being sprayed with ammonia by a 16 year-old youth. In October, an officer from Belgrave Road Police Station suffered a fractured skull when he was knocked unconscious by a man as he tried to arrest two burglars. During the year, 17 officers were attacked with knives.

There were 37 cases of murder recorded in 1993, a reduction on the previous year, of which 34 were shown as detected. 3 recorded cases of manslaughter were also detected.

***

This was the year that white shirts were introduced for male Constables and Sergeants and culottes were added to the uniform of female officers, who could choose between wearing them, skirts or trousers.

***

For public-order purposes the Force continued to maintain a commitment to the training and availability of 40 Police Support Units (PSUs) which was far in excess of the ACPO recommended commitment of 24 PSUs.

The Operational Support Unit continued to provide the backbone of this approach, with a dedicated unit of 1 Chief Inspector, 3 Inspectors, 13 Sergeants and 123 Constables, who were divided into 13 serials based in the east, west and central locations of the Force. 11 of the serials were aligned to Divisions as signified by their radio call-signs.

As of the 31st December 1993, the Force Dog Section had an actual strength of 88 officers made up of 2 Inspectors, 10 Sergeants and 76 Constables. The Force had a total of 95 dogs trained for general purpose and explosive purposes.

The Mounted Section consisted of 37 fully trained horses, and 41 officers, 6 of whom were females.

1994

Operation 'Portdale'

Figures for drivers breath-tested during the festive period revealed that 1,500 such tests were administered, of which 246, or 16.4% were positive.

In January 1994, 4 men were killed when a light aircraft taking them back to the Isle of Man from a business trip in the Midlands, crashed on waste ground near Bloxwich, narrowly missing overhead power lines, a housing estate and the nearby motorway.

The first air disaster in the region happened just minutes after the twin-engine, 6 seater plane, had taken off from Birmingham International Airport.

Over 50 officers were engaged in the subsequent operation to secure the scene and to gather evidence.

***

On the 28th February 1994, a football league fixture took place between Wolverhampton Wanderers and West Bromwich Albion. Disorder broke out at the end of the match which was dealt with by members of the Operational Support Unit, supported by the Mounted Branch and Divisional officers. As a result, 62 people were arrested, and 4 officers slightly hurt.

Figure 141 Courtesy of the Express & Star

Also, in February, Chief Fingerprint Officer Ray Broadstock was called to Singapore to testify at a murder trial. Seen as one of the world's leading authorities on fingerprints and Chairman of the Fingerprint Society, Mr Broadstock had been invited by Singapore Police to review some of the evidence in the case and to reveal his findings in court.

In the same month, officers removed videos and books worth £100,000 from 4 bookshops in Wolverhampton Town-Centre. The operation was co-ordinated by the newly-formed Commercial Vice Unit.

***

In March 1994, a month-long operation by 13 officers at Bromford Lane was concluded after 52 arrests were made and 60 crimes detected in the Bromford, Shard End and Firs Estate areas after a 'hotline' was set up for members of the public to phone in with information.

***

In June, Coventry-based Constable Peter Rooke and police dog *'Sabre'* received the *'Police Dog Action of The Year'* trophy for saving the life of a 90 year old man who was confused and had gone missing from an elderly people's home. After hours spent searching the area in appalling weather conditions, they were making one last search of fields when *'Sabre'* picked up a scent. He then found the man's jacket in some undergrowth and finally the man himself, who was lying in a ditch, unconscious and suffering from hypothermia.

Also, on the 11th June, the Annual Neighbourhood Watch Conference was held in Birmingham where a magazine called *'Scan'* which was produced by the Streetly Neighbourhood Watch scheme, won a prize in a national competition to find the best community publication in the country.

***

In July 1994, a pilot scheme was commenced at Walsall Police Station to set up a Divisional Crime Bureau and a dedicated Intelligence Cell. Up to 40 staff, some providing 24/7 cover, were involved in the 3 month scheme handling 30,000 reported crimes a year with criminal intelligence analysts trained to identify 'hot spots' and emerging patterns and trends, as well as prolific local and cross-border offenders.

In July 4 officers who were shot at by an armed-robber in Birmingham City Centre in 1992 were awarded the Queens Commendation for Brave Conduct. Constable Paul Dean and Constable Evan Mytton had approached the man after he had robbed a service station. He threatened to shoot them, and a violent struggle ensued during which time the man fired his weapon. It was later found to be a blank-firing replica, but the shot left one of the officers with flash-burns to his face. The offender was finally overpowered with help from Sergeant David Murcott and Constable Ian Padley and he was later sent to prison for 8 years.

***

On Tuesday 9th August 1994, at 12.35pm, the body of 84 year-old Second World War veteran Clarence Haddon Cooper, was found at his semi-detached home in Alexandra Road, Palfrey. He was found after a Walsall Council 'meals on wheels' volunteer failed to get an answer at the house and alerted police.

Clarence Cooper died from asphyxiation after being stabbed 12 times, and had a handkerchief forced so hard into his mouth that his lips were bruised, and his tongue cut. He was found lying in bed, in a front ground-floor room, with his arms above his head, and covered by a quilt. The house had been ransacked, and burglary became an early potential motive after it was discovered that there been a break-in at the house only 5 days before.

It was a savage and senseless crime, committed against a vulnerable man, who used a walking stick. He had served his country as a bugler with the Staffordshire Regiment but after surviving violent conflict in North Africa and Burma, had died a slow and painful death in his own home.

A team of 48 officers were involved in various capacities, which included house-to-house enquiries, and over 200 witness statements were taken. There were early indications that local youths had targeted Mr. Cooper, and harassed him regularly, and there was a clear feeling from investigators that the answers to this crime would be found not far from his door.

On Friday 12th August 1994, 9 people were detained during raids in Palfrey and Caldmore, and property believed to be stolen recovered. The 9 were interviewed about the murder, and outstanding burglaries in the area, as Detective Superintendent John Plimmer made further appeals for information. 6 further arrests followed, with all being released on police bail pending further enquiries.

On Wednesday 24th August 1994, 4 significant arrests were made in relation to the murder of Clarence Cooper, again in the Palfrey and Caldmore areas. They were not amongst those previously arrested, and were also suspected of committing burglaries in the area.

On Thursday 25th August 1994, two 17 year-olds, and a 16 year-old, were charged with the murder. All 3 lived not far from the victim. Ultimately they were tried at Stafford Crown Court 6 months later, together with a 48 year-old man from Manchester, who was also charged with 'conspiracy to commit burglary.' He was in a *'Fagin'* style relationship with the other 3 accused.

Figure 142 Courtesy of the Express & Star

***

Co-author Michael Layton, by this time a Detective Chief Inspector, recalls his involvement with the first 'sting' operation of its type in the West Midlands:

'On Friday 2nd September 1994, I had an early morning planning meeting in Birmingham with managers who ran a covert unit, to progress issues relating to 'Operation Portdale', and four days later had a similar meeting with the National Criminal Intelligence Service. I wanted to make use of their facilities and to work in partnership with them in developing intelligence that we hoped to obtain.

The concept of the operation, which was to be the first 'sting' operation of its type outside the Metropolitan Police Force area, was quite simple. We were going to buy property from criminals that had already been stolen, and in due course identify and arrest the offenders. We already had 'flyers' printed and cards advertising for TV's, videos, mobile phones, and computers, together with a contact telephone number. Little would the criminals know that the person answering the phone would be one of three undercover police officers, who would be using a van kitted-out with technical equipment to capture all the transactions on video and audio.

In May 1994, the Metropolitan Police had completed a similar operation, resulting in the arrest of 42 persons, and the recovery of stolen property valued at £125,000.

Police in Walthamstow had set up a second-hand shop and found that three-quarters of the property they purchased was stolen.

We had done some research and were satisfied that what we were proposing was legal. In May 1992 there was a stated-case before the Court of Appeal, Criminal Division which we felt that we could rely on.

From the 4th October 1994, I was responsible for the day-to-day control and management of 'Operation Portdale', and I was able to gain a great deal of experience in the control of undercover officers, and to use the skills developed on other major Operations such as 'Red Card'. It was not long before the thieves started to 'take the bait.'

In the early days we did some leaflet drops in four selected 'hot-spot' areas for crime in Mossley, Blakenhall Heath, Beechdale and Bloxwich. We kept a record of where the leaflets were posted, but avoided the addresses of known criminals, so as to negate accusations of acting as 'agent provocateurs' by counselling, inciting, or procuring the commission of a crime. The undercover officers were encouraged to find their own targets as too much information could prove to be dangerous for them.

Their cover stories or 'legends' were designed to show that they were from the Leicestershire area, and exporting goods to Eastern Europe. Therefore they would not have been expected to possess much local knowledge.

As part of their 'cover story' the undercover officers always tried to get a receipt signed for the cash handed over. Where possible the criminals were encouraged to sit in the front seat of the van, whilst this was completed. Taped to the dashboard in front of this seat was a postcard of a naked woman, which always attracted admiring looks and comments from 'customers'. What they didn't know was that there was a 'pin hole' camera, behind the picture, and as they signed receipts we had a nice full-front facial picture of them.

We had hidden cameras running constantly in the van which covered every angle. In particular the undercover officers always encouraged people to help them to load up so that we could get good video of them holding the property. The rear walls of the vehicle were papered with pictures of 'Page Three' models which always attracted attention and meant that we got some good shots as they were scrutinized!

During the operation we infiltrated teams of professional thieves, burglars and receivers of stolen property, who were talking openly to the undercover officers, almost bragging about their activities.

During the covert evidence gathering phase of the operation, stolen property valued at £30,000 was recovered which included video recorders, stereo systems, TV sets, cannabis, and £5,000 worth of counterfeit currency, as well as a £1,000 worth of counterfeit goods. All this was achieved for an outlay of £5,214 spent by the undercover officers in purchasing the items.

On Wednesday 7th December 1994, a 5am briefing with arrest teams took place, at 8 locations in Walsall. We had briefed a core group of senior officers the day before and they were required to give the briefings to the teams, which had to be 'short and sharp' so that all of the officers would be in place and ready to execute their warrant at 6am. We couldn't risk losing prisoners, or evidence, by giving people the opportunity to phone each other, so it was critical that they were all ready to go at the same time.

We had 53 targets to go for, and 53 arrest teams. During the course of the operation we had prepared 78 target packages on suspects, but in some cases we had not been able to positively identify the offenders, or build the evidence to the level required to have sufficient grounds for arrest.

We even had a large Cargo van with a driver on standby at Park Lane Traffic Headquarters in order to assist with the removal of recovered property. Two dog handlers were on standby in the event that we needed to deal with any dangerous dogs found in houses, or to act as a deterrent should any target become aggressive with any of the teams. As it was, 'the shock and awe' style of the operation meant that most people came very quietly.

Throughout the day, in the final phase of the operation, 46 search warrants were executed at houses, pubs, and business premises in Walsall, Willenhall, Blakenhall and Bloxwich, involving more than 230 officers, with more than 60 police vehicles. The pub used by our undercover officers, as a regular meeting place, was amongst them, and whilst we were not that confident of recovering stolen property, we had to try to stop criminals using it as a 'base' from which to conduct their activities.

Plain-clothes police officers storm into a house .

Dawn swoop on homes

Hundreds of police swooped on 47 properties in a series of dawn raids across Walsall today in a massive anti-counterfeiting and burglary operation.

More than 50 people — including husbands and wives — were arrested and £90,000 worth of fake and stolen goods seized.

Police estimate a haul valued at £250,000 will eventually be recovered and handed back to bur-

glary victims. The co-ordinated raids swung into action at 6am.

Officers, armed with search warrants, used sledgehammers to force their way into homes, pubs and businesses in Walsall, Willenhall, Blakenall and Bloxwich.

Counterfeit money, perfumes, videos, electrical equipment, designer clothing and weapons were recovered.

The operation, led by Detective Superintendent John Plimmer of Walsall crime bureau, targeted

known criminals across the borough. Today's arrests follows a two-month undercover investigation and is the second phase of the operation to combat increases in burglaries.

Between October 3 and yesterday, officers posing as buyers set up a van with hidden cameras and recording equipment to gather information on suspects. "Word of mouth" among criminals publicised the van was open for business in stolen goods.

Figure 143 Courtesy of the Express & Star

Chapter and vers
for raid suspects

The raids across Walsall followed a two-month undercover operation. Reporters Paul Hinton and Debbi Gardner and photographer Tim Sturgess joined the police teams

It was a case of poetic justice when the long arm of the law caught up with two suspects at a house in the Delves area of Walsall.

Dc John Shelley and Det Sgt Alan Shakespeare led a team of six officers in a 6am "wake-up" call at the smart three-bedroomed house in the shadow of the M6.

Just one neighbour's curtain twitched as the full force of the law — in the shape of a 20lb sledgehammer — splintered the front door.

The element of surprise was essential for the success of the early morning mission as officers raced up the street and surrounded the house.

Seconds later four arresting officers, a TV camera crew and a Press photographer had bounded up the stairs and burst into the main bedroom.

Possible charges

A startled husband and wife, with a babe in arms, were arrested in their bed in the full glare of powerful television lights.

Both faced possible charges in connection with a series of offences including handling stolen goods and burglary. Downstairs, officers stumbled on a Christmas grotto of goods, all thought to be counterfeit.

The haul included a stock of chart-topping Power Ranger videos, Polo jerseys by Ralph Lauren, Georgio and Samsara perfumes and Armani watches.

Five minutes after his rude awakening, a hastily-dressed man in his mid-20s, shadowed by the two poetically-named officers, was on his way to Green Lane police station for questioning.

The mother-of-two followed later, but only after brewing up a pot of tea for officers as they carried out a thorough search of the house.

By 6.30am the baby and a young boy were up and dressed and the TV was on. Almost an everyday breakfast scene.

Almost 50 other people received the early morning call as police officers swooped on their homes as part of the borough-wide crime crackdown.

Sgt Graeme Pallister with some the goods at Brownhills pol

Figure 144 courtesy of the Express & Star

Over 50 persons were arrested in total, and stolen property recovered in excess of £120,000, as well as a small quantity of drugs, nearly £2,000 worth of counterfeit currency, £10,000 worth of counterfeit goods; £500 worth of alcohol on which no excise duty had been paid, was also seized.

A total of 70 primary offences were cleared, and an additional 150 offences later cleared following prison visits with some of those convicted.

During the month of November 1994, 35 offences of burglary dwelling house were recorded, whilst in December 1994 following the conclusion of the operation only 12 were recorded in one of our 'hot-spot' areas.

The operation had been a major success, and put the local organised criminal community on the 'back foot'. We had not played by 'Queensbury Rules' and they didn't like it.'

***

On the 10th September 1994, disturbances broke out during a world title boxing match between Nigel Benn and Juan Carlos. The Operational Support Unit played a role in the subsequent post-incident investigation.

Verdicts of unlawful killing were recorded in September on 3 members of the same family who were found stabbed and beaten to death at their home in the Northfield area of Birmingham in December 1992. It was a murder described by some of the investigating officers as the worst that they had ever witnessed. The case had remained under investigation, and whilst at its height some 90 police and support staff were involved, and 30 arrests made, no-one at that time had been formally charged with the murders.

On the 12th September, police had to close Wolverhampton Town-Centre due to the size of crowds who had come to pay their respects at the funeral of former Wolverhampton Wanderers and England football team captain, Billy Wright.

***

In October, the Underwater Search Unit was called on by West Mercia Police after a 19 year-old fell into the River Severn at Ironbridge and failed to surface. After failing to find him in the immediate vicinity officers persevered into the hours of darkness until the last pair of divers, using their last air tanks, found the man's body 160 yards away.

***

In November, Special Constable David McLeod suffered two stab wounds in the chest when, with regular officers, he was called to an address in the Acocks Green area of Birmingham. A man had already injured two youths by the time that police had arrived, and he was seen to run to a nearby house. The officer bravely pursued him and was stabbed at the front door. He made a full recovery.

***

On the 8th December 1994, an incident occurred in *'Rackhams'* Store in Birmingham City Centre, when a man armed with a knife went on the rampage on the ground and first floors. 9 members of staff and 6 members of the public were later taken to hospital with stab wounds and another 5 admitted suffering from shock.

A 30 year-old man from Aston was overpowered and arrested by officers who raced to the scene, and Sergeant Jim Lavery, PC Morris Watson and Scenes of Crime Officer Keith Hart were later recognised for their actions.

Figure 145 Courtesy of the Express & Star

Figure 146 Courtesy of the Express & Star

***

In December 1994, 150 officers were mobilised from across the Force following the crash of a Boeing 737 cargo aeroplane near Coventry, killing 5 people on board. They remained at the site for 10 days whilst the Air Accident Investigation team carried out their work.

At 9.55am on Wednesday 21st December 1994, the plane clipped an electricity pylon, caught fire, and plunged into woodland on the fringe of the Willenhall housing estate in Coventry. It brushed rooftops as it fell, and burst into flames on impact. The 5 people on board, 3 Algerian crew, and 2 British stock handlers were killed.

The Algerian-registered plane, owned by *'Air Algerie'* and on hire to *'Phoenix Aviation',* was on its way back from Amsterdam, after dropping off a cargo of livestock. It had initially been diverted to East Midlands Airport due to bad weather but had eventually taken off for Coventry Airport.

Officers deployed to the scene from across the Force cordoned off the area during freezing weather conditions, and carried out an extensive search of the crash site resulting in the *'black box'* flight recorder being recovered later in the day.

For the first 2 days following the crash 6 serials of 9 officers were on duty at any one time.

Figure 147 Courtesy of the Express & Star

***

In December, a police officer was lucky to escape serious injury after he lost his footing and fell 20 feet into the River Rea in Balsall Heath whilst chasing a suspected burglar. Constable Nicholas Mills jumped over a fence and some bushes before falling into a concealed culvert. He suffered spinal injuries, and the emergency services took 45 minutes to rescue the officer, who eventually made a full recovery.

In the same month, 5 West Midlands Police officers commenced a 6 month secondment to the Western European Union police force in Mostar, Bosnia, as part of the initiative to unify the police force in the city.

Again in December, a joint operation involving the West Midlands Police Commercial Vice Unit, Warwickshire Police, the Regional Crime Squad, and the National Criminal Intelligence Service, resulted in 49 warrants being executed at houses and commercial premises, and hard-core pornography valued at £250,000 recovered.

***

At the end of the reporting period, and for the first time in 4 years, crime reduced - by 4.6%, with a total of 308,584 crimes recorded, whilst there was a 22% increase in calls from the public.

Chief Constable Ronald Hadfield, reflecting on the reduction in crime, commented in his Annual Report, *'The last two years have been a time of unprecedented change for everyone, but we now have a well-equipped and progressive Force ready to take us forward into the next century. I am grateful to all the staff for their co-operation and support that have made these changes possible.'*

The detection rate fell from 26.8% to 25.1%.

A total of 44 murders were recorded, of which 43 were detected.

To support these investigations, in 1994 the Home Office Large Major Enquiry computer system was used on 35 major enquiries. As a result of an establishment review, a Sergeant and 6 Constables were returned to operational duties from the HOLMES Department, to be replaced by civilian index supervisors.

Also, during the period, a campaign called *'Doorstoppers'* was launched, aimed at prevention in partnership with major utility & service companies to combat 'Bogus Official' offences. As part of the campaign, a Code of Practice was created.

Another operation, *'Cheetah',* targeted mobile phone theft. It was started on the *'F'* Division but then rolled out force-wide, co-ordinated by the Force Intelligence Bureau. It led to the examination of 1,564 phones in possession of arrested persons and numerous offences being disclosed.

During another operation *'Clough',* the Stolen Vehicle Squad investigated the use of forged log books. Over 50 vehicles were identified and £250k of stolen vehicles recovered. Overall, the Stolen Vehicle Squad recovered £3.4 million pounds worth of stolen vehicles during the reporting period.

Drugs continued to be a major challenge in the fight against crime. In one joint Drug Squad operation with Thames Valley Police, heroin with a street value of £100,000 was recovered. This led to 4 other operations where £200,000 heroin was recovered and the discovery of a plot to assassinate a Birmingham couple using heroin as a down-payment. Following an undercover operation, the suspect was arrested and later sentenced to 12 years imprisonment at Birmingham Crown Court.

During this period the longest ever sentence for crack-cocaine dealing was given, as a Birmingham man went to prison for 15 years.

***

Violence continued to raise its 'ugly' head during the year. By way of example, at a football match between Aston Villa and Turkish side Trabzonspor, about 70 supporters ran onto the pitch at the end of the game and fought briefly, but effective action by police officers and club stewards prevented a mass pitch invasion. Trouble after the match was quelled by 100 officers outside the ground, including the Mounted Branch. A total of 19 Villa fans and 19 Turkish supporters were arrested for public order offences.

Assaults on police officers reached 1,320, versus 1,676 the previous year.

In one case, CID officers were making routine enquiries at a bank in Smethwick when they realised that a robbery was taking place. They approached two men who were dressed in boiler suits and balaclavas and there was a violent struggle. They overpowered the offenders, but a third man then appeared and threatened the officers, discharging a shotgun at the counter shield, and injuring one officer beneath the eye.

In another case, PC David Mullaney suffered serious head injuries whilst on plain clothes duty in Coventry City Centre, whilst investigating a man acting suspiciously outside public toilets. After following him inside he was punched and kicked around the head and body.

Elsewhere PC Tracey Meredith was run over by youths who had been interfering with motor vehicles in a Birmingham car park. She was carried on the bonnet of a car for several yards, receiving bruising and cuts to head.

Finally, after PC's Jamie Checkland and David Brooks had arrested a suspected thief in Castle Vale, a second offender returned with 6 others, who assaulted the officers, inflicting cuts and bruising.

***

This period saw the installation of a further 27 sites where speed cameras were installed, making a total of 59 sites in all in the Force. For the first time 'stingers', (devices to halt vehicles by puncturing tyres), were provided to traffic officers, and used on 35 occasions during the reporting period.

***

The number of operational tasks performed by the Air Operations Unit increased from 2,644 in 1993 to 2,865 in 1994, an increase of 8%. The Unit assisted in the arrest of 352 people, of which nearly half were attributed to the use of thermal imaging equipment.

In 1994, the Underwater Search Unit became a serial of the Operational Support Unit, whilst retaining their primary role as divers. They conducted 297 operations in the Force area during the year, and 13 in other Force areas. To assist with searches, they also acquired an underwater search camera capable of taking high-resolution images in poor conditions.

During 1994, the West Midlands Police were responsible for the policing of 24 Royal visits, including 2 by HM The Queen, and 7 by HRH The Princess Royal.

From its inception in 1979, the Special Support Unit functioned as a dedicated surveillance unit for the Force as a whole. During 1994 they conducted a total of 249 operations, resulting in the arrest of 133 persons for offences including armed robbery, drug dealing, and burglary.

At the same time Divisionally based observation teams (DOT'S) conducted in excess of 1,000 operations.

***

In 1994, the Force supported moves by the Commission for Racial Equality to encourage more people to report racial incidents. This led to 444 such incidents being reported in 1994.

***

The ongoing Force reorganisation had a major impact on the Force Surveyors Department as 9 Divisional Information Rooms were created, and the Force Control Room at Bournville Lane was completely refurbished. Work also began on Coventry's new £3,600,000 million police station at Chace Avenue in Coventry.

A new purpose-built Dog Training Centre was also completed in 1994 at a cost of £1.500,000, and was the first building of its type to receive a *'Secured By Design'* award.

1995

Murder Mayhem

In 1995, the West Midlands Police was one of the largest employers in the West Midlands with a work-force of nearly 10,000 people and an annual budget of £340,000,000 A reduction in supervisory ranks and a moratorium on promotions for a year had contributed to a successful recruitment campaign. A total of 530 new officers joined the Force, nearly a third female, leading to an overall increase of 270 Police Constables after retirements and other factors had taken place.

31 of the new recruits were from ethnic minorities, reaching a total of 3.75% of the establishment of the Force and the highest in the Country.

Female officers also made up 18.5% of the establishment of the Force, again the highest of any Force in the UK.

During the year, 33% of civilian staff changed jobs or had their job descriptions amended, as the Force led the country in terms of civilianisation.

A new Command and Control system was introduced into the Force during the first year of another new Police Authority for the West Midlands Police, which was required to perform a more strategic role in determining local policing objectives under powers provided by the Police & Magistrates Act 1994. The new body consisted of 9 local Councillors, 3 magistrates and 5 independents.

There were new requirements for the Force to produce performance indicator information, which included key objectives set by the Home Secretary, as well as measures identified by the Audit Commission, Her Majesty's Inspector of Constabulary and the Association of Chief Police Officers. A leaflet *'Your Service, Our Standards'* was formally launched setting out the standards of service that the public could expect from the police.

During the year, all officers up to the rank of Inspector were issued with rigid handcuffs and extendable 21-inch 'Casco' batons, as assaults on police officers exceeded 1300. A 26-inch version of the baton was issued to over 100 teams.

The number of Armed Response Vehicles was increased from 2 to 3 on a 24/7 basis and for the first-time officers were authorised to carry sidearms openly in a holster.

As the profile of the Force changed, so did the make-up of the West Midlands itself; 348 square miles in total, with a population of 2,550,907, of which 15% came from visible ethnic minorities, and 22% under the age of 16 years, whilst 18% were over retirement age.

Some 11.5% of the working population were unemployed whilst 60% of the working population travelled to work by car every day.

***

In January 1995, West Midlands Police were asked by the Birmingham Coroner, Dr. Richard Whittington, to report on the circumstances surrounding the death of Frederick West at Winson Green Prison on New Year's Day. A post-mortem had revealed that the cause of death was due to hanging. He was on remand awaiting trial following the recovery of 12 sets of human remains at a house in Gloucester.

***

On the 6th February 1995, the Force Clothing Store was centralised at new premises near to Birmingham City Centre and the whole department was computerised.

As the Force continued to make advances in the use of technology, another system costing £1,000,000 called *'ASSURE'* began being rolled out to Administrative Support Units. The computer package featured a large database containing details of court cases and appearances, road accidents and warrants, as well as a library of 2,000 offences and charges.

***

In February 1995, officers seized weapons and drugs worth £2.5 million in two raids.

At one warrant in Ladywood an AK47, Winchester .22 repeater rifle, CS Gas canister, Stun Gun, 300 rounds of ammunition and £35k of Ecstasy, amphetamine and cannabis were found. It was the first seizure of this type of assault rifle in the Force area.

Elsewhere in Ladywood and Edgbaston, local officers staged a crackdown on street prostitution and kerb crawling, resulting in 41 men being summonsed to appear at Birmingham Magistrates Court.

***

In March 1995, Constable Stephen Rowe and police dog *'Jamie'* were awarded the *'Police Dog Action of The Year'* trophy for disarming a former psychiatric patient, who had been threatening staff with a 6" knife in 1994 at Highcroft Hospital in Erdington. Police officers' initial attempts at calming the man had been met with further violence as he picked up a heavy desk and threw it at them. The police dog was then deployed, and despite being attacked, managed to bring the man under control, although PC Rowe suffered serious injuries in the prolonged struggle which took place before the man was finally subdued.

Now retired, Steve Rowe recalls:

'Jamie' was a German Shepherd aged seven years and had been a police dog for about five years. The man who was threatening staff and other patients was in a relatively small room and it was a very dangerous situation. Ideally, we would have liked to wait for some shields to arrive, but I realised that we just didn't have time and released the dog who managed to hold onto one of his arms, but he still had the knife hand free.

I knew that I had to act quickly to stop him from stabbing the dog, so I started grappling with him, as other officers joined in as well. Before finally subduing him, I was stabbed in the arm and suffered some broken ribs which left me off work for three months. The man was later sent to a secure mental health unit.'

***

In March, the new Dog Training Centre in Holly Lane, Balsall Common, was officially opened by His Royal Highness Prince Michael of Kent, President of the Kennel Club. 50 local schoolchildren joined the Chief Constable Ron Hadfield and members of the Police Authority in welcoming him.

***

A total of 86 people were arrested, and 132 offences cleared after a month-long operation in April to combat street robbery and burglary in Harborne, Handsworth, Ladywood, Great Barr and Birmingham City Centre. Stolen property valued at £100,000 was also recovered.

A new approach was adopted by officers from Thornhill Road, who used two female officers to act as decoys to catch street robbers who preyed on elderly victims. The officers volunteered to be 'aged' by 40 years using wigs and make-up before walking in known 'hot spot' areas with teams of officers covertly deployed nearby. To avoid allegations of entrapment the tactic was made known in the media beforehand.

***

On the 11th May 1995, 6 addresses in the Black Country and Birmingham were raided resulting in the recovery of £60,000 worth of hard-core pornography by the Commercial Vice Unit as part of Operation *'Dara'*.

***

During the year, the West Midlands Police highlighted the financial and operational costs of major incidents within the Force using one case as an example.

On the 11th May 1995, a body was found in the Chelmsley Wood area. A murder incident room was set up at Solihull Police Station which was staffed by 8 civilians and 33 police officers.

On the 21st May 1995, a further 28 police officers were assigned to the enquiry.

On the 26th May 1995, two suspects were charged with the murder, but the Incident Room did not close until the 8th December 1995, as prosecution files were prepared.

The total cost of just this one investigation came to £133,479.

During the year, the Force dealt with 51 murders, 43 attempt murders and 4 cases of manslaughter, as well as scores of other 'major' incidents.

Of these, 48 murders and 5 manslaughters, (one case from the previous year), were detected. In addition, 95% of all reported kidnapping cases and 73% of all reported rapes were detected.

On the 'F' Division alone, covering Birmingham City Centre, 19 cases of murder and 1 manslaughter were dealt with during the financial year 1995/96, of which 17 were detected by the 31st March 1996.

By that date 6 major incident rooms were still running on the Division, using 45 CID officers from the Division's total complement of 98 CID officers, who were supplemented by another 85 CID officers from other Divisions.

***

On the 16th May, the West Midlands Police launched a year-long burglary campaign at 'Tally Ho' Police Training Centre, in an event which was attended by the Chief Constable and the Minister of State for the Home Office, Mr. David Maclean.

***

On the 19th May, an armed robbery occurred at a branch of Lloyds Bank in Wolverhampton. PC Roger Moon was on routine patrol when two schoolgirls ran up to him and told him that a robbery was taking place. As the officer approached the bank two men ran out, and as he tried to pursue them, shots were fired, before they made good their escape. Following a lengthy investigation 3 men were arrested.

***

On the 2nd June, Operation 'Suncrown' was mounted on the 'F' Division following concerns that 1,400 street robberies had occurred in a 3 month period. The initiative led to a 33% reduction in robberies, and by the end of the year had led to 170 arrests.

***

In July 1995, officers covering the Stoke Aldermoor area of Coventry launched Operation 'Maramasco' which resulted in the execution of 14 search warrants and 8 arrests. It resulted in a 67% reduction in local burglary offences with one individual admitting 255 offences.

On Saturday 15th July 1995, over 100 officers blocked off 6 streets in Digbeth as part of Operation *'Aberhill'* as they sought to tackle the problems of road-racing in the area, which attracted up to 100 vehicles and 600 spectators. The activity had achieved 'cult status' with some participants, but high-speed racing on ordinary roads had led to several accidents. In due course 150 people appeared in court charged with a variety of offences.

***

On one weekend in 1995, the Borough of Walsall suffered from two fatal killings in the course of just 24 hours.

On Friday 20th October, a 17 year-old teenager died after a fight erupted during the early hours, outside the *'Zone and Ethos'* nightclubs in Bentley Mill Way, Darlaston. The victim was attacked by a number of individuals and 5 people were subsequently charged with his murder.

Figure 148 Courtesy of the Express & Star

The second murder occurred outside a *'Kentucky Fried Chicken'* in Bridge Street, Walsall when a 30 year-old man was attacked and subsequently died from head injuries.

4 men were subsequently charged with his murder, of which 3 were later convicted.

BRAWL DEATH MURDER NO 2 IN TWO DAYS

MAN was murdered in Walsall after a fight outside a takeaway restaurant – the second murder in town in two days.

Paul Andrew Adshead, aged 30, died from head injuries.

It was claimed that his head was rammed into a shop window.

Two other men, aged 20 and 27, were badly injured in the disturbance outside the Kentucky Fried Chicken restaurant in Bridge Street at 12.30am.

Shopowner Karen McAllsonvey, who lives in a nearby flat, said girls moving in the Kentucky told her that men held Mr Adshead and rammed his head against the window.

Police said there are no links with the murder of 17-year-old Merrick Nightingale, who died in a fight at a burger van in Beesley Mill Way, Walsall, early on Friday morning.

Police officers and a passer-by attempted to resuscitate Mr Adshead, but he was dead on arrival at Walsall Manor Hospital.

Mr Adshead, of Paterson Place, Stow Oak, Brownhills, died from head injuries, police said.

Taxi driver Mohammed Amin, chairman of Walsall Taxi Association, witnessed the resuscitation attempts.

MASSAGE

"There was blood all over the road. The police and ambulance crew were there for a long time doing those beat with mouth-to-mouth and heart massage," he said.

Four men were arrested soon after words and three other men detained today. All are from the Walsall area.

A spokeswoman said: "This is being treated as a murder inquiry. We believe the parties involved did not know one another."

The two injured men had head stitches and were released from hospital.

A spokeswoman for Kentucky Fried Chicken said today: "It was an incident the shop and did not involve any-one who had been inside."

The family of Merrick Nightingale, from Tipton, today said he could have been attacked on extres.

His sister Dallas, aged 22, of St George's, said: "He had never been to a nightclub before. I believe it was a case of mistaken identity."

Twelve people were arrested after his murder near to the Same and Elbow nightclub. A West Midlands police spokesman said five 16-year-olds and a youth, 17, were still in police custody.

Last night detectives released three girls, aged 14 and 15, without charge and together three men aged 17, 19, and 24 on police bail.

● First victim Merrick Nightingale

Figure 149 Courtesy of the Express & Star

***

In 1995, concerns were raised about the increasing use of firearms by criminals in offences related to the drugs trade, albeit they still only represented just 0.4% of total reported crime.

In October, officers on the *'D'* Division launched an investigation into 3 separate shooting incidents which occurred in a few days – one armed robbery and two attempt murders – which were believed to have been committed by the same person. Following an intensive surveillance operation, a man was arrested at gunpoint, and found to be in possession of a loaded weapon.

During October 1995 alone, the Drugs Squad executed a total of 25 search warrants resulting in 22 persons being arrested, and drugs worth £131,890 being recovered, as well as a stun-gun, CS gas cannisters, a hand-gun and 15 rounds of ammunition.

***

Also, in October, Operation *'Santiago'* was set up following a sharp increase in the theft of high-powered motor vehicles from the *'L'* Division. In the previous 6 months cars valued at £8,000,000 pounds had been stolen. 13 officers worked on the operation which resulted in 225 arrests. The Airport Police at Birmingham recovered several stolen vehicles from the long-stay car parks which were being used by some thieves as storage areas.

***

In November 1995, during a football match between Millwall and Birmingham at St. Andrews football ground, major disturbances took place, as well as in the city centre. During confrontations with police officers and supporters, a police horse, *'Lochinvar',* was stabbed in the head, and PC Maxine Brook suffered a broken arm.

During the financial year 1995/96 the Operations Support Unit, numbering 132 officers in total, policed 140 football matches at which they made 660 arrests and ejected 156 persons.

***

In November, a recruitment campaign aimed at increasing the number of applicants from ethnic minorities, which had been running for 18 months, won a prestigious national award.

Advertisements were featured in the local press, radio, and on the sides of buses, and posters were distributed to mosques, colleges and community centres. 500 audio tapes, recorded in Hindi, Punjabi and Urdu were sent to places of worship containing a message to the parents of potential recruits about the positive benefits of joining the police.

***

On Tuesday the 5th December 1995, more than 60 officers executed warrants on addresses in Walsall as part of Operation *'Christmas Cracker'*. Stolen property, valued at more than £5,000 was recovered and 11 arrests made.

In the West Midlands, 91 arrests were made, and stolen property valued at £39,000 was recovered as 133 addresses were raided. At one address officers found £8,000 worth of designer clothes which had been stolen from the *'Clothes Show Live'* at the NEC.

Figure 150 Courtesy of the Express & Star

The operation was part of a nation-wide initiative; in the biggest ever crack-down on burglars with 12,000 officers conducting 4,000 raids in 40 different Force areas.

***

On the 17th December 1995, PC Robert John Dallow, aged forty-one years, died after a patrol car he was a passenger in was involved in a collision, while pursuing a stolen car suspected of having left the scene of a burglary in Oldbury.

Just after midnight, PC Dallow was in a police vehicle being driven by another officer, who was subsequently convicted of dangerous driving, sent to prison for 3 months, and banned from driving for two years.

The police vehicle, travelling at high speeds, hit an entirely innocent motorist, Neil Homer, just two days after his twentieth birthday. He had been waiting at traffic lights and was struck by the police car as he started to cross the junction as the lights turned to green in his favour. Both Neil Homer and Robert Dallow lost their lives in the crash.

This tragic loss of life opened a debate on whether the guidelines on police pursuits should be reviewed.

West Midlands Police Officer Simon Jones recalls:

'I was on 'E' Unit at 'K2' Smethwick at the time. Under normal circumstances I would have been in the police vehicle that gave chase on that night, but we swopped around a couple of days before.

A report came in that a burglary was in progress at a community centre near Windmill Lane, Smethwick, and 'Bob' Dallow and his partner picked up on a stolen vehicle, I think it was a blue Escort, as it left the scene. There was a chase all around the back streets and then eventually onto main roads.

I was in another vehicle, paired up with a colleague, and as we listened to the commentary over the radio, we tried to get closer to the pursuit. At some point the pursuing police vehicle crashed into another car at some traffic lights and the stolen vehicle managed to escape.

We were on the scene very quickly and the driver of the police car was out of the vehicle and in shock with cuts to his face. Bob was still trapped inside the vehicle and my partner got inside next to Bob and held him, whilst I checked the other car, but tragically the driver inside was dead.

In the days following the incident several car thieves came into the police station voluntarily to be interviewed as they wanted nothing to do with what happened. Eventually the person driving the stolen car was brought in by his father.

I was one of the 'pall-bearers' at Bob's funeral and the deaths had a devastating effect on the shift. It is something I will never forget, and I still sometimes dwell on the circumstances to this day. If I was to sum Bob up, I would say he was someone who was everyone's friend – someone who was always there to help. It was just his way.'

(Postscript: In July 2018, the wife of Robert Dallow gave an address during a memorial service organised by *'Care Of Police Survivors'* as part of its annual family weekend at the National Memorial Arboretum. After the service the families and guests made their way to *'The Beat',* the avenue of trees dedicated to each Force, where roses and wreaths were laid in memory of fallen officers.)

Figure 151 PC Robert Dallow, Control Room, Wednesbury Police Station, 1984, courtesy of Lynne Sedgley

Figure 152 PC Dallow's plaque, National Memorial Arboretum, courtesy of M Layton

Figure 153 PC Dallow's plaque in the grounds of 'The Beat', National Memorial Arboretum

***

At 5am on Wednesday 20th December 1995, as part of Operation *'Hailes'*, OSU teams, together with members of the Force Drugs Squad, the National Criminal Intelligence Service, and supported by Dutch Police, executed search warrants at 21 homes in Walsall and Cannock, resulting in the recovery of cannabis valued at £350,000

21 arrests were made, and at one house enough cannabis plants to fill a skip were removed, whilst similar raids took place in Avon and Somerset and Merseyside.

On the same date, a 4 week national knives amnesty commenced. It was sponsored by a national newspaper following the fatal stabbing of a London teacher, and resulted in 1,318 knives and other weapons being handed in at police stations across the West Midlands.

***

On Christmas Eve a man was shot in the back near Hill Top Golf Course in Handsworth and seriously injured. A man and woman were later arrested and charged in connection with the incident.

On the 27th December, a man was shot dead by two masked intruders at his home in Handsworth.

On Friday 29th December, a 22 year-old employee at the *'Netto'* store in Small Heath ran amok with 3 knives and stabbed a total of 10 people. He was chased by a security guard, and the father of one of the victims, and was about to turn on them when two police officers arrived on the scene. They managed to disarm the man who was initially charged with 10 attempt murders but following the death of one of the victims he was later further charged with murder.

***

In the 12 month period commencing April 1995, the Force made a total of 49,975 arrests of people for 'notifiable' offences.

Of these, traffic and motorway officers were responsible for 8,437 arrests, of which 3,099 were for criminal offences. Traffic officers dealt with 78 fatal road accidents. During just one 2 week campaign on a single stretch of road in Birmingham, a total of 1,145 drivers were caught speeding.

In the same period, officers responded to 913,536 incidents, which was an increase of 60,000 on the previous year. A total of 161,023 immediate response calls were made which represented an increase of 40% over the previous two years.

In terms of crime a total of 320,046 offences were recorded, an increase of 5.9% with vehicle crime up by 16% and robbery – mainly street offences known as 'muggings' up by 17%. The overall detection rate was 23%.

51 murders were recorded over the reporting period, of which 48 were detected.

***

During the year the Underwater Search Unit conducted 239 diving operations and took delivery of a 'Pioneer' multi-rigid hull boat costing £11,000. Made mainly of polythene, it had a drop-down front to give divers better access to the water, as well as sonar and radio.

In relation to the vehicle fleet, the Force took delivery of Ford Mondeos to carry out 'First Response' roles. A new Range Rover and Volvo Estate was tested for police usage as well as Ford Scorpions being brought into service.

***

In just one example of how individual officers could make a considerable impact on policing, PC Terry Knott, with 31 years' service, was awarded a Chief Constable's commendation for making 445 arrests over a 21 month period, whilst working on a vehicle squad on the Western side of the Force.

1996

Another Death in The Line of Duty

In January, Detective Superintendent Tim Salt, the Head of the West Midlands Police Fraud Squad, and Detective Sergeant Peter Rowan, an expert on credit card fraud, travelled to Saudi Arabia to advise bankers, police and businesses on fraud.

Some weeks later Detective Chief Inspector Terry Street, Deputy Head of the Squad, travelled to Uganda as part of a delegation organised by the Oversees Development Association to advise government officials on anti-corruption strategies.

***

On the 21st January 1996, a London man was shot in a car park outside the West Indian Federation building, opposite Winson Green Prison, and received leg injuries. Several people were charged in connection with the incident.

Also in January, a factory unit in Birmingham was raided and one tonne of cannabis with a street value of £10,000,000 recovered. It was the largest seizure of its type ever in the West Midlands and resulted in 3 arrests.

In the same month a man was arrested in possession of 2,000 ecstasy tablets worth £30,000 which was found to contain a dangerous cocktail of stimulants and anaesthetic drugs.

***

In February 1996, over 100 offences of burglary were committed in the Four Oaks and Sutton Coldfield areas of the West Midlands. A 9 day Operation, *'Hook'*, was mounted, resulting in 9 arrests and 63 offences being detected. Stolen property valued at £5,000 was recovered and burglary offences dropped by 60% in the area.

***

In the early hours of Saturday 17th February 1996, the body of a 26 year-old man was found lying in a pool of blood by a police officer near to Heath Road in Darlaston. He was thought to have been hit with a concrete post and suffered severe head injuries.

After first phoning a local newspaper, a 23 year-old from the Wednesbury area, gave himself up and was charged with the murder of his cousin.

Also in February, a 24 year-old man was shot dead whilst sitting in a car outside an empty building in Hockley, which was being used for an illegal drinking party. 6 people were later charged with his murder.

In the same month a 27 year-old man was fatally wounded with a handgun whilst sitting in his car outside a café in Dudley Road, Winson Green.

On Monday 11th March 1996, an armed robber, described as having a *'face like a bulldog'* held a revolver to the heads of two women at a jewellers in Walsall before stealing £2,000 in cash and a large quantity of jewellery.

The following day the police took the unusual step of publishing a photograph and the name of the suspect, aged 40 years, who was wanted for 6 violent robberies at banks where a pistol had been brandished. The suspect was known to use disguises and at times had dressed up as a woman.

A significant reward was offered by the British Bankers Association for information leading to his arrest, and 10 days later he was found asleep in the back of a lorry on a lorry park in Pleck and arrested.

***

In February and March 1996 alone, the Force Drugs Squad executed 30 search warrants resulting in 33 arrests and the recovery of more than £2,000,000 worth of drugs.

One of the warrants involved the recovery of more than 6 kilos of heroin, and the arrest of 4 men, whilst in another, 3,500 ecstasy tablets were seized with a street value of £90,000.

At the same time, one of the Government's 'flagship' policies, *'Tackling Drugs Together',* came into being, with the creation of multi-agency 'Drugs Action Teams' in which the police were key players.

***

On the 28th April 1996, Inspector Vanessa Rosemary Carroll, aged thirty-five years, was killed in a road accident while with the British Police Unit in Bosnia.

Vanessa Carroll joined the West Midlands Police in September 1979 and was posted to Chelmsley Wood. She received a commendation early in service from a Judge for her bravery in chasing and detaining a violent offender who had already seriously injured two police officers.

She was promoted to Sergeant and posted to Queens Road in 1985 and then to Inspector in 1995 when she returned to Chelmsley Wood.

Vanessa was an enthusiastic sportswoman who was the captain of the Force's netball team, a cross-country runner and basketball player.

Vanessa was in Bosnia as part of the Western European Union Police Mission, a multi-national group, based in Mostar, reviewing policing arrangements and how the local police could be unified.

She was fatally injured in a road traffic accident when she was forced to swerve to avoid an oncoming car and was thrown from her vehicle.

Debbie Menzel was a close friend of Vanessa, and summed up her thoughts when contributing towards an article from the *'West Midlands Police Heritage Project'* as follows, *'I consider it a great privilege to have known her. Vanessa was a very talented lady and a wonderful friend. I think about her often and will never forget her. She was one in a million.'*

Debbie added: *'All the officers on the 'L' Division had to do six months at the Airport as soon as they had got their two years in. Me and Vanessa were already on the same shift at Chelmsley Wood and we ended up going together to the Airport for 166 days and we counted every one of them! The below photograph is my favourite of the two of us together.'*

Figure 154 Debbie Menzel (L) & Vanessa Carroll (R), circa 1982, courtesy of D Menzel

Figure 155 Vanessa Carroll's plaque, National Memorial Arboretum, courtesy of M Layton

Figure 156 Vanessa Carroll's plaque in 'The Beat', National Memorial Arboretum

***

In May 1996, Operation *'Jericho'* was set up to tackle 'street robberies' in Sandwell. In the first 2 weeks, 69 arrests were made as robbers were displaced into the hands of covert teams.

Throughout the year more than 8,000 offences of robbery were recorded across the Force area.

***

In June, the European Football Championships were held throughout England and thousands of European supporters visited Birmingham to watch 4 matches played at Villa Park, where between 24,600 and 34,300 fans attended each game. Some 600 officers were deployed to the events, with just 96 arrests in total.

***

At 3.15pm on the 8th July 1996, a class of 3 and 4 year-old children were enjoying a 'teddy bear's picnic' in the grounds of St Luke's C of E Primary School, in Blakenhall, Wolverhampton, whilst being supervised by Lisa Webb, a nursery teacher.

Outside, a man armed with a machete attacked 3 mothers, who had been waiting outside the school, before entering the school grounds and threatening the children.

In a desperate attempt to protect the children, Lisa managed to grab a child under each arm whilst others cowered under her skirts. She was slashed by the attacker on her arms, head and back as 3 children also suffered injuries in a concerted attack which lasted 8 minutes.

The attacker then made off but was found a short time later hiding in a block of flats nearby by police officers.

This incident occurred just 4 months after the Dunblane massacre in which a teacher and 16 pupils were killed, and sent shock-waves throughout the local communities.

Figure 157 Courtesy of the Express & Star

Figure 158 Courtesy of the Express & Star

The following year Lisa Webb was awarded the George Medal in recognition of her bravery.

The person responsible was later detained in a hospital indefinitely under the Mental Health Act, after he was diagnosed with severe schizophrenia.

***

In the summer of 1996, a new 'Integrated Custody Information System' was piloted at Wolverhampton with a view to rolling it out to the rest of the Force during 1997. Its main function was to streamline the process of booking prisoners into custody suites and save operational police time by reducing duplication of effort, at a time when up to 130,000 persons in custody were being processed in a 12 month period.

***

In July 1996, Sir Ronald Hadfield left the Force, to be replaced by Edward Crew in August of that year. Following his retirement, Ron Hadfield was appointed as a consultant in training and people management. He passed away in 2013.

Edward Crew had previously served in the Metropolitan Police, Kent County Constabulary and as the Chief Constable of Northamptonshire Police. He was awarded the Queens Police Medal (QPM) in 1990 and was appointed as a Deputy Lieutenant in 1997 before being knighted in 2001.

***

In September 1996, a 14 day initiative took place in the Balsall Heath area of Birmingham. In 1995, following the establishment of a 'street watch' scheme in the area, numbers of prostitutes working in Balsall Heath fell by 98%. During the 1996 operation, there were 22 arrests of the remaining prostitutes, in addition to 25 'kerb-crawlers', and 40 letters were sent out advising other drivers regarding their conduct.

***

In October 1996, sector officers in Handsworth received reports about a local man having young boys visit his house. It was established that 2 men with access to the premises were convicted paedophiles and as a result, Operation *'Fever'* was mounted.

During the operation, one of the men moved to Hereford, so a joint operation was set up with West Mercia Police. The young boys were subsequently interviewed by Family Protection Unit officers and 2 men arrested and charged with indecency offences. One was later sentenced to 6 years imprisonment, and the other to 4 years.

***

In November 1996, 24 kilos of cannabis and 7 kilos of amphetamine were recovered following a raid on a house in Sutton Coldfield. A brother and sister were charged with conspiracy to supply drugs.

For the financial year 1996/97, a total of 4,229 people were dealt with for drugs offences, of which 3,771 involved 'personal' use, two-thirds of which resulted in a caution.

Of significance, a four-fold increase in the use of heroin was reported, as nearly £2,000,000 worth of the drug were recovered. Increases were also seen in the supply of 'crack-cocaine' as well as the cultivation of strong cannabis called 'skunk'.

As a result of Drug Squad operations, drugs with a 'street value' of nearly £5,000,000 was recovered.

**

Operation *'Street Strike'* was launched across the Force in November 1996 for 5 weeks, targeting offences of robbery, nuisance behaviour, violence, damage and drugs. It resulted in a 15% fall in recorded crime compared to November 1995 and 7,122 arrests. It was the first Force-level co-ordinated operation of its kind to be adopted.

**

On the afternoon of Wednesday 20th November 1996, after a domestic dispute with his parents, David Howells went into a Co-Operative Supermarket in the Ward End district of Birmingham armed with a knife. He handcuffed the manager and threatened to kill him.

Firearms officers attended and Howells was fatally shot as the incident unfolded. It was the first time that shots had been fired by West Midlands firearms officers since the Unit's inception.

The incident was subsequently investigated independently by the Metropolitan Police supervised by the Police Complaints Authority. A Coroners Court later recorded a verdict of 'lawful killing'.

**

In 1996, the West Midlands Police Air Operations Unit conducted 2,400 flights, assisted with 300 arrests and recovered stolen property valued at nearly £500,000, which included 82 stolen vehicles. They had also been instrumental in finding 7 vulnerable missing persons.

**

At the end of the financial year 1996/97, crime fell by 8.2% during the year, as a total of 293,789 offences were recorded. The detection rate was 24% which was brought about mainly by changes in the recording of primary and secondary detections.

More than 9,000 offences of violence were recorded during this period which included 32 murders and 22 manslaughters.

By the end of the financial year all the cases of manslaughter had been detected as well as 26 of the murders.

A total of 1,301 police officers were assaulted during their duties, with 262 classified as serious, and 46 attacks on female officers.

Crimestoppers received 3,131 calls which resulted in 103 arrests, and the recovery of stolen property valued at £40,000 and drugs valued at £114,000.

In the same 12 month period, nearly 400 road safety campaigns were launched as well as 370 speed campaigns and 21 'drink/drive' campaigns, the latter of which resulted in 21,945 breath tests, of which 17.1% were either positive or refused.

A total of 117 fatal accidents occurred whilst 1,610 people were seriously injured and 7,602 slightly injured in road accidents.

In terms of Neighbourhood Watch it was confirmed that 8,584 local schemes involving 340,000 homes, schools, businesses and pubs were operating.

9,615 persons were reported missing from home during this 12 month period, of which 99.6% were found or returned home.

1997

The Pioneers of Change

On a typical day during this period the force dealt with 2,496 incidents, including 1,266 '999' calls and 85 false alarms. A total of 805 crimes were reported, including 3 relating to firearms, 26 assaults, 114 stolen vehicles, 133 thefts from vehicles, 235 burglaries, 22 robberies, 26 road traffic accidents involving injury, 38 domestic violence incidents, 26 missing from home reports, 344 arrests, 348 prosecutions, 50 cautions, and 4 officers assaulted.

***

At the beginning of March 1997, the Force launched a 4 week operation code-named *'Wheel-Strike'* that targeted all forms of vehicle crime, which at the time accounted for nearly one-third of all crime in the West Midlands area. It was estimated that 5 cars were being stolen every hour, with the UK having the worst record for vehicle crime in Europe.

The operation led to 1,800 vehicle related arrests, and for the first time *'decoy vehicles'* were deployed which led to 19 arrests, whilst in some areas dog-handlers were deployed in 'fast-response' vehicles. One such team used a Volvo T5 estate-car, crewed by a traffic officer and dog-handler, who together made 28 arrests.

In March 1997, a total of 3,000 vehicles were stolen, compared to 4,322 in the same period in the previous year, a drop of 23%.

***

At 6.15am on Monday 10th March 1997, a series of road traffic accidents took place close to Junction One of the M42 motorway in foggy conditions with visibility down to 75 metres in places. Over a distance of one mile, a total of 117 vehicles were involved, 35 of which were destroyed by fire, resulting in one fatality.

A short time later a second series of accidents occurred on the opposite carriageway involving 42 vehicles and 2 further fatalities.

A total of 60 casualties were dealt with, 8 of which were seriously injured.

The accidents were dealt with by 18 officers from the Central Motorway Police Group and 10 local officers.

The motorway was closed until 5.50am the following day for repairs whilst an enquiry team was set up to investigate the circumstances.

***

Retired officer Michael Patrick Cole served on the Central Motorway Police Group between the 3rd August 1993 and March 2001, when he transferred to H2 OCU as a result of a tenure policy which was introduced in the Force and affected many officers in specialist posts. He has fond memories of his time on CMPG where officers on the Group displayed a distinctive badge on their uniforms to identify them.

Figure 159 PC 2909 Cole in unmarked BMW 535 heading out on patrol from CMPG HQ, courtesy of M Cole

Figure 160 PC Cole in jacket displaying the CMPG badge, courtesy of M Cole

Figure 161 PC Cole & CMPG vehicle, courtesy of M Cole

***

As of the 31st March 1997, just 4% of serving police officers were from visible ethnic minorities, which was still among the highest levels in the Country.

As part of an ongoing campaign to recruit more such officers, a poster-campaign was mounted on 35 billboards throughout the West Midlands, an initiative which was the first of its kind.

Out of a total of 411 new recruits taken on during the year, just 20 were from ethnic minorities.

In terms of female officers, as of 31st March 1997, a total of 19.3% of serving officers were female and 27% of new recruits for the year were women, the highest of any Force.

As of the same date the Force had a total of 945 Special Constables against an establishment of 1,100.

***

On the 1st April 1997, the West Midlands Police undertook a massive reorganisation, as 21 Operational Command Units (OCU's) were created, to replace the previous 9 geographical Divisions. The new OCU's were created to deliver a local policing model, each of them headed by a Higher Range Superintendent (the equivalent of a Chief Superintendent).

Chief Constable Edward (Ted) Crew said at the time, *'For some colleagues the pace of change has been breath-taking and for some, particularly at senior level, there is a feeling of soreness. Continuing devolution of decision-making, and the recognition that policing should be locally delivered, has reduced the need for Superintendents and Chief Inspectors. A substantial number of these colleagues have chosen to leave us and have done so with dignity. They have served West Midlands Police with distinction and deserve all our gratitude.'*

The new strategic approach was badged under the title contained within the Force's crest namely, *'Forward in Unity',* and was aimed at replacing what was regarded as a bureaucratic, hierarchical, divisional structure, by using 3 key principles of, 'Purpose, People and Priorities' as the corner-stones of future policing plans.

'Purpose – To protect life and property; To provide a high quality police service, 24 hours a day; To work with the community and other agencies to improve safety, security and quality of life; To maintain the public's respect for our role in upholding the rule of law.

People – Our people are our greatest asset in achieving our purpose; our people should be open, honest, fair and courteous, both to the public and each other; our people's hard work, creativity and unique contribution is valued; our people are required to act with integrity and loyalty to our purpose. Allowances will be made for honest mistakes; our people can expect training for their role and the opportunity to develop their skills.

Priorities – To make effective use of our police and civilian support staff; To prevent and detect crime; To protect and reassure the community; To provide the best possible response to calls from the public; To develop and maintain partnerships and improve community safety.'

Senior management posts were reduced, leaving the Force with the lowest management overhead costs in the country, and the savings from this exercise were reinvested in new Constable posts.

The Force was about to embark on a mixture of 'zero tolerance' 'performance-related' policing, and 'problem orientated' policing, whilst maintaining the overriding tradition of policing communities with consent.

The view of Chief Constable Edward Crew was that there were too many specialist departments, and that there were complicated command chains with too many senior officers, who had little influence or accountability for the service being delivered.

In future the emphasis was going to be on increasing the number of well-trained, well-equipped, and well-briefed officers patrolling the streets.

***

Terrorism returned to the West Midlands on Thursday 3rd April 1997, and Friday 25th April 1997, when bombs were placed on the M6 Motorway by the Provisional IRA. Extensive disruption was caused and the motorway was closed as police officers searched for devices.

Police officers and members of the Armed Forces put their lives at risk searching for, and disabling, a viable high-explosive device.

A coded message was received at two Walsall hotels, from a telephone box in Manzoni Gardens, Birmingham City Centre, which warned of a bomb that had been placed under the M6 motorway at Junction 9.

At the height of the rush-hour, the motorway and an adjacent railway line were closed causing widespread disruption. As searches were being carried out one detonator exploded but the bomb itself, which contained high-explosive, failed to explode, although it remained unstable. Another device found under an elevated section had to be defused by an Army Bomb Disposal officer, Warrant Officer Aminul Islam, from the Royal Logistics Corps, who was later awarded the George Medal for bravery.

Despite knowing that PIRA was most likely to have placed the devices, he removed his protective suit and helmet to climb onto scaffolding under an elevated section of the M6 to reach the devices.

They contained 2 pounds of commercial high-explosive and the motorway itself remained closed for 30 hours.

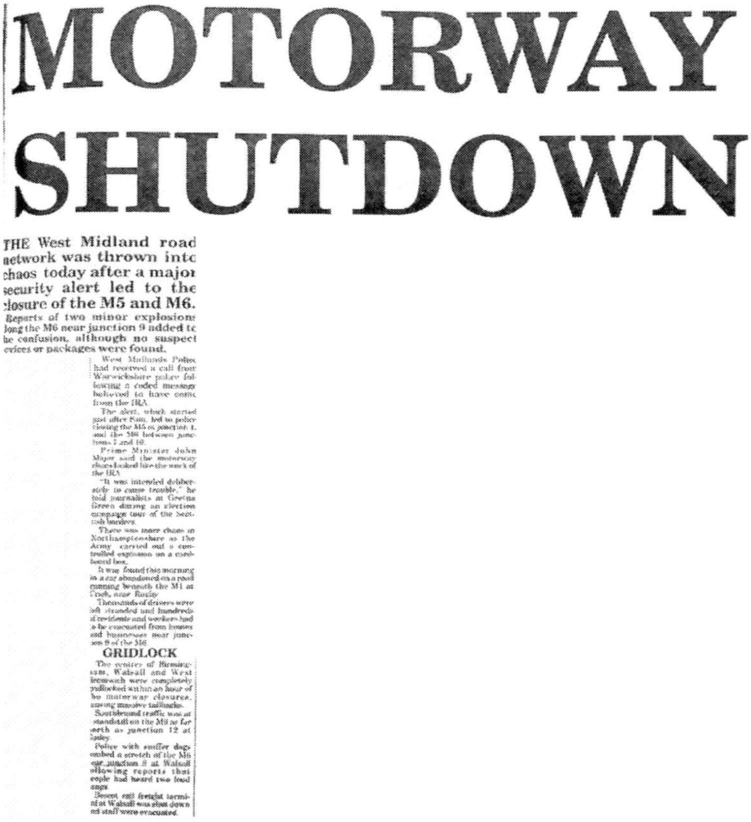

MOTORWAY SHUTDOWN

THE West Midland road network was thrown into chaos today after a major security alert led to the closure of the M5 and M6.

Reports of two minor explosions along the M6 near junction 9 added to the confusion, although no suspect devices or packages were found.

West Midlands Police had received a call from Warwickshire police following a coded message believed to have come from the IRA.

The alert, which started just after 8am, led to police closing the M5 at junction 1, and the M6 between junctions 3 and 10.

Prime Minister John Major said the motorway chaos looked like the work of the IRA.

"It was intended deliberately to cause trouble," he told journalists at Gretna Green during an election campaign tour of the Scottish borders.

There was more chaos in Northamptonshire as the Army carried out a controlled explosion on a cardboard box.

It was found this morning in a car abandoned on a road running beneath the M1 at Crick, near Rugby.

Thousands of drivers were left stranded and hundreds of residents and workers had to be evacuated from houses and businesses near junction 9 of the M6.

GRIDLOCK

The centre of Birmingham, Walsall and West Bromwich were completely gridlocked within an hour of the motorway closures, causing massive tailbacks.

Southbound traffic was at standstill on the M6 as far north as junction 12 at Cannock.

Police with sniffer dogs combed a stretch of the M6 near junction 8 at Walsall following reports that people had heard two loud bangs.

Bescot rail freight terminal at Walsall was shut down as staff were evacuated.

Figure 162 Courtesy of the Express & Star

Figure 163 Courtesy of the Express & Star

On the Friday 25th April 1997, two explosive devices went off close to the M6 again, near to Junction 10, in the Shortheath area, as the IRA attempted to bomb a 100 foot, 132,000 volt, electricity pylon. Some commentators at the time said that if the pylon had fallen across the motorway it would have led to tremendous loss of life.

During the incident, some residents from the Beechdale Estate were evacuated from their homes to TP Riley School in Bloxwich, as part of a pre-determined plan. The school was the designated North West Walsall evacuation centre, and after being put on standby at 10am they received around 60 local residents. They were eventually allowed home in the late afternoon, but not before a controlled explosion at 12.30pm in relation to the second device.

***

In April 1997, the Force announced that armed crime had risen from 952 offences in 1994/95, to 1,374 in 1996/97, an increase of 44%. Concerns were raised about increases in the flow of weapons arriving from Eastern Europe and China.

***

In April and May, major crime investigations were commenced following an attempted murder and a murder on the E2 OCU (Kings Heath). Operation *'Selito'* was set up after a woman was attacked in the hallway of a block of flats. She remained in a critical condition in hospital for 9 days, and a man was subsequently arrested and charged with attempted murder. He was later sentenced to 8 years imprisonment.

Operation *'Extreme'* was set up following a disturbance near a local pub during which one man died and another was seriously injured with a hammer. 6 men were arrested and charged with murder and attempted murder.

Also in May 1997, two men forced their way into a building society in Erdington and forced staff to hand over cash after threatening them with a hand gun. As they tried to leave, the manager tried to prevent their escape by damaging their 'getaway' car. The offenders shot at the manager narrowly missing him, before escaping. A media appeal, including one made on the *'Crime Stalker'* programme, led to the arrests of the suspects.

***

In June 1997, the Labour Home Secretary made a speech at the annual Police Federation conference in which he said that the Government was going to be *'tough on crime and tough on the causes of crime'*, and announced plans to reduce the burden of paperwork on officers.

The Force played its part by renaming the *'Books & Forms Committee'* the *'Doing Away with Books & Forms Committee'*. In its early days of operation around 200 forms were scrapped and 80 moved to a 'rarely used' folder.

***

On the 27th July 1997, the West Midlands Police Air Operations Unit celebrated 10 years of operation. During that time they had recorded 19,000 flying missions and been involved in the arrest of some 2,500 suspects.

***

In August 1997 the West Midlands Black Police Association was officially launched.

Racial tension, including that which followed the murder of Stephen Lawrence in London, still created challenges for recruitment from visible ethnic minority groups, and the Association provided officers with both a local and national voice.

As the BPA became established, they were able to contribute towards policy, legislation, recruitment processes and police officer training with a focus on diversity, as well as attracting more officers to specialist departments.

In addition, they helped with target setting for recruitment and progression of officers, as well as providing expert advice on external issues such as 'stop and search' and deaths in police custody.

This is the story of one officer's career in the West Midlands Police and how he eventually became one of the founders of the West Midlands Black Police Association.

Paul Antonio Lewin was born on the 27th January 1959, in St. Mary, Jamaica, and together with his twin sister, Paulette, was brought up in Jamaica until the age of 5 by his grandmother, before leaving the island to come to England. Paul's parents had previously left Jamaica in search of a better standard of living. The family settled in Smethwick, in the West Midlands.

Paul attended Waterloo Road Primary School before passing his eleven-plus for grammar School. Whilst at school he aspired to become either a Police Officer, Physical Education Teacher or a Chef.

Having completed his education in 1975, he applied and was accepted as one of the first minority Police Cadets in his home town force. At the age of 18 years he joined West Midlands Police Force where he worked as a uniform beat Constable as well as performing plain clothes covert duties.

Paul, after showing early promise, was promoted 5 years later to the rank of Sergeant and then Inspector. He held several managerial positions within the organisation including District Uniform Inspector, Intelligence Bureau Manager, Diversity Trainer and Head of Force Equalities.

One of Paul's many policing highlights was his contribution as a founder member and later Chair of the West Midlands Black Police Association (BPA), the first such Association to be formed outside London.

Paul Lewin recalls:

'The reason I joined the Police Service at such a young age was that traditionally I saw the police as –

a) Trustworthy – The gatekeepers of the criminal justice system

b) A disciplined service - in standards of behaviour

c) Law enforcement – they were locking up the 'bad guys'.

In explaining the background to the creation of the Black Police Association it is important to delve into history.

On the 22nd June 1948, pioneers from the Caribbean arrived in Tilbury, Essex on board the 'Windrush' ship, marking the beginning of large-scale West Indian immigration. Those arriving between 1948 and 1971 became known as the 'Windrush Generation'. Many highly-qualified first generations were denied access to professional jobs and became manual workers, cleaners, drivers and nurses. For decades, those most visible by the colour of their skin, or by different cultural habits, suffered both overt and institutional racism. This directly hindered their access, retention and progression in public and private organisations.

The late 80's and early 90's then saw members of the Black communities move into prominent positions as a result of hard work, education and/or community support.

Despite this shift in demographic and societal involvement of black people, it was clearly established that parts of British Society maintained attitudes and perceptions which were either misinformed or just plain wrong, leading to black communities being disadvantaged in terms of access to opportunities and rewards.

In April 1995, I took up the role of Head of Equalities and recognised the erosion of the image of the police within the black communities, who frequently articulated the following issues for their mistrust of the police: -

a) Internal scandals - corruption/malpractices

b) External incidents - miscarriages of justice, ('sus' law and the use of 'Stop & Search')

c) Non-acceptance of 'Institutional Racism' by most police staff.

The above led to the Black community developing deep feelings of doubt and suspicion about the service. This manifested itself in them questioning the ability of senior managers to understand, let alone, act upon the concerns and issues facing the community. In their experience, there was a collective reluctance for the service to change.

These were challenging times for the police service, who simultaneously, were attempting to recruit more black and ethnic minority officers into their ranks from these communities, without appreciating the depth of resentment, which also questioned the principles of 'policing by consent'.

The demand for permanent internal organisational change, was pivotal, if the service was to truly regain their trust, ensuring quality of service to the community was proportional and effective.

A gathering of a handful of black members of staff in August 1995, was to become the foundation of the BPA. Ironically, most black staff decided to boycott the meeting, citing:

(a) White colleagues being suspicious of their motives if they were to become associated with the group.

(b) They felt they would be shunned within the organisation and would be forced to leave the service.

This was a common theme amongst staff in attendance, who all felt that internal organisational change was needed. The group's consensus was that the key requirement for changing the culture lay not in the recruitment of more black members of staff, but in changing the working environment of those staff already within the service.

These views struck a chord within me. I too, had been perceived by my black colleagues as 'cultured and progressive', drawn into the white privileged policing hierarchy, more concerned with protecting our own rank and status, than caring about the masses. In essence, I had become a 'token'.

The group identified six key areas ('Dismantling Barriers') for immediate attention:

1) *Challenging and educating the dominant culture to ensure proper implementation of existing policies.*
2) *Securing proper equality of opportunities across all policing activities.*
3) *Establishing black 'role models' for all black staff.*
4) *Pro-active involvement in 'core' decision making*
5) *Building confidence within Black Communities.*
6) *Recognition of the BPA as 'part of the solution' to effective policing in a growing multi-cultural society.*

A presentation was made to the then Assistant Chief Constable, which was endorsed and accepted by Ted Crew, Chief Constable.

I do not want to give the impression that it was plain-sailing for the embryonic BPA, who's newly formed Executive Committee worked tirelessly in their own time with very little recognition. We had to overcome many obstacles in pursuance of our objectives. The Force was not our only impairment, as other Staff Associations, who might have helped in the early stages, hindered us instead - this was to later change.

In August 1997, the official launch of the BPA took place at Tally Ho Training Centre, with the following mission statement:

'The West Midlands Black Police Association seeks to eliminate racial discrimination within West Midlands Police and work to assist ethnic minority officers and support staff in achieving their potential within the organisation. The Association is committed to helping the WMP deliver a fair, effective professional service'.

Just days before, the BPA was thrown into the 'spotlight', when on the 31st July 1997, the then Home Secretary Jack Straw, ordered a Public Inquiry to be conducted by Sir William McPherson and entitled:

'The Inquiry into the matters arising from the death of Stephen Lawrence on the 22nd April 1993, in order particularly to identify the lessons to be learned for the investigation and prosecution of racially motivated crimes'.

The announcement of the inquiry heightened pent-up frustrations within the community, giving them a legitimate platform to 'voice their concerns', in demanding changes within society. Prominent members of the Black Business Community contacted West Midlands Police senior hierarchy to invite a senior manager to address their monthly meeting, where concerns and fears surrounding institutional racism would be expressed. The community took it as a deliberate slight by the police when informed that 'no senior officer would be available'.

A late invite was made and accepted by the BPA to attend the meeting. This meeting was to change everything for the BPA, of which I was now Chair.

I have never addressed such a great hostile packed audience before and it was an exhilarating experience. By the time the meeting concluded late that night, Kirk Dawes (Deputy Chair) and myself had managed to turn the initial 'boos and jeers' that greeted us, into staunch supporters of our Association.

The Association was now firmly ensconced and rooted within the community and could now confidently move forward and be seen as 'part of the solution' to effective policing in a growing multi- cultural society.

On the 24th March 1998, the Public Inquiry Hearing in the Stephen Lawrence Inquiry began.

On the 13th November 1998, Hearings in the Inquiry came to an end, fittingly in Birmingham, where the views and work of the BPA in harmonising 'Community and Police' relationships were recognised and acknowledged.

In late1998, I returned to uniform operational duties at Walsall, where I worked for Mike Layton, one of the most open-minded, and forward-thinking Chief Superintendents. BPA's strategies were pro-actively incorporated at 'core decision-making' policing tactics.

The approach contributed to the H2 Operational Command Unit not only achieving the highest reduction and detection of crime, but directly led to the highest increase in the recruitment of black and Asian staff from the wider community. The OCU was recognised and held up as 'best practice' across the Force.

In terms of a legacy success or otherwise, the BPA should not only be judged on the visible increase of black and minority ethnic staff at all ranks within the service. Our legacy should be seen as 'the journey travelled' to become a catalyst for social change. There will always be a sense of pride in our professionalism, commitment and determination to overcome barriers to achieve our goals.

Our legacy has been about learning from the past, living in the present in order to build and improve for the future. I am proud that we did our best. Ultimately, this will be for others to judge'.

Figure 164 Paul Lewin, courtesy of P Lewin

Figure 165 Paul Lewin & Prince Charles, courtesy of P Lewin

***

Retired officer Pamela Burrell-Clayton recalls her experiences:

'Looking back, the decision of a young black woman to join the police in the early eighties was unusual. No one really talked about it as a viable career for a black person, and it was certainly a shock to the local community when I signed up. I was inspired to join by the local Constable. He was part of a police sports team who played "Tug of War" against a foundry team, which included my father. The Constable would visit our house to enjoy my mother's Jamaican home cooking! I remember having admiration for him and becoming interested in the police. I also got into the habit of attending community and police public meetings from the aged of sixteen.

There was some resistance to me joining up from the local church community, who tried their darnedest to put me off. This was a time of racial tension in the UK, and the West Midlands in particular, but I was absolutely determined to be a law enforcement officer for the British police.

The interview may have been a cinch, but the intense discipline of the training process was a real culture shock. Drill Sergeants seemed to be constantly shouting at me, and my tendency to smile a lot got me into trouble on countless occasions.

Following training I was posted to a station in the inner-city. I was greeted by a senior officer who flapped his lips at me. It was like a scene from 'Love Thy Neighbour'. Meanwhile the local residents remained suspicious of the new black police woman and called out "Coconut!" and "Bounty Bar!" as I patrolled the street, intimating that I was black on the outside but white on the inside. I was caught in the middle: Facing racism from inside the job and being branded a traitor by some of my own community.

With a strong resolve and help from girlfriends and peers, I managed to remain positive and enjoy a successful and productive career.

After a few years as a beat-bobby I became a Family Liaison and Domestic Violence Officer. In this role I'd provide advice and support to the victims of crime and their families. Obviously, this required me to deal with people in a sensitive and compassionate manner. I also had to deal with victims of crime who were also potential suspects, so maintaining balance and neutrality was also essential.

I then moved on to the Police Training Department, where I became a Detective Trainer. In addition to delivering training to both new and experienced police investigators, I also designed multiple training programmes, including specialised Family Liaison and Enhanced Witness Interviewing Courses.

I also enjoyed the opportunity to collaborate with industry professionals, including a world-renowned psychologist, to produce educational material for the training department. Diversity and Cultural Training was a vital part of what we taught. I felt that it was, and still is, important for the Police Service to understand the communities they serve.

In order to implement all that information, research and training, the logical next move was to go to the Major Investigations Unit, where I completed my thirty-year career as a Detective Investigator. Here I worked as an Advanced Interviewer of significant witnesses and perpetrators of serious crimes, including sexual abuse, domestic violence and murder. I enjoyed the fast-paced nature of the work, and the satisfaction that comes with a successful prosecution at the end of a long case. I do not however, miss the tragic circumstances and situations I was a witness to.

West Midlands Police has given me a great deal, not least, my husband! I was dealing with a stolen motorcycle, and we contacted the owner who had reported the bike missing. He came to where we had recovered the vehicle and had the cheek to ask me out! Well, I accepted, and shortly afterwards we were married. As all partners/spouses of serving officers know, he was also married to the police service. He endured my long and erratic work hours for many years.

I owe a great deal to West Midlands Police and the opportunities presented to me during my service. While there were challenges (being a woman in the police is not easy, being a black woman in the police is even more difficult), I am extremely proud to have served as an officer for three decades, and grateful to the police force for giving me that chance. It changed my life and played a large part in defining who I am today.'

Figure 166 Courtesy of P Burrell-Clayton

Figure 167 Courtesy of P Burrell-Clayton

Figure 168 Courtesy of P Burrell-Clayton

***

On the 11th August 1997, it was announced that Special Constables working in the West Midlands would in future wear the same hats as regular officers i.e. helmets for male officers and hard bowler-hats as worn by female officers.

Jason Clarke joined the West Midlands Police Special Constabulary in early 1994 and left in 2005 after becoming the Divisional Officer for H2 (OCU) Special Constabulary based at Bloxwich in Walsall – the highest ranking Special on the area. These are some of his personal recollections:

'I was posted to Bloxwich Police Station in the mid-1990's and, when able to, I enjoyed going out on foot patrol with another Special, Martin Troke. He was a very conscientious Special and like me would never, 'look the other way'. Consequently, a foot patrol when paired together was always going to be eventful!

On one foot patrol, I remember we were on the Beechdale Estate in Bloxwich. The Beechdale was a classic 'council' estate with a mixture of housing and residents. As in common with most estates, it had its fair share of anti-social behaviour problems. One such problem was motorbikes being ridden by, predominantly, young men and teenage boys. The bikes would be ridden on canal tow-paths and waste ground, as well on public roads and pavements. The manner in which these motorbikes were ridden made them a clear danger to the pedestrians.

The bikes being ridden were also generally, unregistered and uninsured and their ownership was also questionable.

We came across one such a motorbike early one evening not too far from a pub, the 'Three Men in a Boat', I think it was called. I think the errant motor-biker spotted us about the same time as we spotted him. Unsurprisingly, our shouts of, 'stop-police!' were ignored and the rider made off along the pavement. With the flat caps we wore in those days in hand, we gave chase! The rider had a good 150m head start on us and, to be honest, I didn't expect to catch him. Continued shouts of, 'Stop!', however, must have unnerved the rider and in his panic to get away from us, he lost control on the gravel of the pub car park, and dropped the motor bike onto its side. We saw him struggling to right it and hastened our pursuit. Seeing us approaching, the young rider, who was no older than fifteen years, fled into the pub.

We arrived at the bike, slightly out of breath, and also a little unsure of next step we should take. We were always told not to enter a pub unless necessary and to always tell 'control', by radio, before doing so. I'm sure I recall correctly that the motor bike was a 'scrambler' type with no rear number plate, not road legal and possibly stolen. We decided to secure the motor bike, and radio control for further advice, prior to, hopefully, entering the pub and apprehending the rider.

Before we could make the radio call, men started coming out of the pub to confront us. They seemed to have taken offence to us pursuing the motor bike and 'causing' the rider to crash. Whilst we stood guard over our seized motor bike the crowd got larger and more aggressive.

Our radio calls would have requested 'back up' or such similar term but whether we inadvertently mentioned the magic word, 'assistance', or a controller, fearing for two relatively inexperienced Special Constables thought more resources were necessary, half of the combined Willenhall and Walsall units turned out to us!

On hearing the approaching sirens, the hostile crowd seemed to slightly lose its blood- lust. Martin and I were still surrounded and getting pushed but the steam was gone from them. As the police vehicles arrived I remember waving my flat cap in the air so we could be seen! The crowd started to drift away, no doubt encouraged by the arriving officers.

One of the first officers to arrive was a police dog-handler. He got out of his vehicle and with his dog on a long lead, made his way towards us. It was amazing to see the dog work, it created a completely clear area the radius of its lead, barking and jumping towards anyone who got within reach.

The police dog's arrival completely cleared the crowd who all, except for a few 'brave' individuals, returned to the pub. The motorbike was safely stowed aboard a police van and, deciding that the youth riding it was probably long gone by now, a judicious withdrawal was advised as the most appropriate course of action. This episode taught me the danger and unpredictability of an intoxicated crowd, the effectiveness of a well-handled police dog and, most importantly, that the police-family is a strong one and when one of its own is threatened, Special or Regular, it pulls together.

On another occasion I was on another Bloxwich foot patrol, I don't remember who I was paired with but, we took in the King George V Playing Fields. Most of our foot patrols were tasked with tackling the problems of anti-social behaviour. Children would congregate in the park in the evenings and drink and cause damage to the park buildings.

In the park, there was a wooden pavilion. I don't recall its specific purpose, but it contained tables and chairs and a small store room. On patrol in the park, we came across the pavilion. There was a small group of children, in their mid-teens, sitting outside the pavilion. We noticed immediately that the wooden door to the pavilion had been broken open. Making sure the children outside didn't leave, I carefully looked inside and saw tables and chairs strewn around but also noticed a tin of white paint had been tipped out onto the floor. After this paint had been spilt, at least one person had walked through the paint, leaving clear foot-prints.

I went back to the group of children and asked how the door had come to be broken, and who'd been inside? I was answered by protestations of innocence and a complete lack of any knowledge of the damage inside. I then asked each child to show me the soles of their shoes. Just as I'd hoped, one boy had white paint covering them. With a sense of excitement, I cast my mind back to my training and the 'Points to Prove' of an offence. If someone trespasses and commits damage, I thought, that's a burglary! Far more impressive to arrest for burglary than 'mere' criminal damage! Therefore, asking the young lad to stand, I arrested him then and there for burglary, my first arrest for that offence.

I radioed I had one under arrest for burglary and could I have transport back to the station.

On getting back to Willenhall Police Station, the circumstances of the arrest were explained to the Custody Sergeant and the lad's detention was authorised for the purposes of interview. At this point an appropriate adult was going to be needed, in this case, a parent. Listening to the lad give his full name and address, something rang a bell in my head. I'd been to that address earlier today! My day-time job was as an engineer in the family business and I'd repaired the washing machine in that house. Sure enough, a short while later the father of the lad came to the station and after a slightly puzzled look, he remembered where he'd seen me before, in his kitchen that morning!

The interview took place and I believe the lad confessed to being inside the pavilion but denied actually causing any damage or being the one who broke the door. I believe he was probably dealt with by means of a caution. That would have been the end of this incident but a few weeks later, at work; we had a phone call from the father of the lad. His tumble- dryer was broken and he asked if I could come and repair it. He held no ill-will against me. His only request was for me to attend at a certain time, when his older son wasn't going to be home, as he didn't much like the police!

Recruitment for Special Constables was very effective and in the late 1990's H2 OCU had more Specials than any other OCU in the West Midlands Police. I think it would be fair to say this was down to the OCU Commander at the time Chief Superintendent Michael Layton.

To aid recruitment, a civilian member of staff, Neelam Puri (now Kumari) was recruited to work within the H2 Human Resources department. Neelam was able to work during the day when most Specials were carrying out their day-time jobs and as such, could be available when Specials were not. She also assisted at weekends, attending local events, with Specials to recruit to our growing team.

The OCU as a whole also attracted a large number of applicants from B.M.E groups, despite the fact that the local communities were predominantly white. At one stage nearly forty Special Constables were from Black or Asian backgrounds including the first Bangladeshi female officer.

This large number of Specials, over a hundred in total, was a huge resource for the OCU. Most Friday nights, historically one of the busiest 'policing' nights and therefore both a popular and useful night for Specials to be on duty, there were often more Specials on duty than Regular officers.

On other occasions we put large numbers, up to fifty Specials, on the streets to tackle anti-social behaviour in 'hot spot' areas, and it was very effective. We also had specific days, generally on a Sunday when all of the Specials available for duty took over the normal policing duties from shift officers, attending incidents and dealing with all manner of jobs.

The local press wrote of the hard-working volunteer Specials, giving up their time to help their local communities and over time H2 became an OCU of 'Best Practice' on how Specials should be recruited and deployed. It was a great time in my life, being given the chance to serve the public, and one which I will never forget.'

***

On the 21st August, the longest-serving officer in the West Midlands Police retired after nearly 40 years police service. John Carter, a Superintendent, aged 58 years, was based in Wolverhampton.

The untimely death of Diana, Princess of Wales, at the end of the month, led to many large gatherings and commemorative events in the Force area, many of which required a police presence.

***

At the beginning of September the Government introduced the Sex Offenders Act which required those with convictions for sexual offences to register their details with the police.

In the West Midlands it was estimated approximately 200 people needed to do so, with just half having registered within the first 14 days of the legislation being enacted.

***

Just after midday on Sunday 21st September 1997, police officers were called to Davies House in Sandbank, Bloxwich, where they found Darren Steemson, aged 29 years, perched precariously on a wall on the roof of the 11 storey building.

He was threatening to throw himself from the roof, and efforts by his mother Diane, who lived in the tower-block, to talk him down prior to police arrival had failed.

Sergeant Christopher Johnson took her and her husband to safety as other officers cordoned off the area. The officer was later commended for his actions.

Two trained police negotiators were called in and spent much of the day and night talking to Steemson as he sat with his legs dangling over the edge, wearing just jeans and a T-shirt and wrapped in a red and white blanket.

Hundreds of people watched the drama unfold in the streets below, as the Fire Service also stood by.

Figure 169 Courtesy of the Express & Star

At 3pm, officers visited a nearby house in Croxdene Avenue, in Bloxwich, where his wife, 27 year-old Angela Steemson was found dead in one of the bedrooms. A post-mortem examination revealed that the mother of three had died as a result of asphyxiation, due to strangulation, using a curtain tie-back which was tied around her neck in a reef knot.

At 5am on Monday 22 September, an opportunity to grab Steemson presented itself and he was arrested after keeping police at bay for 18 hours. He was examined by a Police Surgeon and detained until it was determined that he would be fit to be interviewed.

The initial negotiating team included Detective Chief Inspector Ellie Baker, DCI Alan Hyslop, and Chief Inspector Adrian Pickard. A second team arrived at 2am including Detective Superintendent Dave Unwin, DCI Andy Hunter, and Detective Inspector Dave Ford.

During the negotiations the team had to find the right balance between being honest with Darren Steemson versus not confirming the fate of his wife. Ellie Baker was subsequently quoted in the press as saying that Steemson had said to her, *'I know she's dead. The way I left her. She's the only girl I ever loved and I can never get my life back to what it was.'*

The suspect had spent hours lying on the edge of the roof but at this moment in time he sat up for a brief moment and was grabbed by Detective Superintendent Unwin who pulled him away from the edge of the roof and, together with DI Ford, they fell about 8 feet into a pit in the roof.

All of the officers were subsequently commended for their actions.

Co-Author Stephen Burrows recalls:

'I was the Senior Investigating Officer for this death, and it was a very tragic case. Darren Steemson was convinced that his marriage would end because he was going bald. They had known each since the age of sixteen years and married in 1990. He was obsessed about losing his hair and feared that his wife would taunt him.

He later pleaded 'not guilty' to murder but admitted manslaughter on the grounds of diminished responsibility. His plea was accepted by Judge Clive Taylor who sentenced him to five and a half years in prison.

It transpired that Steemson had sought psychiatric help in 1996 for his mood-swings and clinical depression, and that his wife had been advised to stay at a refuge for wives at risk but had refused.

He had a morbid fear of hair loss and was fearful that his wife would leave him if he went bald. She had also allegedly called him a 'wimp'.

On the 20th September the couple had apparently argued after Mrs. Steemson had been to a wedding reception, and according to his version of events had threatened to leave him. The murder followed.

The defence barrister Roger Smith, in mitigation before sentencing, said, 'Shortly before the killing Mrs. Steemson had teased him about his hair loss. She had poked fun at him and teased him about his hair about which he was so sensitive. It hurt so much that she was contemptuous and she referred to him as a wimp. She had fallen out of love with him and he was desperately keen to keep her. The whole relationship went downhill with him striving, perhaps too much, to retain the affection which did not exist.'

I do vividly recall that whilst the negotiators were trying to persuade him to come down off the roof some of the people watching were shouting for him to jump! Literally hundreds of people lined the pavements and waste ground below the tower block for hours. Some were curious about the outcome but a few actually tried to goad him to jump. At a height of 120 feet up there would have been only one outcome.'

***

At the end of September the Force announced, following a 3 month amnesty, that 3,000 high-calibre handguns had been voluntarily handed in after new Government legislation in the wake of the Dunblane shootings.

***

In October 1997, the Force was further reorganised into a sector-based structure designed to reflect the natural geographic and demographic boundaries within an area, and the rigid shift system abandoned. Each of the sectors was to be headed by an Inspector who was encouraged to direct activity based on an intelligence-led approach.

In the same month the 'Commercial Vice Unit' was renamed the 'Paedophile and Pornography Unit' to reflect the nature of its work more accurately. The Unit enjoyed considerable success in prosecuting people involved in circulating pornography on the internet as well as seizing material worth £1,000,000.

***

In November, Operation *'Strike-Back'* was conducted on a force-wide basis, targeting offences of burglary. This operation led to a 21% reduction in offences compared to the same period the previous year, and a doubling of the detection rate. A total of 1,058 people were arrested and stolen property worth almost £3,750,000 was recovered.

In something of an ironic twist, Chief Constable Edward Crew was himself the victim of a burglary at his home in Lickey Hills, whilst he was away at a police conference.

During the year the largest single *'Secured by Design'* award in the UK was given to Birmingham City Council for a refurbishment programme of 2,500 homes.

***

At the end of the reporting period 1997/1998, drugs valued at £14,600,000 were seized in the Force area, and more than £48,200,000 pounds worth of stolen property recovered. To achieve this level of success, officers made a total of 130,652 arrests, as overall crime fell by 8.8% on the previous reporting period.

During the same period the Force also investigated 38 murders, 4 of which were on the G2 OCU (Wednesfield). In another case a man died following an unreported assault two weeks previously. Operation *'Maritsa'* was mounted from Rose Road Police Station in Harborne which led to the arrest of a 15 year-old youth who was charged with murder and later ordered to be detained at Her Majesty's pleasure.

Another case was dealt with at Walsall after a body was found floating in the lake of Walsall Arboretum which resulted in a number of people being arrested and charged with murder.

In total, 37 cases of murder were detected during the period and officers also investigated 9 cases of manslaughter.

During the same period the Force also policed 104 football matches, 16 Royal visits, and investigated 100 fatal road traffic accidents.

In 1997/98, the Air Operations Unit went from strength to strength. Operating from Birmingham International Airport using a twin-engine 'Aerospatiale Squirrel' helicopter, which was fitted with a high-quality video camera and thermal imager, it allowed observers to monitor 'live' incidents and assist in searches for missing persons and stolen vehicles.

The profile of the Force Firearms Unit also increased as they dealt with 48 spontaneous incidents, one of which entailed safely detaining a man armed with a sawn-off shotgun who had threatened the occupants of 3 armed response vehicles.

In the same period, they also dealt with 256 pre-planned operations which included a 3 week operation that involved officers working undercover to investigate a gang carrying out armed-robberies. The offenders were arrested just prior to carrying out a raid on another sub-post office.

Following reorganisation of the Force, the Underwater Search Unit was retained as an additional serial of the Operational Support Unit and during the year was deployed 124 times to search for weapons and missing persons, during which 12 bodies were recovered from waters.

Despite the deployment of CS spray to officers, the number of assaults increased to a total of 1,360. Of these assaults, 345 were of a serious nature, showing an increase of 83 compared to the previous period.

In an effort to improve officer safety, trials began in the use of personal body-worn armour, with those vests tested in 'pilot' schemes half of the 15lbs weight of those kept in immediate response vehicles.

***

'Operation Roper' referred to an enquiry by the Force's Major Investigation Teams and was set up after two men from London, with international criminal connections, carried out offences of murder and armed robbery in the Force area. They were later arrested and sentenced to life imprisonment.

***

During this period the West Midlands Police also became 'market leaders' in the development of DNA techniques, working closely with the Forensic Science Service. The Force held DNA profiles of 12,567 criminals on a national database and had achieved more than 2,000 'hits' on 'suspect to scene' and 'scene to scene' matches.

1998

The G8 Summit

In January 1998, the Force announced the purchase of the computer system known as *'ICIS'*, (mentioned previously), costing more than £5,000,000 which was designed to cut down on paperwork relating to the criminal justice system. At the time the Force was still using paper custody records and on occasions up to 35 forms needed to be completed for a prisoner in custody.

***

In April, Sergeant Adrian Allsopp and PCs Andrew Pooler and John Miller were called to a tower block in in Highgate where a man was threatening to jump from the 11th floor. This was just one of several such incidents which occurred at tall buildings in the city and all resulted in police bringing the victims to safety.

On Sunday 12th April, police were called to Marklew Close, on the Friezland Estate, Brownhills where a 41 year old man had been found with fatal stab wounds. The man's dog 'Benny' was also found with knife injuries outside the address.

A 52 year old man was arrested on the 15th April and charged with murder. Of note, was that the concern of the public for 'Benny', equalled, if not surmounted that for the victim!

***

On the 11th May 1998, the Eurovision Song Contest was held at the National Indoor Arena in Birmingham City Centre, which entailed detailed preparations for 2 weeks beforehand.

As well as regular general searches, equipment and material weighing 4,000 tons was either scanned or physically searched by police officers before it was allowed into the building.

Despite a hoax bomb call being received during the live broadcast the security arrangements in place ensured that there was no disruption to the event.

One of the officers on duty for this event was PC Paul Richards, from H2 OCU, working with an explosives search dog *'Daniel'*.

Figure 170 'Daniel the Spaniel's' Identity Card for Eurovision, courtesy of P Richards

Figure 171 PC Richards & PD 'Daniel' on course at Stafford HQ, 1996, courtesy of P Richards

The following weekend, the Force carried out its biggest-ever security operation code-named *'Global Future'* when Birmingham hosted the G8 Summit at the International Convention Centre, attended by leaders of the world's most influential countries.

The summit lasted for 3 days and was preceded by a year's planning as well as an extensive search-regime at several venues and hotels.

During the course of the event the Force also successfully policed a number of rallies which attracted local and international media attention. These included facilitating a peaceful demonstration of over 100,000 people who were lobbying for the removal of Third World debt repayments, and containing the activities of a more disruptive group, 'Reclaim the Streets', who held a rally in Birmingham City Centre on the 16th May 1998.

The latter demonstration resulted in a request for Mutual Aid from surrounding Forces, the first such request since 1985. Although there was some violent disorder, and more than 30 arrests were made, the demonstrators were contained and there were no serious injuries to police officers or protesters.

Up to 1,200 officers were deployed to the conference on each of the 3 days, with officers working 13 hour shifts. In an innovative move they were provided with a CD-ROM briefing package.

Retired officer Simon Westwood recalls his involvement with one particular aspect of G8:

'The leaders of the G8 group of the richest nations had decided to use the centre of England for their annual meeting between 15th and 17th May 1998, the year lending itself to the logo that was adopted; '19G8'. There were various venues, including the new International Convention Centre in Birmingham City Centre and Weston Park in Staffordshire. All the participants would be flying into Birmingham Airport – BHX – which is actually in Solihull.

Needless to say, the various police forces involved, especially the West Midlands, went into overdrive and the amount of planning that went into it was staggering. Each OCU had a liaison officer appointed and for the 'L' OCU, that was me. I was the Inspector Co-ordinator at the time, so there was no way I was going to dodge that bullet! The Operations Department officer assigned to the 'L' OCU was Sgt Bal Sidhu and we established a mutually supportive relationship.

I had also been appointed as the Traffic Inspector for the OCU and given responsibility for dogs and quite a few other bits and pieces - I never got bored!

The amount of paperwork, e-mails and meetings increased steadily as the date grew nearer.

The plan called for quite a large number of Bronze Commanders and I found myself nominated as the 'Landside' Bronze Commander for the Airport. My good friend Inspector John Pegler, an Airport Inspector who I got on brilliantly with., was appointed the 'Airside' Bronze

In many respects, we had it fairly easy; just the small problem of getting all the delegates in on the first day and then getting them all out again at the end. In the middle, we were still required to remain as the Bronzes but, if everything went okay, we should have nothing to do – a very rare state of affairs.

Part of the plan required 'L' OCU Traffic to patrol the entire perimeter of the Airport which we were, of course, singularly ill-equipped for. The fleet manager organised about eight - rather tired but serviceable – ex-CMPG Range-Rovers. Having looked at some of the ground they would have to negotiate, and considering that it had to be done 24/7, the Fleet Manager agreed to fit extra lights. All this was done in short order.

Driving off-road is not something that is practiced on advanced car courses, so I contacted Land-Rover and asked if they could see their way clear to getting all of the 'L' OCU Traffic Officers on their 'Jungle' track for a day. They readily agreed and so all the Traffic officers learned how to drive off-road.

In order to put out so many vehicles round-the-clock, I had to draft in other officers who were advanced drivers but were not on Traffic. This led to a motley crew of Traffic, Response Unit, Resident Beat Officers and Admin people crewing up together.

The plan started to come together, but the principal problem was the deluge of e-mails received from Headquarters. Few had any relevance to what I was doing, but those that did frequently altered what had gone before and it seemed that myself and Bal were always on the phone or he was sitting in my office and telling me to ignore this or that change to the plan. The briefing book that was produced was a masterpiece and was packed with good information and illustrations.

In addition to Land-Rover helping us out with the off-road training, they had provided the Force with many vehicles. I found myself presented with a brand-new Range-Rover in a deep burgundy colour. The first I had ever driven and I admit to falling in love with it immediately. Sadly, I have never been able to justify the purchase of one since. I became re-acquainted with later versions when I was on CMPG and nothing has changed my view that they are magnificent vehicles.

The major problem for me and my 'airside' counterpart was that the first leader to arrive would be the POTUS, Bill Clinton. It wasn't as though we could see how it went with a delegate, such as Jacques Santer, EU Commission President. No, we had to start with the most powerful person in the world.

As an avid aircraft enthusiast, I was well aware that 'Air Force One' is unlike any other aeroplane and the rules that surround it and where, when and how it flies are unique.

Not only was it going to be the first in, it was landing at dusk. Although the weather had been very good, as the sun went down, a mist, bordering on fog, had started to descend.

The plan called for the aircraft to land and the Principals to be greeted by various welcoming parties. The cavalcades would then form up 'airside' and with a heavy escort, leave the airport and drive straight up the A45 Coventry Road.

A problem with sight-seeing pedestrians manifested itself on the into-city carriageway of the A45 between Goodway Road and Glencroft Road. The pavement here is quite narrow and was rapidly filling with sight-seers, with a real concern that they might spill out onto the carriageway. I was informed by Control that they were sending a van-full of Special Constables to line the route there and to make sure everyone stayed on the pavements. I was uncomfortable with this as these officers had not received a briefing.

They were deployed and I drove up to make sure all was well, and largely, it was. I turned at the gap in the central reservation and noted a traffic car parked near the A45 on the road leading to Hatchford Brook Golf Club. I then drove down the A45 and just saw 'Air Force One' coming in to land as it appeared out of the murk and watched it touch down safely.

All we had to await now was the President's cavalcade to come up the Coventry Road and drive into the city centre. I returned to the only place where it seemed we might have potential issues; the Coventry Road opposite the Golf Club. I was standing chatting to the officers in the Traffic vehicle, PCs Heather Perry and John McCausland. We were listening to the developments and progress concerning the 'airside' cavalcade. Eventually, we heard that the cavalcade was moving.

The Traffic Motorcyclists, known as the 'Scruffies' were all Special Escort Group (SEG) trained. I knew that once they started moving, the whole idea was for them not to stop until they reached their final destination. Anything that may have interfered with this was seriously bad news.

The first bike came through reporting back on any potential issues. The Specials had done a good job of keeping the pedestrians in check. An event then occurred which still leaves me utterly baffled. A police personnel carrier came down the out-of-City carriageway and turned across the central reservation opposite where we were with the traffic car. The vehicle then continued to drive until it was completely across both lanes of the into-City carriageway, when it stopped -it was now completely blocking the carriageway. The very same carriageway that was going to be filled with the US President's cavalcade within a few short minutes!

I shouted into the radio to get the vehicle moved, but Heather and John in the Volvo sped off and drove through the gap in the central reservation. I think it was John that leapt out and spoke urgently to the driver of the van. I saw the reversing lights come on and the van reversed out of the carriageway. It could not have been more than twenty seconds later that the first of the close-escort bikes came along that carriageway at speed, followed by the President and his fleet of blacked-out limousines.

The rest of the arrivals passed uneventfully. Indeed, when the last of the leaders had landed, it went very quiet at the airport. 'Airside' Bronze, John Pegler, took me around the gigantic C-5 Galaxy aircraft and also took me to 'Marine One'. This was the President's helicopter, a 'Sea King'. It was staffed and guarded, as the name suggests, by US Marines.

We were 'greeted' by a substantial Marine who never stopped smiling as he gave us a well-rehearsed chat on the President's transport and we were invited to take as many pictures as we wanted from where we were. It was very politely pointed out that we weren't to go any closer.

All the action was taking place in Birmingham and Staffordshire. I divided my time between meetings with John Peglar and making contact with the officers patrolling the perimeter. All that remained were the various dignitaries leaving the airport. Bill Clinton was not one of them. 'Marine One' collected him from somewhere in Birmingham and flew him out. I can't remember when 'Air-Force One' left or where it went.

Sunday, May 17th 1998 was a beautiful hot spring day. Just a question of making sure the roads around the airport and the perimeter itself were all clear. Various dignitaries flew off without any issues - then came the Japanese delegation.

Those of you who know BHX will remember that before the runway was extended, the A45 was quite close to the runway threshold. It was also fairly straight. Directly opposite the end of the runway was a track leading to some dwellings. These were demolished to make way for the runway extension. This track was a favourite place for aircraft spotters and I didn't want them there in such numbers as to cause a problem. The prevailing wind meant that the aircraft would be taking off in that direction, as opposed to taking off over Marston Green.

I had learned from John Pegler that the Japanese delegation were next to go. I had parked my vehicle across this trackway. I was with the Duty Sergeant and PC's Simon Lusty and Peter Thorpe, who were patrolling off-road. They had decided to place themselves in amongst the approach lights. They were, therefore, directly underneath the flight path. The Sergeant and I were slightly to the left and a bit closer to the A45.

We could see the tail fin of the Boeing 747 carrying the large 'Hinomaru' emblem. The aircraft was moving towards the far end of the runway for its take-off. What we did not know at the time, was that the entire delegation was on this aircraft, along with most of the luggage. They were going to do what have never been done before, which was a non-stop flight from Birmingham to Tokyo.

Jumbo-jets were still a very rare sight at BHX as the runway was not really considered long enough for a fully-loaded one. This was fully-loaded with over a quarter of a million litres of Avtur fuel! We could see that the aircraft had started rolling. We could see more and more as it bore down towards us. I was acutely aware that it had gone past the 'point of no return' and yet showed no sign of wanting to be airborne. I remember thinking that if this went wrong; I was going to have a ring-side seat for an air-crash; at least for the few seconds that it would take for the fireball to get me.

After what seemed like an eternity, the nose-wheel lifted. By this time, it was scarily close to the end of the runway. Mercifully, the main wheels lifted and it just scraped over the boundary fence, scaring the life out of a few drivers on the A45. Quite what was going through the minds of Peter and Simon ensconced as they were right in the path of this behemoth, I'm not sure. It cleared them and the lights – but not by very much - and gradually gained height and flew away to the north-west, much to our relief. That was 'Japan One'. They had another, identical, aircraft, imaginatively called 'Japan Two'. This was carrying very little and floated off about half-way down the runway.

Shortly after this, the whole operation came to an end. John invited me over to the old Airport Terminal. The airport management were having a bit of a 'do'. This was the first time I had been in the building since I had been taken there by my Grandmother on a number of occasions when I was a very small boy to watch the aircraft taking off and landing. This was probably the start of my love affair with aviation.

If memory serves, the airport management had given the old building interior a proper makeover and the room where the 'do' was taking place was not only sumptuous but commanded a fabulous view over the airport. Filling the view outside the window was the USAF C-5 Galaxy.

Much though I would have liked to stay, it was time to go back to Solihull Police Station and hand back my beloved Range-Rover. It was a most successful operation with just a couple of issues that ran the risk of disaster; but then I suppose that's true of most operations.'

Figure 172 Elmdon Airport Terminal building, 1998, courtesy of S Westwood

Figure 173 Simon Westwood & John Peglar, 1998, courtesy of S Westwood

Figure 174 Wayne Knight, Andy Nixon & Simon Westwood, 1998, courtesy of S Westwood

Figure 175 'Air Force One', courtesy of S Westwood

***

On the 3rd June 1998, Peter Hastings was re-arrested for the murder of his friend Mrs Jean Bellis, who had been found dead at her home in Kingstanding with multiple stab wounds on the 13th April 1993

Although Hastings had already been arrested twice for this offence in 1993, and had actually been charged with her murder, after consultation with the Crown Prosecution Service the charges against him were later withdrawn.

However new scientific techniques revealed fresh evidence which Hastings was unable to refute; DNA testing had identified a strand of Mrs Bellis' hair on Hastings' belt, along with 5 small drops of blood on his shoes which had effectively been sealed in place under layers of shoe polish.

He was later convicted of murder and sentenced to life imprisonment.

***

In June, Birmingham hosted the Lions Club International Convention, the largest conference of its type in the world, which included 15,000 delegates coming into the city centre for their traditional parade.

Also, in June, a 91 year-old pedestrian, who was knocked down on a zebra crossing, by a driver who failed to stop, later died in Walsall Manor Hospital. An Incident Room was established, and following a huge public response a vehicle was recovered at a car dismantlers in Walsall and a local man arrested and charged with causing death by dangerous driving.

***

Again, in June, concern was raised at Force level about the lack of advancement for officers from ethnic minority groups, and in particular Black officers.

At that stage West Midlands Police had 294 serving officers from B.M.E. backgrounds, which although just 4.1% of the total strength, was in fact the highest of any other Force at the time where the national average was just 2%.

***

In August, a murder investigation was set up after the body of an elderly woman was found at her home address in Coventry. A local man, aged 22 years, was subsequently arrested and charged with murder.

***

In September, the body of Father Paul Orchard, the Roman Catholic priest of St. Hubert's Church in Warley, was discovered in his presbytery. He had been assaulted and stabbed several times. A local man was subsequently arrested and charged with his murder.

On the 18th September, two men armed with a weapon resembling a shotgun carried out a robbery at a service station in Smethwick. Descriptions were circulated and despite the possible danger, officers carrying out a search of the area stopped and arrested them.

***

At the end of September, Prime Minister Tony Blair highlighted that between 1982 and 1996, crime had risen nationally by 58% and emergency calls increased by 181% whereas police numbers had risen by just 3%. It was estimated that crime was costing some 50 billion pounds annually.

A new 3 year crime strategy was announced and the police were asked to adopt a twin-track approach, that of *'order maintenance'* which was known more widely as *'zero tolerance'*, backed up by a *'problem solving'* or *'intelligence led'* approach to 'hot spot' areas. These arrangements were set to become the forerunners for the Crime and Disorder Act which would require a mandated approach to partnership working between the police, local authorities and other agencies.

***

In October, HM the Queen visited Castle Vale, which was undergoing major refurbishment.

There were a total of 13 Royal visits to the West Midlands during the year, including a visit to the new Birmingham Children's Hospital, which Her Majesty renamed *'Diana Princess of Wales Children's Hospital'*.

In the same month, the National Exhibition Centre staged its largest ever Motor Show with more than 750,000 visitors to the event, which experienced very low levels of crime.

In October, PC's Keith Guthrie and Jennifer Smith were on patrol in Birmingham City Centre when they were made aware of an incident whereby security staff, from a nightclub, were threatened with a firearm by two men. The officers chased the suspects and arrested them in possession of an imitation firearm. One of them went on to admit 14 armed robberies.

***

In November, a gang of people forced their way into a 6th floor flat in Halesowen and attacked the occupants. During the disturbance, which was drug-related, a young woman fell to her death from a balcony. Two men were later charged with her murder.

In the same month, two officers called to help a man threatening to jump off a building in Coventry found him on scaffolding 70 feet above ground. By handcuffing each of his wrists separately, and hanging on to the other end of the handcuffs, the officers managed to support his weight for 30 minutes before the fire brigade arrived.

It would be impossible to catalogue every act of personal bravery by officers, but another example occurred during this year when Sergeant Kerry Blakeman and PC Dave Williams were on patrol when they were directed to a house fire in the Stoke area of Coventry.

Retired officer Kerry Blakeman recalls the incident well:

'It was a 2-10pm shift on M2 sub-division at Chace Avenue in Coventry. I was one of the late-turn 'response' Sergeants and one of my officers on the 'Zulu' asked if he could have a couple of hours off. With no suitably-qualified drivers available to cover his time off, I volunteered to double-crew the 'Zulu' with PC Dave Williams.

It was only a couple of hours until the end of the shift - what could possibly happen in those two hours?

The radio burst into life, 'persons reported trapped, house fire Terry Road, Stoke.' Dave and I looked at each other – we were literally around the corner. Dave activated the sirens and blue lights and before we knew it, we arrived outside the premises, where smoke was billowing from the house. We were first on the scene.

We jumped out of the car and started banging on the front door – there was no reply, but we could hear moaning coming from inside. At this point I thought back to my initial training going through the 'smoke-house' at Coventry fire station.

I was conscious that I needed to force entry but worried about the potential flash-over as I kicked the door in, but there was no time to waste. I literally kicked the front door in with one boot and threw myself to the floor to avoid a flash-over. Being a terraced house, the lounge was immediately in front of us.

As smoke was billowing from the house, I could see a settee directly in front of us which was on fire. We could hear the moaning coming from somewhere in the house. I shouted into the house "Get on the floor, get on the floor!" hoping that the person would hear us. Instinctively we knew we had to try and rescue whoever was in the house. We crouched down, chins next to the floor and start feeling our way through the lounge, then to our amazement at the other end of the settee we found a semi-conscious lady on the floor.

Dave and I managed to drag the lady back towards the front door by her ankles and just as we got outside into fresh-air the Fire Service arrived and then shortly afterwards the ambulance.

The lady was treated by the ambulance for smoke inhalation and taken to hospital. I just remember coughing and coughing and looking up at Dave, I knew looking at him we were both thinking "what have we just done?"

We were both honoured to later receive a Police Authority Commendation for rescuing the lady from the house fire.'

***

On the 30th November 1998, a shooting incident outside a nightclub in Handsworth resulted in one man being killed and another being seriously injured. Enquiries by the Force's Major Investigation Team resulted in 4 people being arrested and charged with murder, attempted murder and firearms offences. As part of the investigation, officers raided a house in Aston and recovered 2 loaded machine pistols complete with silencers, 2 hand guns, one of which was loaded, and ammunition.

***

On the 5th December 1998, the body of a man was found in his flat in Caldmore, Walsall. A suspect was later arrested in London and charged with murder.

Also in December, a man was taken to wasteland in Sutton Coldfield, where he was attacked with a hammer and knife, and left for dead. Enquiries led to the arrest of 5 people who were charged with attempted murder and kidnap.

Again in December, officers from the 'Paedophile and Pornography' Unit co-ordinated, Operation *'Warstock',* which was aimed at disrupting a major pornography distribution network in Birmingham. 6 addresses were raided, and 8 persons arrested, resulting in the recovery of over 4,000 videos and 1,400 magazines.

During the course of the year, the Force detection rate for murder was 100% which included the murder of a young man who died during a disturbance in Coventry, after being punched and kicked. Operation *'Quality'* resulted in 4 men being arrested and charged with murder.

During the 1998/99 period 52 crimes of homicide were reported. Of these, 48 were recorded as murder, and the remaining 4 as manslaughter. All 48 cases of murder were detected.

During a 3 month weapons amnesty in Coventry, members of the public were invited to deposit unwanted weapons in containers at 12 sites around the city. A total of 1,106 were surrendered including knives, machetes, axes, 28 firearms and 2,000 rounds of ammunition. The amnesty was a joint initiative between the police, city council and *'Coventry Evening Telegraph'* as West Midlands Police increased their efforts at developing partnership approaches.

During November and December, Operation *'Scrooge Strike'* took place across the Force area, aimed at disrupting the market in stolen goods during the pre-Christmas period. As a result 483 people were arrested for handling stolen goods and property valued at more than £1,500,000 was recovered. More than 1000 offences were detected, and burglary and vehicle crime offences fell dramatically.

1999

Operation 'Strike Out'

On Thursday 14th January 1999, police attended a flat above shops in High Road, Shortheath, Willenhall during the early hours, where they found a 16 year-old boy with stab wounds. Despite efforts to save him he died hours later.

A 23 year old man from Bilston was arrested days later and charged with murder.

At 8.30am on Wednesday 20th January 1999, officers searching a lock-up in Darlaston recovered cannabis with a street-value of more than £1,000,000, a record recovery of drugs in the Borough of Walsall, consisting of 108kg of cannabis resin and herbal cannabis.

Two men were later arrested on suspicion of conspiracy to supply controlled drugs.

***

On the 14th February 1999, Operation *'Fontina'* was set up to investigate the fatal stabbing of a 24-year-old man at the home of a woman in Wednesbury, who was also wounded. 5 days later a 28 year-old man appeared at West Bromwich Magistrates Court charged with murder and malicious wounding.

***

On Thursday 11th March 1999, Operation *'Strike Out'* was launched at dawn, with 200 officers searching 43 homes in the Walsall area. The operation, led by officers from H2 OCU, was the culmination of 4 months of targeted policing activity, which included some undercover tactics.

More than 38 arrests followed, as stolen property in excess of £40,000 was recovered. This included electrical goods, bikes, tools, garden equipment, car parts, a firearm, and drugs.

Figure 176 Courtesy of the Express & Star

In March 1999, the West Midlands Police Mounted Branch was disbanded after a long and proud history of service – a sad moment for many.

Retired officer officer Roy Shotton, by then still a member of the Force Firearms Unit, recalls that the stables were refurbished at Park Lane and taken over by the section.

In describing how the expertise of the Firearms Unit had developed over the years he recalls a particular robbery operation of which he was a part:

'There was information that a robbery was going to take place at the Queslett Road Post Office in Great Barr. A surveillance team was deployed to follow the targets.

We had an observations post near to the post office, and a team inside to stop them gaining entrance as we didn't want a hostage situation.

We had another team in a van, and I was deployed in a car with a colleague to do a 'hard-block' on any vehicle being used in the robbery. In due course the three suspects turned up in a Range Rover and did a drive-past the post office.

They then went to a stolen Honda Civic car and came back and parked up behind us. Two suspects got out, one of whom was carrying a shotgun, and made towards the post office whilst the getaway driver stayed inside the stolen vehicle. The code-word was given for action to be taken and the post-office doors were slammed shut before they could get inside. At the same time we reversed hard into the getaway car and finished up getting into a violent struggle with the driver as he fumbled on the floor of the car, and grabbed a handgun, which we initially had great difficulty in wrenching from his hands. Other Firearms officers intercepted the other two, as they tried to run back to the car, and all three were taken into custody. No shots were fired and it was all captured on video. It was a really professional job and what we were trained for. All three pleaded guilty and finished up getting ten years in prison each.'

***

At the end of the reporting period for 1998/1999, the West Midlands Police Authority also published its Annual Report. In the Foreword, Councillor Bob Jones, the Chairman, commented that a number had people had asked the question as to what the Authority did. His response was to quote the Chief Constable Edward Crew who somewhat 'tongue in cheek' had described it simply as a *'supportive irritant'*.

The number of people arrested for 'notifiable' offences reached 90,521 for the 12 month period ending March 1999. Included within those arrest figures were 208 dealt with by the Force Drug Squad which related to the recovery of drugs with a total street value of nearly £8,000,000.

In the same period the Force received 583,619 emergency calls and dealt with a staggering 1,042,585 incidents – the highest on record.

These figures included dealing with 83 fatal road accidents.

Likewise West Midlands Police detected 94,268 offences in the same period, which represented a 39% increase on the previous twelve months, a record in the Force's history.

Across the Force area, 97 'hot spots' were identified through analysis and were designated for targeted policing.

This was a period of time when the West Midlands Police was seen as being a police force 'on the move' despite all of the ongoing challenges it still faced.

The first 25 years of West Midlands Police, and the period covered by this book, ended as the new millennium began. Looking back over the last eighteen and a half years, it is plain to see that the principles of courage, commitment, sacrifice and 'sense of duty' that permeate this book have continued.

Sports & Social Activities

In 1976, the West Midlands Police Club catered for a variety of interests throughout the Force area, ranging from rugby and boxing to choir singing and chess – 33 separate sections promoted their particular field.

In 1977 a Force tie was created bearing the colours of the constituent Forces of the West Midlands Police at the time of amalgamation, and part of the arms of the Borough of Wednesbury, the oldest Borough in the conurbation. The ties were sold through the Sports and Social Club.

***

Tally Ho Police Training Centre & Social Club

For decades the activities of the West Midlands Police Sports and Social Club have been centred on *'Tally Ho'* Police Training Centre in Edgbaston, Birmingham where the bar, meeting room and banqueting facilities, coupled with changing rooms and sports-ground facilities have fostered many groups over the years.

In the banqueting area top cabaret acts regularly played to large audiences, and *'Pay Day Discos'* became legendary!

In 1985 alone there were 40 sections, and the activities of the Sports Office at *'Tally Ho'* expanded as a selection of crested goods were available to purchase. The sale of diaries, Christmas cards, cabaret show tickets, and the organisation of trips to places like Belgium and Florida kept the staff busy, as well as the administration of the Force Lottery Scheme.

Figure 177 Courtesy of M Layton

In this book a few memories of some of the groups engaged in sports and social activities are captured, but they do of course represent just a snapshot of the numerous groups and teams which have sprung up since 1974, many of which still survive and prosper to this day.

Between April and October 1994, the Sports and Social Club underwent a refurbishment and extension, and was renamed the *'Tally Ho Sports & Conference Centre'*.

The development was officially opened by Her Royal Highness the Princess Royal on Wednesday 8th February 1995. All the sports clubs which met at the centre were represented among the 270 people who attended the event.

***

West Midlands Police Pipe Band

In 1977, the band had a very successful year, entering 4 pipe-band contests with considerable success including being the holders of the *'All England Shield'*. In addition they carried out 8 further engagements, which included the Lord Mayor's procession in Birmingham, and the Cheshire County Police Day, plus carnival events and Remembrance Services.

In 1978, the band won 11 trophies during competitions and enrolled its first female piper, Police Cadet Ann Proud.

In November 1979, the Pipe Band travelled to Frankfurt in Germany as guests of the Frankfurt Police, and in November 1981 they took part in a Festival of Remembrance.

David Rischmiller is a retired West Midlands Police Officer and was a member of the Pipe Band for many years. He recalls some of its history:

'The Birmingham City Police Pipe Band was founded in 1962 by a small group of Scots and Irish police officers, part of that recruited influx into the region of suitable candidates from far and wide who were required to help police the streets of the City, and who found employment and a home there.

Most were already players, some from previous military experience, and this nucleus was soon supplemented by suitable civilian players in the area who were recruited into the band. This combination of players from within the force, together with members from the local community, continued throughout the band's existence.

In those early days when positive extra-curricular activities were actively encouraged by the Force, the band received good early support from the then Chief Constable Sir Edward Dodd and the Watch Committee. The Special Constabulary also had a 'whip round' to purchase the band's first mace which was eventually given to the Police Museum. Early uniforms were provided by the seamstresses of the Stores Department who adapted police night tunics to suit. The band was fortunate that this active support continued throughout its existence, no doubt as recognition of the positive impression of the Force that it created on a very wide stage.

The purpose of the band in the early years was predominantly to represent the force and this continued throughout its existence alongside its later competitive success.

Birmingham was twinned with Frankfurt in 1966, and a regular, almost annual tour of that twin-sister commenced soon afterwards. Strong links were forged between the band and the Frankfurt Police as a consequence.

In 1974, as a consequence of the national re-organisation of police forces, the band became the West Midlands Police Pipe Band.

Through the Band the Force has been represented across Europe and through its competitive period even wider around the world. The band toured Berlin in 1986 prior to re-unification and also conducted a seven-day tour of Tuscany with the band of the Irish Guards in the late1990's.

In addition to Frankfurt, the band toured wider Germany, Belgium, France, Italy and The Netherlands, and was particularly proud to be selected to play at the International service at the Thiepval Memorial on the Somme at the 80th Anniversary commemorations of that battle in 1996.

It should be recognised that piping and pipe bands is a very competitive business, some bands never compete but very many do and our involvement served to encourage improvements in playing standards, acted as a wider stage on which to represent the Force, and encouraged the recruitment of players, a number of whom subsequently went on to have good careers in the Force, with a number rising through the ranks.

Pipe Band competitions are regulated worldwide by the Royal Scottish Pipe Band Association which ranks bands into six adult grades, with promotion and relegation a consequence of competitive success.

At the peak of its own competitive success in the early 2000's, the West Midlands Police Pipe band achieved promotion to Grade 2, which is just below Grade 1, which is populated mainly by semi-professional outfits.

The band competed at major competitions around the country and once in Belgium, including the premier World Pipe Band Championships which was screened by the BBC and is literally a World-attended event. As a consequence it is no exaggeration to say that the band bought the Force name to the attention of pipers, drummers and spectators across the world.

In 2012, the band voluntarily folded as a consequence of the retirement of a number of key individuals. It was also a fact that the Force finances were under severe pressure as a result of the public sector austerity climate, and despite the members being entirely volunteers it was considered by the Band unreasonable that the necessary finance to operate the Band should be sought at a time when people were losing their jobs. We were an independent group and as such received no external funding.

In personal terms I joined the Band at the age of twelve in 1976. I had expressed an interest in learning, and my father being a 'Cop' knew most of the guys. I went down and accompanied the Band to Richmond in Surrey where the Band won the All-England Championships.

There followed the most almighty 'session' which although only twelve gave me an insight into the 'conviviality' I could expect which surrounded this activity. My timing was perfect as an old retired piper Charlie Campbell joined as tutor and a small class soon developed around him. Four members of that class are still very close friends to this day. I joined the Police Cadets in 1980 graduating to the Regulars in 1982. I retired in 2012 having spent thirty-six years in the Band.'

Figure 178 Pipe Band, pre 1974, courtesy of D Rischmiller

Figure 179 Pipe Band pre 1974, including Derrick Capper & Philip Knights, courtesy of D Rischmiller

Figure 180 Dave Rischmiller, courtesy of D Rischmiller

Figure 181 Pipe Band at the Brandenburg Gate, Berlin, 1968, courtesy of D Rischmiller

Figure 182 Pipe Band on the steps of The Reichstag, Berlin, 1986, courtesy of D Rischmiller

Retired officer Rodney Simpkins recalls:

'I joined the Pipe Band in 1974, and I think that the first event I ever took part in was a garden fete in Solihull. The band was full of 'characters' with a great sense of camaraderie and friendship. Over the years I played at big events in Germany, Belgium and France. Unfortunately, in about 1989 I broke my ankle and could no longer march properly, so had to give up playing. I stayed on as Treasurer until 1995 and used to organise the annual 'St Andrews Dinner'. It was the one night of the year when the men out-dressed the women! I have fond memories of the Pipe Major Harry Shepherd, who was a PC working in the Jewellery Quarter, and the likes of John Stephen who was the Drum Major for a long time.

I do recall on one occasion a band member Percy Keenan asked if someone could come along to his daughter's wedding in Kings Norton to pipe her out of the church. He was told that everyone was committed so it wouldn't be possible. What he didn't know was that the whole Pipe Band had agreed to turn up and were there to his great surprise when they left the church.'

***

Coventry Division Band &
West Midlands Police Brass Band and Corps of Drums

The Band was formed in Coventry in 1928, and at the time it was known as the *'Coventry City Police Band'*.

In 1979, the Coventry Division Band celebrated its Golden Jubilee with joint performances with the Male Voice Choir and the Choral Society, together with the Pipe Band.

The membership of the band was 24, and the Music Director then was PC Derek Paxton, a serving police officer on the 'M' Division, who was a Marine bandsman for 14 years before joining the police.

The West Midlands Police Brass Band was re-formed in late 1980, and in addition to playing at concerts it continued to develop its parade-ground techniques. The band also assembled a Corps of 12 drummers to add to the existing 25 musicians.

In 1992, the band became known as the *'West Midlands Police Brass Band'*. Its current Musical Director *'Barney Barnes'* has a long history in military, wind and brass bands.

In March 1993, the West Midlands Police Brass Band & Corps of Drums surprised Mrs. Ethel Scott with an impromptu concert to mark her 70th birthday. Friends and family looked on as the band played her favourite tunes outside her house in Rubery. Her daughter had arranged the surprise with Band secretary, Sergeant Gerry Perks.

Retired officer Tommy Myers was a member of the West Midlands Police Corps of Drums and recalls:

'I was a member of the Corps of Drums, which was part of the West Midlands Police Band, for about 10 years. The band was always well received by the public wherever it performed and became a very valuable 'public relations' tool. My favourite engagement was at Ryton where we entertained the officers enjoying their 'dining in night' followed by the passing-out parade the following day. We were always very well looked after by the training staff with meals and free beer! I think my proudest moment was performing at the NEC alongside the massed military bands in front of a capacity audience - nerve racking but very enjoyable. 'Barney' Barnes has been the band's conductor for many years. Below are just a couple of photos of some members of the Corps of Drums relaxing before performing.'

Figure 183 Corps of Drums at the Royal Show, mid 1980's, courtesy of T Myers (far left)

Figure 184 Corps of Drums preparing for an event, courtesy of T Myers

Retired officer Paul Quinney comments on the below photograph:

'The picture below was taken at the Corvey tattoo in Germany in 1987. From left to right are Joe Burdiken - RIP, Mick Banks, Larry Quinn, Linda Murphy, me, Dennis Sinclair, and Tony O'Donohue. The Corps of Drums was started by Coventry officers in the late 1970's and joined up with the Coventry Police Brass Band when they fulfilled local engagements.

The Band and Corps of Drums then joined together in the 1980's and was joined by other officers and civilian members to form the West Midlands Police Band.

The Corvey tattoo was a one-off, and both the Brass Bands and Pipe Band performed together during displays.

The late PC Derek Paxton was Musical Director for most of the time prior to 'Barney' Barnes taking over. Regarding the drums, prior to 'drummy' Dennis Sinclair, our Steve Jordon and late Roger 'Woody' Wood were also drum-majors of note - both displaying their own unique sense of humour and immaculate standards.'

Figure 185 Corps of Drums at Corvey, 1987, courtesy of T Myers

In 1994, the West Midlands Police Brass Band and Corps of Drums paid their own respects on the 50th anniversary of *'D Day'*, when they were invited to play at a service of commemoration held outside the Hall of Memory in Birmingham's Centenary Square.

Lesley Jenkins recollects:

'I joined the band in September 2000, having gone along to help out at one concert as they were short. I have been a member ever since!

I'm not a serving police officer, and have never been, but I do have family connections to the police. I play Principal Cornet in the band.'

Figure 186 Lesley Jenkins, courtesy of L Jenkins

Figure 187 Brass Band, recent photograph. L Jenkins Middle Row, far left, 'Barney' Barnes, front row, centre, courtesy of L Jenkins

***

West Midlands Police Male Voice Choir

The Birmingham City Police Male Voice Choir was originally formed in 1928, but with the outbreak of the Second World War it was disbanded.

In August 1945, a group of 30 officers got together and reformed the choir which, on amalgamation in 1974, was renamed the West Midlands Police Male Voice Choir.

In 1975, the Male Voice Choir, under the direction of Mr Harold Enstone, performed concerts at hospitals, old people's homes and other venues, including at the Town Hall, Birmingham in conjunction with the band of the Irish Guards.

On the 9th October 1976, their annual concert with the band of the Coldstream Guards was held at Birmingham Town Hall.

In 1978, the choir recorded their second long playing record, *'Arise o Sun'*, and also featured in a record release featuring John Inman. Mr Enstone, the Choir Conductor for 8 years, retired due to ill-health and was replaced by Mr Philip Smith, who was the Head of Music at a comprehensive school in Wolverhampton.

In 1991, the choir sang as part of the Midlands Massed Male Voice Choirs at the opening ceremony of the British Olympics Association which was held at the International Convention Centre.

One long-standing member of the choir was Cyril John Worton, and his daughter Janet Worton recalls:

'My father was a Birmingham City Police Special Constable, as well as being a member of the choir for many years. He finally retired from the choir and, to use his phrase 'hung up his blazer', on the 15th February 1996. Sadly he is no longer with us.

I remember that at the end of each concert the choir would sing 'Good-Bye' by Walter Reisch and wave white handkerchiefs at the audience. It was sung as a tribute to my father at his funeral.

Figure 188 WMP Male Voice Choir 1987, courtesy of J Worton

Figure 189 WMP Male Voice Choir presenting charity cheque, 1991, courtesy of J Worton

Figure 190 WMP Male Voice Choir at the International Convention Centre, 1991, courtesy of J Worton

In August 1994, the choir recorded a happy birthday 'jingle' for the Tony Wadsworth Breakfast Show on BBC Radio WM, giving listeners wishing to send a birthday greeting over the air the option of a West Midlands Police version. The 45-strong choir recorded the song during a rehearsal at Police Headquarters.

In 1997, Sergeant Christopher Grove was awarded the MBE for services to the choir.

***

West Midlands Police Football Section

Retired officer Bryan Dorrian recalls:

'I joined Birmingham City Police as a Police Cadet in September 1969 at the age of sixteen years and joined the Football Section which was managed then by PC Keith Norman, an ex-Aston Villa professional. The team played in the Midlands Combination League.

In 1974, on amalgamation, the team was renamed the West Midlands Police Football Section and we continued to play in the same league, and the Police Athletics Association Trophy.

A little-known fact was that in recognition of my rigorous style of play I became known as 'Billy' on the field which was a reference to Billy Bremner, the legendary Leeds player with a rather determined tackle!

I wasn't the only player with a nickname. I regularly played with Roy Tinkler, Tommy Reardon and Tony Taylor as well as Dave 'Snap' Butterworth. I won't go into how he got the nickname but he also had a rigorous style.

In 1998, the Chair of the Veterans F.C, Mick Rose, nominated me for the Force's 'Holbrook Trophy' in the following terms, 'Brian was a Birmingham City Police Cadet in 1969, making the Force X1 in 1970 and signing amateur forms with Aston Villa in the same year. As captain of the cadets Brian won League, Cup and PAA competitions for two consecutive years and also broke into both the English and British Police Squads. In 1971 he made his debut for the English Police against Scotland at Portman Road, Ipswich, winning 2 – 0. As an amateur Brian played for two seasons in the Villa youth team, alongside Brian Little, Jimmy Brown, and Bobby Macdonald. A strong centre-half, Brian was lined up for his debut for Villa reserves versus Liverpool, until a certain Tony Hateley was announced as the Liverpool centre-forward that day. Brian was withdrawn and turned out for the Force instead; he sustained a double fracture of the leg and his professional ambitions were curtailed.

Brian joined the regulars in 1972, going on to captain the Force, English and British Police teams, travelling the Country and Europe until he broke the same leg again in 1977. Nevertheless his playing career continued and he became Coach to the Force reserves until 1997, with the birth of the Veterans Section, which Brian has since captained throughout.'

I was subsequently jointly awarded the trophy jointly with Andy Hinton – a proud moment in my footballing career.'

WEST MIDLAND POLICE FOOTBALL TEAM
SEASON 1974—75.

STANDING   M. WILLETTS, D. TAYLOR, B. DORRIAN, T. REARDON, D. ELLIS, G. CLOUGH, D. DELDERFIELD, T. TAYLOR, L. ARUNDEL, J. THORNTON, A. HOLMES.

SITTING   R. TINKLER, J. HART, B. JONES (Secretary), M. BUCK (Chairman), K. NORMAN (Manager), T. BROWN, N. TIMMS.

Figure 191 Courtesy of B Dorrian

Figure 192 Bryan Dorrian, 1974, courtesy of B Dorrian

Roy Tinkler recalls another highlight in the team's history:

'In 1988 we played the PAA Cup Final at St Andrews and beat the Royal Ulster Constabulary on penalties after a 1-1 draw. Colin Brookes was the manager at the time and I was 40 years of age on the day and it was 20 years on from when I appeared in another PAA Cup Final when we lost to Grimsby Police 1-0 in 1968.'

Figure 193 PAA Cup-winning team, 1988, courtesy of R Tinkler

***

Cricket Section

Birmingham City Police had an active cricket section, as recalled by Roy Tinkler, who joined the Force in 1967 and subsequently achieved over 50 years of representing the police by continuing to play until 2018, long after retirement. He was also very active in the football section. He recalls:

'For many years the cricket team was captained by Bob Flack who was the 'opening bat' and whose father Bert was the Head Groundsman at Warwickshire. In 1974 it became the West Midlands Police Cricket Section. We used to play 42 games a year.

Another stalwart of the cricket team was my good friend Ron Morris who joined the police on the same day as me. When we both retired in 1997 we also played in the 'Veterans' team and Ron continued his involvement until 2012. The 'veterans' started in 1984 and played 'friendlies' in and around the Midlands area as well as going on an annual tour. Tariq Somra was the captain for years and Tony Hunter was also a regular player.

In 1979, a cricket match to commemorate the memory of PC David Green was played, in which the West Midlands Police faced a team drawn from the Caribbean plus Asian players captained by Alvin Kallicharan'.

Roy continues, *'In April 1991 we went on a three week tour of Trinidad, Tobago, and Barbados where we played 3 games against the police, and 3 against civilian sides. There were 34 of us altogether including Mick Foster, who was chairman of the section.'*

Figure 194 West Indies tour 1988, courtesy of B Smalley

Figure 195 Jersey tour, 1995, courtesy of R Tinkler

***

Rugby Section

In 1977, Inspector Blick won the *'Holbrook'* Trophy after being a major contributor to the rugby section for many years. Described as being a *'sportsman of the highest character and ability, and now, probably in his last season of police 1st class rugby.'*.

Retired officer Ron Morris recalls:

'I played in the rugby team from 1967. It became the West Midlands Police Rugby Team in 1974 and I continued to play until 1978 when I stopped due to a shoulder injury. As far as I recall Dave Blick was never the captain but he was a key member of the team and played in the second row. Dave Millichamp was the team captain for years and played as a 'prop'. Simon Hussey was the Secretary for years. We played lots of 'friendly' games as well as playing against teams from the military in Germany. We also played in the PAA winning a number of cups.'

***

Ladies Hockey Section

Retired officer Debbie Menzel recalls:

'I joined the West Midlands Police in 1980 and was posted to the 'L' Division. The Force Ladies Hockey Section had been in existence since 1974 and I became a member and played on the left wing. It has always been a hugely successful team which regularly played in Police Athletics Association Cup games. I became the secretary of the team in 1988 and remain so to this day, even though I retired from the police in 2010. We won the PAA Cup in 1988 for the first time and went on to win it 3 years in a row. The team has continued to be successful even in recent times.'

Figure 196 PAA Cup-winning hockey team, 1988, courtesy of D Menzel

***

First Aid

In 1975, all new recruits joining the Force received initial training in First Aid, and revision classes were conducted by Police Sergeant Tom Hurley (RIP), the Force First Aid Instructor.

The *'Proctor'* Cup provided opportunities for Divisional First Aid teams to compete against each other, and at a national level teams competed in the St John Ambulance High Grade Competition.

In May 1993, the Force had significant success in a national competition to find the country's top police first-aid teams. The men and women's teams both came first in their categories – the first time any force had achieved the double. They won the *'Pim'* Trophy and the *'City of London Rose-bowl'* respectively. The open team took third place.

***

Police Bars

Bars situated on police premises were a feature of the Force for many years until the late 1990's, when the Force pursued a policy of closures, often to provide office space for staff devolved to OCU's. They provided a 'safe space' for officers to 'wind down' at the end of a shift and were very much a part of police culture.

By way of example, there was a bar in the basement area of Steelhouse Lane Police Station, which, in keeping with those in the rest of the Force, regularly played host to police pensioners, and provided a fitting venue for promotion and retirement functions.

Retired officer Peter Court reflects on another such bar:

'I lived in Little Park Street Coventry Single Quarters in the 80's. The bar was my living-room. Many celebrities performing at Coventry Theatre would come and give us a show – 'Cannon & Ball' were there in their prime.

I met my wife at Coventry Police Club, as she fell off a stool!

After a 2 X 10 shift, you just had half hour on week-days to down a couple of drinks before going home.

The social life was amazing. Coppers who had retired 20 odd years ago were still welcome, mixing with the 'new breed' and passing on their stories and wisdom. More importantly it was a place for all 'coppers' to be together, relaxing and sharing their problems, and achievements.'

***

Awards & Medals

During the period covered by this book, scores of police officers and police staff won recognition at the very highest levels for carrying out their duties, many involving acts of courage and commitment which went well beyond the call of duty. It has been impossible to mention everyone, but the list reflects the outstanding work carried out by members of the Force on a routine and regular basis.

George Medal

1990 – DC L Jakeman

Queen's Gallantry Medal

1979 – PC IR Talbot & PC MJ Marden

1990 – DC T Ginn

Queen's Commendation For Brave Conduct

1974 – Un-named officer

1977 – PC DMG Wardle

1978 – WPC M Elcock

1979 – PC JA Bixter, PC BJ Martin, PC W Smith, PC SH Theaker

1981 – WPC EA Shackell, PC A Bickley, PC MJ Irving

1990 – PC G Carlton (posthumous) Sgt L Yeomans, PC R Kiedron, PC G Oly

1994/95 – Sgt P Dean, Sgt D Murcott, Sgt E Mytton, PC I Padley

Knighthood

1980 – Chief Constable P Knights

1995/6 – Chief Constable R Hadfield

Commander Of The Order Of The British Empire (CBE)

1976 – Chief Constable P Knights

Officer Of The Order Of The British Empire (OBE)

1974 – Assistant Chief Constable JG Morrison

1977 – Deputy Chief Constable G Gaskell

1987 – Assistant Chief Constable T Meffen

1988 – Chief Supt DC Wilson

1996 – Mr J Hillier, Director of Administration

Queen's Police Medal

1974 – Chief Supt FWG Broadbent, Chief Supt PD Peterson

1975 – Chief Supt HGK Longhurst

1976 – Assistant Chief Constable W Donaldson, Chief Supt GK Cockayne

1977 – Assistant Chief Constable H Robinson, Det Supt J Lashley, Chief Supt JS Brown

1978 – Chief Supt EM Unett, Deputy Chief Constable M Buck

1981 – Ex Chief Supt Joe Matthews

1982 – Chief Supt D Bagnall

1985 – Assistant Chief Constable KJ Evans, Chief Supt GC Fieldhouse

1986 Deputy Chief Constable L Sharp

1987 – Chief Inspector BH Jones

1988 – Inspector AL Hislop, Sgt M Hornby

1989 Chief Supt G Trevis

1990 – DS Ernest Evans

1991 – Chief Supt RA Mills, Acting ACC R Longstaff

1992 – Chief Supt D Baker

1993 – Deputy Chief Constable R Adams, Inspector V Neild

1994/5 – Detective Chief Supt M Jenkins, DS J King

1997 – Deputy to the Chief Constable C Roche

1998 – Chief Supt R Jones, Chief Supt M Foster, PC R Nockalls

1999 – PC R Mouzer

Member Of The Order Of The British Empire (MBE)

1974 – Mr AG Wanklin

1977 – Sgt LP Male

1990 – ACC D Ibbs

1992 – Chief Supt C Lloyd

1993 – Miss M Harper

1995 – PC R Smith

1997 – Ex Sgt C Grove

British Empire Medal (BEM)

1974 – Special Supt AE Nickes

1976 – PS JM Booker, PC GE Watkiss

1977 – Special Supt FA Arnold

1978 – PC H Bennett

1979 – PC FH Grant

1981 PC A Harding

1985 – PC D Morgan

1986 – Sgt BA Sharp

1987 – PC V Ferguson, PC PJ Peckover

1989 – DC C Joyce

1991 – DC DG Sargeant, DS C Elworthy

1992 – PC D Jones, PC R Penniket

Police Federation/Sun Newspaper Regional Bravery Award

1997 – PC R Moon

Police Authority Commendations

A total of 345 awards

Royal Humane Society

A total of 148 awards

Society For The Protection Of Life From Fire

***

Officers Who Died Carrying Out Their Duties
'Lest We Forget'

1974 – Constable David Brown

1975 – Constable David Green

1976 – Colin Clive Nichols

1976 – Constable Michael Hewitt

1977 – Constable Bernard Church

1977 - Sergeant Peter James Brett

1977 – Sergeant Louis Bennett

1978 – Constable Brian Phillips

1978 – Constable Phillip Sanderson

1979 – Detective Constable Alexander Forrest

1979 – Constable John Pacey

1980 – Constable David Cameron

1981 – Constable Paul Worth

1982 – Constable Joseph O'Brien

1984 – Constable Andrew Le Comte

1986 – Constable Anthony Hughes

1986 – Constable Jeffrey Barnes

1987 – Constable Martin Laucht

1987 – Constable Geoffrey Collins

1987 – Constable Colin Hall

1988 – Constable Gavin Carlton

1989 – Constable Anthony Salt

1990 – Constable Colin Pursall

1990 – Constable Mark Gumbley

1990 – Special Constable Neil Coleman

1992 – Constable Mark Woodhead

1993 – Constable Philip Kurlinkus

1993 – Constable David Brennan

1995 – Constable Robert Dallow

1996 – Inspector Vanessa Carroll

R.I.P

(Every effort has been made to ensure the accuracy of this list as at the time of publication.)

Conclusion

The 1999/2000 financial year marked the silver anniversary – the 25th birthday, of West Midlands Police, and the words *'courage and commitment'* were the themes chosen to celebrate that anniversary.

The passing of years has witnessed dramatic changes in policing of the West Midlands, not least of which has been a significant increase in workloads, much of it generated by levels of recorded crime.

By way of example, during the last 9 months of 1974 a total of 83,386 crimes were recorded, rising to 314,618 crimes for the reporting period 1998/1999.

***

Figure 197 'Forward in Unity' crest, courtesy of S Burrows

West Midlands Police Museum Group

In March 1993, the new West Midlands Police Museum opened at Sparkhill Police Station. Its collection of exhibits was started by former Detective Sergeant Charlie Elworthy, who worked for many years to set up the museum, originally housed at *'Tally Ho'* Police Training Centre. He died in February 1993 at the age of 72 years. A plaque in his honour was unveiled at Sparkhill Police Station by Chief Constable Ronald Hadfield and the then Chairman of the Police Authority, Councillor Lionel Jones.

In March 1994, the museum celebrated its first anniversary, having that year welcomed 3,300 visitors, including 2,000 schoolchildren. Relying on donations from police officers and members of the public, the museum held hundreds of photographs, documents, crime reports, criminal records, and uniforms. The oldest exhibit was a police truncheon dating from 1827.

Dave Cross played a crucial role in the history of the museum. Known affectionately by his former colleagues in the West Midlands Police as, *'The Vicar'*, sadly he passed away on the 13th December 2016, aged 72 years.

At his funeral the following eulogy was given by a close friend, and former chair of the Museum Group, Tim Godwin:

'In the last years of his service Dave moved to Sparkhill where he took responsibility for establishing and coordinating Neighbourhood Watch Schemes across the 'E3' sub-division. In 1993 he suffered a mild heart-attack some 15 months before he was due to retire. After a short recuperation Dave returned to work and in November 1993, in addition to his normal duties, was asked to help retired DS Charlie Elworthy establish the Police Museum in the old court room at Sparkhill.

The museum opened at Easter in 1994, and Dave managed it until his retirement in 1995, whereupon he was employed two days a week as part-time curator, but Dave being Dave, he rarely did less than 4 days.

He performed this role for 20 years, during which time he developed an encyclopedic knowledge of the history of the West Midlands Police and its constituent Forces: Birmingham City in particular.

During his time as curator, Dave encouraged and hosted hundreds of visits by groups which included schools, colleges, Neighbourhood Watch Schemes, local history groups and academics. He also undertook genealogy research for people from the UK and around the world, regularly answering letters and emails. Dave's advice was often sought on a range of police history-related matters and he regularly appeared in articles and features in 'Newsbeat', local papers and on radio and television.

Dave was passionate about the history of women in policing. He worked tirelessly to promote the often-overlooked contribution that women have made to policing from the early days of the Policewomen's Departments to the present day. He also managed the copying and digitization of the collection of over 7,000 rare Victorian and Edwardian prisoners' photographs, a project of which he was particularly proud.

Dave retired from paid employment at the museum at the age of 67 years but continued to visit on a weekly basis, hosting visits and answering emails and letters. With recent Force changes which require the museum to move to a new home, Dave was at the very heart of this project to preserve the history of West Midlands Police for future generations. He was still attending the museum regularly, even though battling with illness, until 3 weeks before he died.

Dave received 2 Chief Constable's awards for his work at the Museum, the first in April 2014 and the second in June 2016.

In conclusion, whenever we think of all that is good about British Policing, the image of the fictional character of 'Dixon of Dock Green' comes to mind. But for those of us here today, we have our very own 'Dave Cross of Acocks Green', who I'm sure you'll agree epitomizes all that is good about British policing.'

A small group of dedicated volunteers, Deb Menzel among them, continue to work tirelessly to preserve the history and legacy of individuals like David Allen Cross, who started his police service as a regular officer at Bradford Street as PC *'F'* 157.

Figure 198 Dave Cross with Mike Layton, 2016, courtesy of D Menzel

Figure 199 Four members of the Museum Group, Paul & Su Handford, Roger Baker, Debbie Menzel & 'Sid', the dog, courtesy of D Menzel

References/Acknowledgements

Annual Reports – West Midlands Police
BBC News
Birmingham Central Library (Archives Section)
'Birmingham Evening Mail' newspaper
'Birmingham's Front Line' by Michael Layton
Care of Police Survivors Trust
'Coventry Telegraph' newspaper
'Daily Mail' newspaper
'Drug War – The Secret History' by Peter Walsh
'Express & Star' newspaper – Wolverhampton/Walsall
Hansard
'Hunting the Hooligans' by Michael Layton & Robert Endeacott
'Keep Right On' by Stephen Burrows & Michael Layton
'Newsbeat' articles – West Midlands Police
Police Arboretum Memorial Trust
'Policing Birmingham' – an account of 150 years of policing by John Reilly
'Ripon Gazette' online
'Searchlight'
'Shropshire Star' online
'The Independent' newspaper
'The Noble Cause' by Michael Layton & Stephen Burrows
'The Times' newspaper
'Walsall's Front Line – Volume II' by Michael Layton & Stephen Burrows
West Midlands Police Heritage Project
Wikipedia

***

The following serving and retired police officers from the West Midlands Police are especially thanked for their interest and support in the development of this project. We are also grateful to a number of organisations and individuals who assisted in making this book a reality.

Chris Adams – Syndication Editor (BPM Media)
Roger Baker – retired West Midlands Police Officer
Andy Belcher – retired West Midlands Police Officer
Graham Bennett – retired West Midlands Police Officer
Kerry Blakeman – retired West Midlands Police Officer

Angela Bryant – sister of David Green (R.I.P)

Pamela Burrell-Clayton – retired West Midlands Police Officer

Graham Cassidy – retired South Yorkshire Police Officer and son of John Cassidy (R.I.P)

Jason Clarke – former member of West Midlands Police Special Constabulary

Michael Patrick Cole – retired West Midlands Police Officer

Ron Cornwell – retired West Midlands Police Officer

Peter Court – retired West Midlands Police Officer

Barry Crowley – retired West Midlands Police Officer

Grahame Davies – retired West Midlands Police Officer

Paul Dobbinson – retired West Midlands Police Officer

Bryan Dorrian – retired West Midlands Police Officer

Sue Dorrian – retired West Midlands Police Officer

Mark Drew – Deputy Editor Express & Star Newspaper

Tom Duffin – retired West Midlands Police Officer

Tony *'Bunny'* Everett – retired West Midlands Police Officer

Dave *'Fingers'* Faulkner – retired West Midlands Police Officer

Michael Foster QPM – retired West Midlands Police Officer

Steve (Doc) Foster – retired West Midlands Police Officer

Tim Godwin – retired West Midlands Police Officer

Stuart Griffiths – retired West Midlands Police Officer

Malcolm *'Doc'* Halliday – retired West Midlands Police Officer

Peter Hancock – retired Fingerprint Expert West Midlands Police

Bertram (Leo) Harris – retired West Midlands Police Officer

Lesley Hewitt – daughter of Michael Hewitt (R.I.P)

Paul Hooton – retired West Midlands Police Officer

Adrian *'Ada'* Howles – retired West Midlands Police Officer

Lesley Jenkins – Senior Trading Standards Officer & member of WMP Brass Band

Simon Jones – West Midlands Police Officer

Carol Joy – retired West Midlands Police Officer

Tom Kenny – retired West Midlands Police Officer

Peter Keys – retired West Midlands Police Officer

Stuart Knight – retired West Midlands Police Officer

Norman Langford – retired West Midlands Police Officer

Sharon Layton – daughter of George Layton (R.I.P)

Karen *'Kay'* Lenyk nee Weale – retired West Midlands Police Officer

Paul Lewin – retired West Midlands Police Officer & former Chair of the BPA

Dave Mangan – retired West Midlands Police Officer

Ken Marlow – retired West Midlands Police Officer

Debbie Menzel – retired West Midlands Police officer and member of WMP Museum Group

Julie Maley nee Whild – retired West Midlands Police Officer

Paul McElhinney – retired West Midlands Police Officer

David Millichamp – retired West Midlands Police Officer

Bob Moon – retired West Midlands Police Officer

Ron Morris – retired West Midlands Police Officer

Tommy Myers – retired West Midlands Police Officer

Richard *'Rich'* Pearshouse – retired West Midlands Police Officer

Lisa Perry – former wife of Mark Woodhead (R.I.P)

Adam Phillips – Express & Star Newspaper

Tony Price – retired West Midlands Police Officer

Paul Quinney – retired West Midlands Police Officer

Paul Rainey – retired West Midlands Police Officer

John Richards – retired West Midlands Police Officer

Paul Richards – retired West Midlands Police Officer

David Rischmiller – retired West Midlands Police Officer

Chris Rowe – retired West Midlands Police Officer

Derek Rowe – retired West Midlands Police Officer

Stephen Rowe – retired West Midlands Police Officer

Ken Rowley – retired West Midlands Police Officer

Barry John Rudge – retired West Midlands Police Officer

Lynne Sedgley – retired West Midlands Police Officer

Rick Scott – retired West Midlands Police Officer

Roy Shotton – retired West Midlands Police Officer

Mark Simmonite – retired West Midlands Police Officer

Rodney *'Rod'* Simpkins – retired West Midlands Police Officer

Alan Small – retired West Midlands Police Officer

Anya Small nee Layton – former Digital Forensics Manager in West Midlands Police

Richard Small – Head of Forensic Services (West Midlands Police) - seconded

Bob Smalley – retired West Midlands Police Officer

Steve Smith – retired West Midlands Police Officer

Rod *'Smudger'* Smith MBE – retired West Midlands Police Officer

Sharon Spriggs – retired West Midlands Police Officer

'Steve' – an undercover officer on Operation *'Growth'*

Colin Tansley – retired West Midlands Police Officer

Alan Taylor – retired West Midlands Police Officer
Neil Taylor – retired West Midlands Police Officer
Roy Tinkler – retired West Midlands Police Officer
Peter Walsh – Investigative writer and publisher 'Milo' Books
Mark Wardle – former West Midlands Police Officer
Simon Westwood – retired West Midlands Police Officer
Lyndon Whitehouse – retired West Midlands Police Officer
Mavis Worth – wife of Paul Worth (R.I.P)
Janet Worton – daughter of Cyril John Worton (R.I.P)

***

A note from the authors

If you enjoyed this book please take a moment to leave a review on its Amazon page. It will be greatly appreciated. If you want to know more about our Brummie/Midlands books, fiction and non-fiction, please visit and *'like'* our Facebook page *'Bostin Books'* or go to our website **www.bostinbooks.co.uk** .We hope you enjoy them and many thanks for your support.
***

Michael Layton & Stephen Burrows (2019)

Printed in Great Britain
by Amazon

10592683R00181